SODOMY AND THE PIRATE TRADITION

SODOMY AND THE PIRATE TRADITION:

ENGLISH SEA ROVERS IN THE SEVENTEENTH-CENTURY CARIBBEAN

B. R. BURG

NEW YORK UNIVERSITY PRESS
NEW YORK & LONDON
1984

3-86

The clothbound edition of the book was published in 1983 under the
title: SODOMY AND THE PERCEPTION OF EVIL: ENGLISH SEA ROVERS IN
THE SEVENTEENTH-CENTURY CARIBBEAN.

Library of Congress Cataloging in Publication Data
Burg, B. R. (Barry Richard), 1938–
    Sodomy and the pirate tradition.

Bibliography: p.
Includes index.
1. Homosexuality, Male—Caribbean Area—History
—17th century.   2. Homosexuality, Male—England
—History—17th century.   3. Pirates—Caribbean
Area—Sexual behavior—History—17th century.
    I. Title.
HQ76.2.C27B87   1982   306.7'662'09729   82-8310
           ISBN 0-8147-1040-9
                 0-8147-1073-5 pbk.

Manufactured in the United States of America

To Bill Camwell and Alice Watterson

"No interviews!" the pirate cried. "*Especially*
no interviews granted to little girls."
—DONALD BARTHELME

CONTENTS

PREFACE

I have chosen to use the word "sodomy" in the title of this study rather than the more fashionable term "homosexuality." In a literary sense, sodomy fits more comfortably in a seventeenth-century context than homosexuality—a linguistic derivation from the Victorian era—but my reasons for selecting it are practical rather than ornamental. "Sodomy" is unencumbered by scientific meanderings and sundry psychological nuances associated in modern usage with homosexuality, and it is the absence of layered academic or clinical definitions that make it particularly valuable in a title. The antique simplicity and directness of the word are sufficiently intimidating to discourage readers from asking questions about all-male sexuality immediately upon taking up the work that are more appropriately asked and answered in the later chapters.

In Tudor and Stuart England, "sodomy" and "buggery" were most often used interchangeably, and I have used them in that manner. Like many sexual denominators, however, the meanings of the terms are not always clear. At various times sodomy and buggery, as defined by law, included homosexual acts, homosexual child molestation (but never heterosexual child molestation), bestiality, heterosexual anal-genital contact, and assorted methods of homosexual masturbation. In practice the meanings were more precise. Sodomy or buggery, without qualifying explanation, referred only to homo-

sexual acts among adult males. If youths were involved, it was so
stated. Masturbation was called masturbation. Bestiality was always
clearly labeled, and it was explicitly noted when sodomy cases involved women. I have followed this more precise practice. Where
the terms buggery or sodomy are used, they refer only to homosexual
contact between adult males. Any other acts that could possibly be
included under definitions of sodomy are identified by more specific
terms or are fully explained.

Difficulty with definitions is not something confined only to sexual
terminology. In the literature on Caribbean freebooters of three
hundred years ago, there are additional complications. Some works
distinguish between buccaneers and pirates, using the former term
only for sea raiders who had been hunters on Hispaniola before sailing in search of plunder, and by classifying as pirates only those marauders who had never undergone the experience of stalking wild
island cattle and smoking the meat of their prey on a small rack, or
boucan. This distinction is convenient for the first half of the seventeenth century, but by 1660 or 1665 the terms can be used interchangeably, as was done by English residents and governmental officials in the West Indies after the Restoration. The same is true for
the terms privateer and pirate in the last half of the seventeenth century and at least until 1720. The legal distinction between the two
was clearly delineated, but in practice pirate and privateer were often
indistinguishable. Some privateers, most notably William Dampier
and Woodes Rogers, managed to avoid being officially stigmatized as
pirates because of their considerable political acumen and cognizance
of legal niceties, but for most the letters of marque and reprisal, as
the commissions that European governments issued to sanction privateer plundering were known, often made little difference in the
West Indies where legal privateer and illegal pirate operated in much
the same way. This was clearly understood by officials in the Caribbean whether English, French, Spanish, or Dutch; although local
functionaries from each of the countries issued letters of marque and
reprisal or their legal equivalents, all knew that they only gave a veneer of legality to the already operating industry of raiding and plundering.[1]

In dealing with topics as diverse as those necessary to obtain an understanding of West Indian pirates and their mode of life, the aid of dozens of scholars has been indispensable. A number of those who assisted me, several of whom are untenured and naturally disinclined to be associated with any topic that could be considered controversial, cannot be thanked by name. The data and criticism they provided has nonetheless been especially valuable. Others who have helped in sundry ways and need not have reservations about being thanked for their aid in the preface of a book on sodomy are A.L. Beier, Joel Best, Timothy H. Breen, Vern L. Bullough, Michael Craton, Martin Duberman, Richard S. Dunn, Melvin M. Firestone, Stephen W. Foster, Arthur N. Gilbert, Michael Goodich, Arlette A. Hagstrom, Carole L. Levin, Wardell B. Pomeroy, Colin Rickards, Charles Silverstein, Suzanne Stark, and C.A. Tripp, and Retha M. Warnicke. The suggestions, commentary, and advice they have given at various times over the last several years has been essential in formulating my study, but without the encouragement they also provided, the work never would have been completed. David F. Greenberg and Robert C. Ritchie were each kind enough to spend hours examining the manuscript, and their comments enabled me to eliminate a number of errors and speed the flow of the narrative. Any errors that remain are, needless to add, of my own doing.

Arizona State University has been more than generous in expediting my research with a sabbatical leave that enabled me to use the facilities of the British Museum, the Public Record Office, and the National Maritime Museum. They also provided me a summer stipend from the Faculty Committee on Grants-in-Aid. Additional funds were furnished by the Shell Oil Foundation and the National Endowment for the Humanities. The staff of the Alfred C. Kinsey Institute for Sex Research at Indiana University were particularly helpful, but special thanks must be reserved for Mrs. Grace Skinaway and Ms. Margaret K. Riddall, both of whom typed a seemingly endless series of drafts detailing the activities of the buccaneers.

INTRODUCTION

February 1, 1816 was not a noteworthy day in English history. Men worked or played according to their customary patterns, and institutions uninterruptedly functioned at their appointed tasks. The House of Commons received a routine letter from the Duke of Wellington informing the members he had expressed their gratitude for Prussian aid at Waterloo to Field Marshal Blucher. In the afternoon, players of the Theatre Royal at Covent Garden made preparations to perform *Isabella* in the evening. The *Times* reported Princess Charlotte of Wales was indisposed, and James Cooper, with three of his shipmates from the *H.M.S. Africaine*, were executed for buggery. Two other crewmembers, John Parsons and Jack Hubbard, were whipped for uncleanness, a general term then current for deviant sexual behavior. Parsons was given 200 lashes and Hubbard received 170 of the 300 lashes specified by the court. The sentence was not completed because an attendant surgeon determined additional punishment would endanger his life.[1] The harsh treatment meted out by the Royal Navy, where "Rum, Bum, and the Lash" were traditions of long standing, was not something characteristic only of the military in the era of the Napoleonic Wars. It was symptomatic of the abiding concern and profound revulsion to variant sexual practices that was typical of English attitudes in the nineteenth century and after.

Extreme hostility to homosexual acts was a relatively recent acquisition for Englishmen in the closing decades of George III's reign. Two hundred years before, in the early seventeenth century, homosexual acts were rarely condemned by anyone. They were ignored by ordinary citizens, officers of the church, the military, and by leaders of the civil government. Later in the century, after the Civil Wars and the Interregnum, when Charles II was restored to the throne in 1660, homosexual acts and the men who committed them continued to attract little attention. Men who engaged other men for sexual purposes were found on every level of society, from the royal court, through the nobility, in the commercial classes, and on down to the sailors who manned the king's ships and the crews of the merchant fleet. For the most part, Englishmen regarded homosexual behavior as simply another sexual activity, a peculiarity to some, a matter of jest to others, a thing for public cognizance when circumstances warranted, but mostly a practice to be ignored. Even for clerics and moralists profoundly concerned with sexual transgression, homosexual activities were minor matters, no more dangerous than the heterosexual promiscuity they perceived to be corrupting the English nation.

Amid the climate of toleration flourished one of the most unusual homosexually oriented groups in history, the Caribbean pirates who spread terror from South America northward to Bermuda and occasionally into the Pacific throughout the latter half of the seventeenth century. Much has been written of piracy since the time buccaneering flags flew in the West Indian sun and Spanish soldiers or terrified merchant seamen were victims of pirate attacks. But in the years that have passed, the major portion of the literature has been concerned more with piratical deeds than with pirates. Its appeal, one would surmise from the content, is to an audience of small boys, retired naval officers, and others concerned primarily with cannon, cutlass, gore, and decks awash with blood. The emphasis on military matters to the exclusion of all other features of buccaneering life is regrettable, for by paying little heed to the pirate community, the opportunity to investigate one of the unique groups in human history has been ignored.

Attempting to assess the nature of pirate society, tiny communities composed of men far removed from the mainstream of European or English life, would hardly seem worth the effort if it were undertaken only to establish that buccaneers engaged in homosexual acts, an observation previously made by several other authors. The presence of sodomites among those who make their livings from the sea is not a startling revelation. Sexual encounters involving sailors are a part of maritime lore, and fo'c's'le humor abounds with stories of below deck encounters in which salty bosuns initiate tender cabin boys into the arcana of the sea. Yet pirate homosexual practice is distinct from that common either to sailors or to men in other ages and in other societies where masculine sexual bonding has flourished. It differs widely from that of the ancient Greeks, the Knights Templar, the usual practices in seventeenth-century England, and from all-male sexuality in the United States since the gay liberation movement was launched. In diverse cultures at various time periods when homosexuality or homosexual contact was an ordinary social practice or was at least not severely proscribed, it was integrated into prevailing patterns and functioned harmoniously with all other aspects of society. Among pirates, either aboard their ships or while living on isolated West Indian islands, homosexual acts were not integrated with or subordinated to alternate styles of sexual contact. They were the only form of sexual expression engaged in by members of the buccaneer community.

The predominance of homosexual methods of sexual expression alone would not be sufficient to distinguish pirate societies from other particular human groupings. Prison populations rely entirely on homosexual and onanistic practices, and the nature of homosexual social stratification that evolves in penal institutions has been widely studied and imperfectly understood by generations of psychologists, sociologists, and criminologists. While prison and pirate communities are similar in that both are without females, there are also striking differences between the two. Homosexuality and homosexual contact behind bars exists only within a framework of rigidly applied rules and regulations imposed from beyond the ranks of the inmates. Although homosexual activity is often ignored or at least carefully regulated by supervisory personnel, it must still exist within a social structure determined largely by a dominant order that is antipathetic both to the prisoners and to sexual relations among them.

Although homosexual behavior was widely tolerated in late seventeenth-century England and the structure of society encouraged it on several levels, such practices remained only a facet of English life and were thus subject to restriction and regulation by the larger community. This was not the case among pirates in the Caribbean, where the essential features of their homosexual activity, exclusivity and the absence of constraints imposed by a more powerful and unsympathetic society, meant that buccaneer communities could evolve and mature with little or no interference from a dominant, restrictive, and sometimes hostile heterosexual nation. This opportunity to constitute and develop a community where homosexual contact was the ordinary form of sexual expression was unusual enough, but to do it while free from persecution and opprobrium was unique, and although pirates did not indulge in conscious social experimentation, the all-male society they built and sustained in the West Indies for three-quarters of a century was a singular reflection of their peculiar situation.

The use of a subject population from the seventeenth century makes it appear, at least initially, that *Sodomy and the Perception of Evil* is a historical work. Nothing could be further from the truth. The study of history is, as a legion of academicians is willing to point out, much more than description and analysis of past events. Included within the discipline are carefully delineated processes for inquiry, authoritatively prescribed applications of logic, systems for evaluation of evidence, and in most investigations a sharply defined set of goals to be reached from examination of past events arranged in a diachronic panorama. Evolution, process, development, motive and the like— such are the subjects of history, and historical method has been designed over the years to inquire into just these sorts of things. This is all to the good for the study of history, but my own work is very different than that undertaken by historians. It has not been my intent to reconstruct a segment of the past, to analyze its etiology and explain its unfolding, or to communicate the buccaneers' world to the present. I have instead set out to discover coherence in one small segment of human society, the strictly defined male group. Unlike historians with their emphasis on the human conduct recoverable from archival material and other survivals of the past, my study relies heavily on behavioral theory and other devices from the social and behavioral sciences that are often anathema to historians. *Sodomy and the Perception of Evil* has, in fact, been described to me as anti-historical by colleagues rendered apoplectic at the notion of treating the past with modern methods of sociology, psychology, and other social sciences. This study is not anti-historical nor is it an attempt to demonstrate how history can be written by ignoring several of the canons of historical method. It is simply not history. It utilizes the past but does not deal with it. Interdisciplinary sociology might be an accurate descriptive term for those requiring the taxonomy of academic departments to organize their judgments. Speculative social science might also be a convenient label. But whatever term is selected, this study should be evaluated in terms of what it is rather than what it is not.

In the past several decades, students of human behavior have begun to incorporate sex and homosexuality into their work at least in part, as critics have charged, to serve the increasing interest in an earlier generation's taboo. But it is also true that their newly kindled interest is inspired by recent theoretical formulations that provide a framework for investigation into this area that is better suited to the methods of the social scientist than to those of the psychologist or the psychiatrist. Basic to these formulations is the premise that homosexuality is not an inherently pathological condition but rather a variant form of sexual expression well within the range of normal human behavior. Implicit, too, is the understanding that homosexuality is the product of a complex series of situations or combinations of factors. Its etiology parallels the etiology of heterosexuality and involves no pathological predisposition. When these assumptions are used as a basis for investigation, the need to consider homosexual activity a special condition is obviated. Emphasis can be centered on the broader and more illuminating questions of how homosexual conduct is influenced, directed, and even controlled or dominated by societal orientation and how the connotations and expectations surrounding sexual preferences affect behavior of similarly patterned members of groups.

Dealing with piracy, seventeenth-century England, early colonial society in the Caribbean, homosexual preferences, and homosexual activity in a single study requires special attention be given to the overall plan of the book. The task of organization is further complicated because *Sodomy and the Perception of Evil*, unlike many monographs, does not begin at one point and move on a single course through various chapters to a conclusion. Instead, like the hempen rope so familiar to seventeenth-century seafarers, it is brought together out of three separate strands. Chapters 1, 2, and 3 each develop their own premises from the wealth of material available on Stuart England and the English Caribbean. The groups of premises are then spun together in the concluding chapters to form the central theoretical line of the book. Additional data and theoretical formulations based on modern studies of homosexual groups and seafaring communities provide a coating of Stockholm tar to keep the conclusions watertight even in heavy academic weather. More specifically, the initial chapter provides an examination of English perceptions of sodomy, with particular emphasis on the concluding 50 years of the century when pirate homosexual behavior flourished. An underlying premise of the chapter, and of the book as well, is that alternative homosexual behavior is characteristic of societies where homosexual conduct is variously perceived. Chapter 1, then, is the logical starting point for understanding homosexual behavior in Stuart England, containing as it does an examination of critical aspects of the society that produced a homosexual pirate community. The second chapter is a study of the assorted ways men navigated the channels and shoals of English life to reach havens where their homosexual activity was secure and safe. The approach in Chapter 2 is akin to the societal reaction method, a theoretical construct for studying human behavior already in use by some investigators of psycho-social phenomena.[2] It differs only in that while psycho-social methods and their cognate techniques attempt analysis of the individual's sexual situation according to three parameters, the relationship to the heterosexual world, the relationship to the homosexually oriented world, and the individual's psychological situation, the data available on pirates centuries dead make the three-way approach impossible. Modifications must be made to compensate for the lack of data and when compensations are inadequate, the last of the societal reaction parameters must be omitted. In dealing with pirates there is ample material for investigating homosexual relationships with heterosexuals and others involved in homosexual engagements, but the absence of evidence prevents adequate attention from being given to individual problems of sexual adjustment. Still, although this chapter is not comparative in the usual methodological sense and is further limited by the use of only two of the three societal reaction parameters, it is, like the chapters that precede and follow it, postulated on the procedural perspective that the character of homosexual manifestations—like the character of heterosexual manifestations—is shaped largely by the dictates of society.

The third point of embarkation, the discussion of society in the English Caribbean during the latter half of the seventeenth century, provides analysis of demographic material, travelers' accounts, and other sources of information about the nature of life on Barbados, Jamaica, and other West Indian islands during the period. It reveals, not surprisingly, that the tolerant attitudes toward homosexual behavior found in the mother country were present in the islands as well. More important, however, it indicates patterns of population distribution and sex ratios in the West Indies did not merely encourage homosexual conduct as was the case in England. On the contrary, they made it almost obligatory for most residents of the English Caribbean colonies.

The material of the first three chapters is drawn together in Chapter 4. Throughout the chapter's discussion of buccaneer sexuality, the central theoretical factors selected for defining and describing human communities are those dealing with the multiple patterns regulating interpersonal relationships not only between individuals but for pairs and larger subgroups within the entire population. Among pirates, as is generally true within any group, the daily contacts experienced by people in close proximity and the systems for ensuring harmonious operation of life's ordinary routines are well understood by human beings who have mastered the intricacies of their society, although they have never been specifically taught them in the manner that economic skills, love of country or conceptions of the metaphysical are imparted. Outsiders often encounter prodigious difficulties in trying to decipher the subtleties of intra-group relations among tribal peoples, unfamiliar ethnic groups, or national populations whose ways are unfamiliar. In newer areas of inquiry such as human sexuality, where there are only restricted amounts of traditional materials, the well-established procedures used by researchers for discovering political, economic, and an assortment of social relationships are inadequate, and alternative avenues of investigation must be sought. One method to compensate for the lack of usual sources, and that used in Chapter 4, is to adopt the processes of another category of social scientist, the archeologist. Using sources familiar to the sociologist, but extracting data in the manner of field workers digging a site, an archeology of at least one phase of homosexuality can be constructed by finding shards of this and that and with only an occasional artifact discovered completely intact. Like items from excavations of a long-buried place of human habitation, the disassociated and often incomplete snippets of data on homosexual preferences or homosexual contacts are by themselves as meaningless as large aggregations of fragments and material tidbits dug from the earth after centuries of repose. Meaning can be derived from them only by employing archeological procedures, using data derived from observed populations and producing through theoretically based deduction plausible explanations for behavior among inaccessible population groups.

The deductive methodology so widely used by archeologists is, unfortunately, often abused by them. Examples abound of researchers generalizing far beyond what the combination of theory and data can sustain. Ancient cave paintings and interment practices are linked inelegantly with the sociocultural contexts of modern tribal peoples and comprehensive extrapolations of paleolithic religion are proffered to the general public by a cadre of academics who should know better. Modern Indians of the American Southwest are ritually cleansed by the smoke of their council fires and so the same must have been true for the vanished cliff dwellers of Mesa Verde. The large breasts and heavy buttocks on tiny statuettes unearthed in Germany cause them to be labeled fertility figures, while at the same time the scholars issuing such proclamations fail to notice their stone Venuses are probably no more amply proportioned than the average Leipzig hausfrau. The list of similar examples could be continued almost without end, yet despite egregious misuse and blatant over-extension, the technique retains considerable utility. If it is understood that interpreting data in the context of substantial and comprehensive behavior theory produces not proof but raises instead the level of tenability for one or a number of alternatives, then—employing considerable caution and trepidation—some generalizations can be transferred, at least for purposes of testing and evaluating hypotheses. This is particularly true in attempting to examine and analyze the nature and extent of sexual behavior patterns among buccaneers in the Caribbean three hundred years ago. There exist no bulging files of 8″ x 10″ glossies snapped by lensmen with sharp eyes for sodomitical pirates, and while first-hand descriptions, journal accounts, legal records, or even literary evidence would all be desirable, in most cases they are not to be had. Not only did pirates rarely record experiences of any sort, let alone those of a sexual nature, but the total absence of demographic data resulting from the non-reproductive nature of their sexual contacts contributes substantially toward keeping their homosexual preferences and patterns of behavior obscured. As a result, theories of pirate sexuality developed in Chapter 4 will remain in the strictest sense always theories, but at the same time, the most plausible patterns of behavior can be identified and their degree of likelihood evaluated.

The concluding portion of the study deals with pirates and the society in which they lived. Data is available only on a limited number of buccaneers, though thousands of them sailed the Caribbean over seven decades of freebooting, but what survives on individuals and ships' crews provides valuable insight on why they functioned the way they did. It reveals that among the men of this seafaring community, there was no need to hide sexual orientation, and the anxieties, psychological disruptions, and psychopathological difficulties that often result from this type of guilt and repression did not emerge.

ONE

SODOMY AND PUBLIC PERCEPTION: SEVENTEENTH-CENTURY ENGLAND

The England that produced three generations of sodomitical pirates was a land far different from modern Britain or America. Aside from the obvious distinctions created by three centuries of technological evolution, the lives of seventeenth-century Englishmen followed patterns widely divergent from those familiar to men now living. Ideals, values, moral codes, conceptions of mankind, and the very nature of reality were so substantially distinct from those of the present century that one historian was moved to entitle a book on the structure of society three hundred years past *The World We Have Lost*. The author of the study was not employing overstatement to obtain dramatic effect. The nation he described has a strange and terrifying quality for denizens of modern urbanized and electronically bonded civilization. The collections of images that preserve Stuart England for the present form a series of jarring incongruities. Scenes of disorder, frightening cruelty, social, religious, and political instability, perva-

sive violence and profound hatreds are set against a pastoral backdrop
of rural simplicity and growing prosperity, while all is seemingly bound
together by a melange of anti-social institutions straining to mitigate
the centrifugal tendencies of the age.[1]

Of the many features that distinguish the era of buccaneer depredations in the West Indies from the present were the perceptions and
attitudes of Englishmen toward homosexual activity. Unlike the
present day, when sexual contact between members of the same sex
is anathema to large segments of the population in both England and
America, homosexuality was regarded with much less opprobrium in
the seventeenth century. The hostility of the ancient Hebrews to sexual practices beyond the most ordinary heterosexual arrangements and
the destruction visited on Sodom by an offended deity when considered in conjunction with modern hostility toward homosexual
practice has contributed to the notion that an aversion to homosexuality is a constant in human history, or at least in the history of that
portion of humanity that has fallen heir to the thousands of years of
Judeo-Christian tradition. In the case of England three hundred years
ago, however, the idea of virulent hostility toward anal intercourse or
to other manners of sexual interaction between members of the same
sex is controverted by a preponderant mass of evidence. This is particularly important, for an awareness of the place occupied by homosexuality in Stuart Englishmen's great scheme of things is not only
central to understanding the society that produced pirates capable of
engaging in three-quarters of a century's depredations in the Caribbean, but the knowledge of the manner in which homosexual conduct was integrated into national life on every social level provides
essential data for unraveling an aspect of the analytical difficulties
bearing on the evolution of sexual preferences during the Restoration
period and in the decades immediately following.

The earliest English proscription against homosexual acts dates from
the thirteenth century when in *Fleta* it was specified that sodomites
be buried alive. At the same time, other sources prescribed burning
as a fit punishment, but these expressions of law were probably
holdovers from Roman enactments rather than genuine reflections of
sentiments advocated by the legislating classes in Norman England.

There is no indication that such sentences were ever pronounced for sodomy at any time in the several centuries preceding the Tudor period. It was not until 1533, during the reign of Henry VIII, that buggery was made a civil crime—it had been previously subject to limited ecclesiastical censure—but like the Elizabethan law of 1562 against sodomy, it was the result of a struggle for power between the church and expanding secular authority rather than being symptomatic of a developing concern with the need to restrict the varieties of sexual activity practiced by the English.

The laws against buggery and sodomy enacted during the sixteenth century prescribed death as punishment, but their enaction does not indicate legislators necessarily found the offense particularly abhorrent. Capital punishment was routinely specified for felonies by the law. It is true that crimes classed as felonies included the more serious offenses, but Tudor and Stuart officials as well as the general population agreed that many of the deeds for which death was specified were not sufficiently ominous to require execution. While murder, treason, bestiality, and serious crimes against property often brought their perpetrators to the gallows, the minor felonies—such as theft of restricted amounts of money or goods, shipping sheep across the sea, cutting purses, sodomy, or picking pockets—rarely cost anyone his or her life, as least until the application of excessive criminal penalties in the middle of the eighteenth century. The effect of the death penalty in earlier years was to mitigate the severity of the law rather than increase it. When punishment was far greater than the crime, those apprehended were frequently not charged; if charged, indictments were not returned by grand juries, and if trials were held, convictions could not be obtained. The inability and unwillingness to pronounce death sentences for many minor felonies, a practice noticed by writers on legal topics in the seventeenth century and historians of English law ever since, is an indication that the administrators of the statutes were not bent on executing petty criminals for their crimes. They treated the specification of capital punishment for minor offenses not as a requirement, but regarded it instead as a result of historical precedent and the practical requirements of the legislative task. This is evidenced in the case of Nicholas Udall, a sixteenth-century churchman, playwright, and Eton headmaster whose taste for paddling and penetrating the posteriors of his youthful charges did no lasting harm to his career even though his was the first sodomy case to arise after the passage of the new statute against buggery. He was dismissed from the post at Eton but given severance pay equal to a year's salary. Later he became headmaster at Westminster, and in due course received ecclesiastical preferment under both Edward VI and Mary. The ecumenical nature of his sexual preferences evidently made him acceptable to a Protestant king and a Catholic queen. Udall was not prosecuted for his actions and neither were there any other prosecutions under the buggery or sodomy statutes until the next century, indicating further that adoption of the laws was not the result of a need by authorities to rein in legions of homosexuals coursing over the land. Indeed, at the end of the Elizabethan age, Richard Barnfield was composing graceful pastorals on obviously homosexual themes. At one point he softly denied the existence of homoerotic motifs in his work, but went ahead writing more of the same. There were no serious objections to Barnfield's advocacy of love between shepherds and their boys.[2]

The lack of alarm over homosexual practices is additionally apparent in the treatment they were accorded in various manuals intended to aid justices of the peace in the conduct of their official tasks. In a compendium of instructions for the justices, early Tudor author Anthony Fitzherbert devoted only a single sentence to buggery, explaining merely that it was a felony without benefit of clergy. The same lack of concern was evidenced by William Lambarde when he published a manual for instruction of justices in 1582. His *Eirenarcha* was the best of the sixteenth-century handbooks and had enormous influence, going through numerous editions despite competition from similar works by John Goldwell of Gray's Inn and Richard Crompton. Although Lambarde distinguished buggery with man from buggery with beast in his diagram of felonies, the treatment in the text indicated an obvious lack of apprehension. His fifteen-word explanation was narrowly inserted between putting "out the eies of any of the Kings subjects" and "the taking of any maid, widdow, or wife, unlawfully, against her will, that hath lands, or tenements, goods, or chattels." Sir Edward Coke, one of England's foremost legal scholars during the reign of James I, was another who dealt with the legal aspects of buggery. The crime originated, he explained, in pride, excess of diet, idleness, and contempt of the poor. Nowhere did he attempt to connect its beginnings with heresy or any other satanic machinations. It was an ordinary man-made felony. Even the adjectives describing it as "detestable" and "abominable" dated only from the prohibition enacted under Henry VIII, he noted. Coke also sought to extend the definition of buggery to cover at least one heterosexual situation. Being an accessory to rape was to be included under the rubric. At the same time he expanded the definition of buggery he tried to restrict the grounds on which convictions for homosexual acts could be obtained. Penetration was required to establish guilt. Emission alone was not sufficient. When Coke sought to buttress his arguments on sodomy, he found cases of the crime were exceedingly rare. The best precedent he could locate did not involve two men. It was instead a 1608 case of homosexual child molestation, an act that was legally distinct from those involving consenting adults.[3]

With the death of Elizabeth in 1603 and the coming of James I to the throne, there was little likelihood that a wave of prosecutions for homosexuality would ensue. The new king was notoriously involved with a series of male lovers, the most well-known of whom was George Villiers, made an Earl, then Duke of Buckingham for his favors. James was so enamoured of Buckingham that he virtually adopted the Villiers family, distributing royal largess to brothers, parents, aunts, and cousins of his beloved. Not only was England ruled by a misogynist homosexual from 1603 until 1625, but at least one immensely powerful court figure, Lord Chancellor Francis Bacon, was known to prefer a handsome lad to any lady no matter how lovely.[4] His preferences were not concealed during his lifetime nor was any attempt made after his death to restrict knowledge of his sexual proclivities. When political enemies at last gained the opportunity to destroy Bacon, he was certain he would be rescued by James I and Buckingham. The expected benefactors did not preserve him, although the reasons for their failure to do so are not entirely clear. It was thought in some quarters at the time that a charge of sodomy might be lodged against him to make sure he was removed from office, but the king and the favorite duke could hardly allow that. Instead, Bacon was sacrificed to his enemies before they could bring him to account for his sex life. The great seal was taken from him, he was fined an enormous sum, and he was exiled from court for a time.[5]

After the death of James I there was no rush to root out sodomites on any level of English society, and among the gentry, as with those close to the king, it required more than a sex offense to bring a man to justice. John Hockenhull of Prenton was brought before the Chester Sessions on April 21, 1628, charged with buggery, but a more ominous charge of sorcery was leveled against him at the same time.[6] There is no record of the verdict in his case, but it was a rarity. The earliest successful prosecution for homosexuality involving only adults did not come until 1631, half a dozen years into the reign of Charles I. The accused in this instance was a nobleman, Mervin Touchet, Lord Audley, Earl of Castlehaven, and it was apparent from the evidence that more was involved than a simple matter of buggery. Aside from the fact that the accused lord's wife was the sister of the then-deceased Francis Bacon—a relationship that by this time probably contributed little toward bringing about the trial—Audley was also a Roman Catholic. The Earl was charged with more than sodomy. He was accused of committing a series of sex crimes including "Abetting a Rape upon his Countess, . . . Sodomy with his Servants, and Commanding and Countenancing the Debauching [of] his Daughter."[7] He was also accused of voyeurism, child molestation, and buggering the servants who raped the Countess on his orders. Not only was this style of conduct far more extreme than sodomy alone, but the Earl had made his crimes more despicable by his violations of class taboos. He was additionally charged with dispensing lands and large sums of money to his companions in debauchery. The indictment against Castlehaven contained the standard legal phraseology describing sodomy as contrary to nature and a crime not to be named among Christians, but in the judicial proceedings against him almost no attempt was made to label sodomy as more brutish or less natural than rape.[8] The Lord High Steward presiding over the Westminster

Hall trial condemned both crimes as "Great and Heinous," but also cautioned the lords who sat in judgment to make certain that "Reasons and Consciences sway your Judgments, and your Heads direct your Hearts."[9] During the course of the proceeding, rape and sodomy were both described as abominable and felonious, but it was emphatically explained that they were crimes not because of their repellent nature but because they were violations of English law. The only unflattering adjective applied exclusively to sodomy by the Lord High Steward was a moderate "vile" and on the single occasion when the prosecution described the Earl's actions as not to be fit to be named among Christians, it was in a quotation from the legally phrased indictment.[10]

The Earl of Castlehaven was convicted of both crimes, yet the noble lords who decided his guilt did not condemn him equally on each of the two counts. The evidence presented to the tribunal substantiated the facts of the accusations, and in his defense the Earl did not dispute the truth of the testimony. He argued instead that while he had forced his unwilling wife to submit to a series of sex acts, this did not legally constitute rape because she was a promiscuous woman. In like manner he denied being guilty of sodomy since the testimony of witnesses proved only emission but not penetration. The Lord Chief Justice explained to the court that English law was unequivocal on both arguments made by the defendant. The unwholesome character of a woman was no defense against rape, and despite Coke's assertion to the contrary, emission of semen, whether or not penetration took place, constituted sodomy. With all legal questions settled, the 26 peers who sat in judgment were then asked to render their verdict, and each of them pronounced Castlehaven guilty of rape. On the second charge, however, the need for conviction was less immediate for some of the jurors. The majority necessary to vote condemnation of the Earl was available, but it is apparent that if the noble lords had thought sodomy to be as ghastly a crime in 1631 as it was to be considered late in the next century, even eleven of them would have attested to their belief in the defendant's innocence and voted for acquittal.[11]

The trial of the Earl of Castlehaven was not to be the first in a series of sodomy prosecutions. No proceedings for similar but unrelated crimes followed, and sodomy continued to be considered a rare occurrence. The extreme events of this particular case, operating in concert with the political power of the maltreated wife's family, produced the opportunity for zealous English Protestants to bring a Catholic nobleman to trial under circumstances where the Romish-leaning Charles I and his Catholic queen could not possibly exert influence. It was only such a constellation of events that made it possible to prefer charges against Audley.[12]

A decade after Castlehaven's execution another public figure was condemned for sodomy, and again it was apparent more was involved than a sex act between consenting males. John Atherton, Anglican Bishop of Waterford and Lismore, was hanged at Dublin on December 5, 1640. An account of his penitence and his preparations for death was later written by Dr. Nicholas Bernard, a cleric who helped Atherton gain assurance of salvation in his final days. Bernard's pamphlet is concerned with Atherton's humility and his longings for heaven rather than the specifics of his crime, but it reveals that the disgraced bishop was well aware that political transgressions were the true cause of his death. He was being made to answer, he explained, for "too much zeale and forwardnesse, both in introducing and pressing some Church-observations, and in dividing himselfe from the house of Convocation Anno 1634 in opposition to the *Articles of Ireland* then voted to be received."[13] Atherton obviously created some of his own difficulties by serving as local champion for conforming Anglicanism at a time when Puritans were gaining the upper hand, but in fact his errors went beyond those recorded in the pamphlet. During his years of service in Ireland he had made the compound mistake of creating powerful enemies while at the same time becomming the protégé of the Earl of Strafford, a man who was soon to lose the power to protect himself and his retainers. The most dangerous of those in opposition to Atherton was the influential Earl of Cork. He and other leading landowners had some time before been forced by Strafford to surrender portions of their holdings, and later Cork was sued by Atherton in an attempt to make him return lands once owned by the See of Waterford. Under the circumstances, Atherton needed all the support he could muster, but Strafford could hardly protect him even if he had desired to do so. At the very time the convicted bishop mounted the scaffold in Dublin, the Earl was in serious difficulties with the Puritan-dominated Parliament. Within months after Atherton's death, he was charged with treason through a bill of attainder, condemned to death, and executed on May 12, 1641.[14]

The period from 1630 to 1650 in England's history was characterized by disruptions so severe that any attempt to apply the lessons learned in either Castlehaven's or Atherton's prosecutions and use accusations of homosexuality against a major figure for political or ecclesiastical purposes would have been doomed. This was a time when the nation was deeply divided on truly substantive issues, and a charge of sodomy leveled at any participant would have been a peripheral issue. Englishmen were instead vitally concerned with the form of the national church, the collection of revenues, and the apportionment of government authority. Charles I had antagonized large numbers of his subjects, whose hopes for religious reform he had dashed by 1630 with royal edicts demanding conformity to doctrines and ceremonies of the Church of England. Many of the reformers, who were styled Puritans by this time, were rich, powerful, and determined not to accept what they regarded as Romish corruptions as integral parts of their national religion. Their hostility was carried into Parliament, where a large bloc supported the cause of ecclesiastical reform, and their anger over religious problems spilled into the debates on other issues. The king dealt as arrogantly with Parliament as he had with the Puritans, and the members responded accordingly by refusing to authorize the collection of new taxes. Frustrated by its refusal to do his bidding on fiscal as well as on other legislative matters, Charles dismissed Parliament in 1629 and resolved to rule alone. This tactic worked well enough for over a decade, but when the royal attempts to ensure Scottish conformity to the practices of the Church of England led to the disastrous Bishop's War, the king was at last forced to summon Parliament.

Charles had hoped the new Parliament would replenish his bankrupt treasury, but when the members assembled they had other ideas.

Many had served in earlier Parliaments and the eleven years during which they had not met provided ample time to reflect on the elements of tyranny and to nurture their rage. When they assembled at last they railed against the king and his policies rather than producing the new monies he demanded. Charles retaliated by dismissing Parliament a second time, but the empty treasury and a Scottish invasion forced him to summon them once again. The new Parliament lacked legislative experience, but it contained men notable for their leadership ability. Under the direction of John Hampden, John Pym, and Oliver Cromwell, Parliament decreed they could not be dissolved without their own consent, they abolished the king's courts of Star Chamber and High Commission, and ordered that no tax levies be collected without their permission. Charles attempted to halt the flow of events by arresting the legislative leadership, but this failed. Full-scale civil war erupted, and seven years of conflict followed before the parliamentary forces were able to gain complete victory. After their triumph, Parliament began restructuring England. The king was convicted of treason and executed. The House of Lords was eliminated, the Church of England abolished, and religious radicalism was permitted to flourish. During the course of the wars, Oliver Cromwell emerged as leader of the forces arrayed against the king, but after peace was secured, he discovered the truth of what Charles I had learned at so much cost. He found that Parliament was a very difficult body to deal with. After several attempts to govern with them failed, Cromwell gave up the effort and proceeded to rule alone.

During the era of Puritan domination in England, the nation's rulers attempted to restrict what they regarded as the moral transgressions of their people. In addition to alterations in ecclesiastical doctrine and polity, they expended great effort to make patterns of living more in harmony with those prescribed by God. Attempts were undertaken to eliminate dicing, card playing, bear baiting, cock fighting, drunkenness, whoring, homosexual acts, and a whole host of objectionable activities. One of the best contemporary catalogs of these various transgressions is John White's *The First Century of Scandalous, Malignant Priests*. Although written in 1643, before Parliament actually gained control, the book is a veritable roster of sins commit-

ted by members of the Anglican clergy. The most frequent charge
lodged against clerics of the established religion by White was heresy,
as might be expected, but among behavioral lapses the most offensive
acts were drunkenness and whoremongering. Homosexual conduct
was proscribed and a number of ministers were denounced for it, but
these were relatively minor matters according to the author, who was
much more exercised over heterosexual lusting after neighbors' wives,
rape, and adultery. Nicholas Bloxam, a Suffolk clergyman denounced in the volume, was accused of being a common drunkard,
a swearer, a man who neglected his ecclesiastical duties, and was of
lascivious carriage toward several women. He was additionally accused of being an enticer of others to "that beastly vice," but the
exact nature of the final accusation was only implied to be sodomy.
John Peckham, like his colleague Bloxam, stood accused of numerous crimes ranging from drunkenness to opposing Parliament, and
on to adultry and failure to observe the Lord's Supper. Another charge,
that he engaged in heterosexual sodomy, was a minor matter compared with his serious violations of divine command. Even in the
case of a minister who engaged in homosexual buggery eighteen times
according to testimony, his penchant was mitigated in White's opinion by the minister's expression of horror at fathering bastard children. His other offenses could not be so easily excused. Among the
genuinely serious sins were attempted bestiality, drunkenness, baptiz-
ing an illegitimate child, defending imagery in churches, asserting
sins committed after baptism were imitations rather than corruption,
and calling Christ a bastard. The same tolerant attitude toward
sodomy was still found among Englishmen over a dozen years later,
when Lionel Gatford lamented that a cleric accused of either sodomy
or attempted sodomy was made only to stand in a public place with
a paper in his hat describing the offense while ministers with doctrines hostile to those of men in power were forced out of their livings.[15]

The several Parliamentary and Puritan governments that followed
the abolition of the monarchy were minority governments that retained control by the sword. Under Cromwell's direction, they enforced a code of morality alien to most of the people and violated

many of the rights Englishmen had come to regard as their own by the middle of the seventeenth century. Numerous legislative and administrative errors were made during the period and confusion and anarchy seemed to loom in the future. When Cromwell died in 1658, he was succeeded by his son Richard, a friendly, likable country gentleman. Exercising judgment rare among national leaders in any age, the son realized he lacked his father's abilities to govern. He retired voluntarily, surrendering his almost absolute power to the army, and returned to the country to live out his life as a rural aristocrat free from the burdens of power. With the departure of Richard Cromwell, England was left without a government. One of the nation's ablest leaders, General George Monck, forced the reconvening of Parliament to decide what course to follow. After some initial discussion on the advisability of establishing a republic, the Convention Parliament voted to restore the type of government that appeared most in harmony with the commands of God and the wishes of the people. In 1660 the son of executed King Charles I was invited to return to England to rule as Charles II.

The reaction of Englishmen to the decade of harsh and dreary rule of Puritan righteousness coupled with the character of Charles II meant great changes were about to take place, at least on the upper levels of English society. The new king was a notorious womanizer and seeker of pleasure, and his associates as well as members of the upper administrative and economic levels of the social order began to reflect the values of the new sovereign. Along with the reestablishment of the House of Lords and the Church of England, theaters were opened again, other previously proscribed amusements were revived, elaborate fashions of dress were once again worn by those who could afford them, and the enforced gloom of the previous government was dissipated by the new wave of exuberance. Standards of public piety and carriage demanded by the Puritans were abandoned by many in the reaction to the past, and a new sexual liberalism seemed to appear almost as if it had been ordered into existence by King Charles.

How deeply the new morality pervaded all levels of English society is a question with no clear answer. Puritan attitudes could not be expunged by Parliamentary enactment or by royal decree. Among the middling classes that had provided the opposition to the king and to the Church of England, there is little doubt that strict behavioral norms were retained even though political power was lost. These were not people who would acquiesce in the libertine conduct of the royal court or the Anglican aristocracy. They maintained the strains of morality and piety that had been a part of their lives before the Restoration, and they continued to practice their religion even though it had fallen from official favor. This was still an age when two thousand dissenting ministers, most of whom were from the middle classes, gave up their livings for the sake of conscience just as Anglican priests had done a decade earlier. Neither is there any indication that the licentious norms of behavior so often associated with the reign of Charles II extended much beyond the bounds of London. In the market towns and in thousand of villages that were home to nine of every ten Englishmen in 1660, available evidence indicates there was no revolution in attitudes on sexual matters or on any other subjects. Enough addresses and memorials from obscure corners of the nation exist to establish the presence of substantial sentiment for the return of royal government, but beyond this there is little visible indication of changes in the way Englishmen believed or behaved.

Yet the standards of personal comportment of Charles II did influence the life of the upper classes and those that aped them, and here a new freedom on sexual matters was apparent. This is nowhere more obvious than in Restoration drama. The theaters had been considered anathema during Cromwell's time and were closed by official decree. When drama was again legalized, the new social climate required new plays, and a fresh generation of dramatists was ready to meet the demand. The theater of Shakespeare, Massinger, Middleton, Davenant, and Ben Jonson was no longer the stuff that entertained audiences. Although the classical forms instituted by Jonson were retained by his successors, plays that would have scandalized the courts of Elizabeth, James I, and Charles I became mainstays of the Restoration stage. The comedies of popular writers like George Farquhar, Edward Ravenscoft, and George Ethrege explored love and satirized manners with a boldness that would have shocked Jacobean England.

In the frivolous mood of the London stage under the restored Stuart monarch, one of the most successful productions was William Wycherly's *Country Wife*. The hero of the play, a Mr. Horner, masqueraded as a eunuch thereby gaining admission to situations that enabled him to ply his seductive wiles with considerable success. Such situational drama was much imitated and admired by sophisticated audiences that chuckled in amusement at characters like the unfaithful Mistress Pinchwife whose husband was moved to lament:

> The Gallant treats, presents, and gives the Ball;
> But 'tis the absent Cuckold, pays for all.[16]

The dramatic productions of the widely applauded Thomas Killigrew were similar in direction. Killigrew had been a favorite of Charles I in the years before the civil wars, and at least two of his plays had been staged at the Cockpit before 1643. When war came to England, he fought in the royalist army and later fled to the continent to join the exiled Stuart prince. During the years the theaters were dark and ecclesiastical reform stalked the nation, he remained loyal to the House of Stuart. After the Restoration he was again made a royal favorite. Killigrew lost no opportunity to be revenged on those who had brought suffering to him and to the king. In his first play after the return of Charles II, a 1664 comedy entitled *The Parson's Wedding*, he heaped scorn and abuse on Puritans and their notions of sexual morality. He described the days of Cromwell's rule as a time when "a Bailiff trode the streets with terror, when all the Chains in the City were rusty, but Mr. Sheriffs, when the people knew no evil but the Constable and his Watch."[17] It was a decade of "holy war," he said, with London tradesmen and 'prentice boys gone mad from hearing Puritan doctrine preached by a band of "Russet Levites, Apron-Rogues, with horn hands."[18] Jolly, a gentleman courtier in the play, made words do double duty lampooning the fraudulent piety and sexual hypocrisy of a Puritan scrivener's wife who brought a:

> Black-moore from the holy Land, and
> made him a Brownist; and in pure charity lay with him,
> and was deliver'd of a Mag-Pie; a Pied prophet; which
> when the elect saw, they prophesi'd, if it liv'd, 'twould

> prove a great enemy to their Sect; for the Mid-wife cry'd
> out, 'twas born a Bishop, with Tippet and white-sleeves;
> at which the zealous Mother cri'd, Down with the Idoll;
> so the Mid-wife and she in pure devotion kill'd it.[19]

Restoration audiences enjoyed the mixture of scorn mixed with rol-licking wit, and Killigrew gave them their fill. His fumbling Captain when told fornication was a sin roared in reply that "If it be, would I were the wicked'st man in the company," and in a quick exchange of banter when Mr. Constant spoke of a lady who cured a man of venereal disease three times before she married him, Jolly replied "Yes; and I believe some other member (though then ill affected) pleaded more than his tongue."[20] Surely any Puritan, in the unlikely event he were to hear or read *The Parson's Wedding*, would have been aghast at Lady Love-all, a stallion-hunting widow who told her lover, "I'll swear, I could have hang'd you for that Rape, if I would have follow'd the Law; but I forgave you upon condition you would do so again."[21] Neither were the works of Killigrew or Wycherly atypical. Ravenscroft's *London Cuckolds*, exploring the same themes of infi-delity and seduction, enjoyed the highest favor at court, according to Laureate Colley Cibber, and similar plays by a score of dramatists were well patronized by courtiers, members of the upper classes, and by many ordinary Londoners.[22]

The standard themes of Restoration comedy were derived almost entirely from heterosexual situations, with love, courtship, cases of mistaken identity, indiscretion, faithlessness, intrigue, and infatua-tion the usual fare. There were occasional diversions into homosex-uality although this was done by implication rather than by the pre-sentation of explicitly homosexual characters or situations. Sir John Vanbrugh's *The Relapse; Or Virtue in Danger*, first staged at the Theatre Royal in 1696, was a spoof on the purported homosexual tendencies of William III. The effeminate Lord Foppington of the play was apparently a standard homosexual stereotype with outlandish dress and affectation of speech and manner. He was an enthusiastic pursuer of women, but his interest was pecuniary rather than sexual and, significantly, he was never successful in securing either form of gratification. The same was true of John Crown's Sir Courtly Nice,

a character much in the manner of Lord Foppington. Crown styled
Sir Courtly to convey the implication of homosexuality without making his sexual direction a matter of record. The mincing homosexuals
in other Restoration dramas, like Foppington and Sir Courtly Nice,
were in every case foolish rather than noble, and in plays where minor figures were explicitly homosexual, it was not approved. Such
characters were most often the oafs and bunglers of the cast rather
than the heroic figures. There was little doubt of the sexual preferences of Piracquo in Charles Johnson's *The Successful Pyrate*. He was
the "creature" of Lieutenant De Sale and was accompanied on stage
by Jollyboy, Lesbia, and Sir Gaudy Tulip. Although the play was
first presented in 1713, after the high point of creativity in Restoration theater, the moral thrust of the plot remained the same as in
drama staged in previous years. Tulip and Piracquo, who abandoned
their wives and sailed to a womanless island, realize after their arrival
that they want no part of one another. Heterosexuality, they are
brought to understand, is not as unfortunate a condition as they once
believed, and they return happily to their spouses.[23]

Only John Wilmot, Second Earl of Rochester, wrote a play specifically concerned with homosexuality, but as England's foremost sal-
acious poet, playwright, and wit, Rochester was hardly representative
of any literary group. Exceedingly clever on occasion, his compulsive
scatology and elaboration of the vulgar prevented his work from gaining wide acceptance even in an age where audiences laughed aloud
at characters who joked about excrement and parted company with
the jocular farewell "A fart fill your sail." On more than one occasion the Earl was banished from court by Charles II for exercising
wit on the details of royal adultery or commenting on kingly behavior
as he did in one poem:

> Nor are his high Desires above his Strength;
> His Sceptre and his [pintle] are of a length;
> And She that plays with one, may sway the other,
> And make him little wiser than his Brother.[24]

A 1680 collection of his poetry was so offensive that a reward was
offered for information leading to the apprehension of the printer.[25]

Rochester's homosexual tour de force, *Sodom or the Quintessence of Debauchery*, was "Written for the Royall Company of Whoremasters" sometime before 1680. It is thought to have been performed privately before members of the court, but as a *roman à clef* exposing the vice and corruption of the king and his associates it was far too explicit to be presented to the public or even published in England. The first edition was printed in Antwerp in 1684. In the play, Bolloxinion, the King of Sodom, discovered that buggery with boys and men was a far more pleasurable experience than heterosexual activity. He found his new method of obtaining sexual fulfillment so enjoyable that anal intercourse was decreed for all males, and the king's retainer, Borastus, was appointed "Buggermaster-general" to make sure the sovereign will was carried out. Although *Sodom* treated the themes of onanism, bestiality, premature ejaculation, venereal disease, sexual deprivation, and buggery in a lighthearted fashion, like much of Restoration drama, it was essentially a moral tale. Bolloxinion's decree brought debilitating epidemics to the land, and buggery was denounced at last by the royal physician who explained:

> It doth the procreative End destroy,
> Which nature gave with pleasure to enjoy.
> Please her, and she'll be kind: if you displease,
> She turns into corruption and disease.

Bolloxinion rejected the advice, declaring his devotion to buggery, and heavenly fires descended and destroyed the land.[26]

For Restoration dramatists, homosexuality was an activity with theatrical potential but they did not portray it as an acceptable form of sexual expression. It could be used for social and political commentary when placed in satirical form and those indulging in it were buffoons, fools, fops, or dolts. It was dealt with only by implication or in sub-plots and digressions, and while the treatment was usually frivolous, lighthearted, and often witty, there was always an element of derision. Only Rochester dealt with homosexuality as a main theme, but he treated the subject with satirical condemnation rather than with mockery. As an occasional pederast he could hardly do otherwise. The chief objection to damnation made by Bolloxinion,

Rochester's king of Sodom, was not that he would undergo endless torment in lakes of fire and brimstone but that he would be reunited with his queen and linked with her in Hell for all eternity. Nowhere in Rochester's play or in any other Restoration comedy was there an intimation of the hatred and fear that would characterize the attitudes of later ages toward homosexuality. There was a measure of derision but the feeling that this was an abomination or a crime against nature that "no Christian dare to name" was not to be found.

The dangers of projecting characteristics to a population, group, or nation on the basis of literary evidence alone are well known, and even when the literature of an age is interpreted with compound knowledge of the period's authors, techniques of humor, irony, wit, and other writers' devices, the opportunities for error are manifold. Even with correct analysis of character, theme, and plot, Restoration drama can hardly be considered a mirror for life even of the upper classes in the concluding four decades of the seventeenth century. In the same manner, any spontaneous assumption about attitudes toward homosexuality in England during the reigns of the restored Stuarts made on the basis of work by a small number of dramatists would, without substantiation from additional sources, be entirely unwarranted. Yet some of the relaxed attitude of the theater toward sexual behavior trickled down to ordinary citizens. While play-going was primarily an upper-class diversion, there were many from the lower strata who attended with some frequency, and as Puritan writers regularly pointed out, the examples of easy morality provided by dramatic productions had substantial effect on men too young and too unsophisticated to distinguish between theatrical fancy and reality.[27]

The corrupting influence of the drama on all classes of men had long been an article of faith among dissenting clerics and the artisans, merchants, tradesmen, and laborers who followed them. During the reign of Charles I, William Prynne wrote at length of the pernicious influence of the stage and players on public morality. He charged that theatrical performances instigated and abetted "Love-passions, Lusts, Adulteries, Incests, Rapes, Impostures, Cheates, Conspiracies, Treacheries, Murthers, Thefts, Debates, . . . other abominable vil-

lanies, and . . . Adulterous, and Infernall Heathen-Gods."[28] Among
the many vices he cataloged was the acting of female parts by men
and boys. Women were not permitted on the stage in the early decades of the seventeenth century, and this resulted in the encouragement of transvestism among players, both during and after performances. Prynne denounced the practice of males donning female
garb for any purpose. He explained such activities were disgusting,
revolting, and repugnant, counter to the judgments of both pagan
and Christian scholars from earliest recorded history, and contrary to
the revealed will of God. It was a wickedness, Prynne explained, of
"which my Inke is not blacke enough to discypher."[29] In addition,
men donning the raiment of women encouraged the practice of
sodomy, he charged. Not only did "Players and Play-haunters in their
secret conclaves play the Sodomites," but their effeminate manner
and their example encouraged it among the general population.[30] In
proper Puritan fashion, Prynne did not ignore the opportunity to denounce sodomy in his excoriation of transvestism among players, and
he left no doubt that he considered it lewd, unnatural, abominable,
and worse than adultery. But in his condemnation he did not venture
too far beyond that point. He was willing to admit that the lives of
players were characterized by "more than Sodomiticall uncleanness,"
and in his denunciation of the theater, a tirade running over one
thousand pages, the few paragraphs labeling sodomy as one of the
evil results of men dressing as women indicated he was not overly
concerned with it, less concerned with sodomy at any rate than with
the other host of pernicious practices encouraged by actors and the
stage.[31]

Prynne's book, *Histrio-Mastix*, was not intended to persuade the
general reader of the existence of the corruptions it cataloged. It was
written for the tightly organized and highly literate leadership of the
Puritan movement, but the author made it clear to his zealous associates that the dangers of the theater, the pre-Restoration theater in
this case, were visited not only on the upper classes but on Englishmen of every station. This was an institution, he argued, that would
corrupt not simply through the downward percolation of its evils but
by offering its vile precepts and damnable examples to all. By the end

of the century, when the theaters had reopened and Restoration plays regularly delighted audiences with sexual escapades, there were still some who continued to denounce the stage. In a 1706 tract aimed more for the general reader than for an exclusive brotherhood of ecclesiastical reformers, the sins of the drama were carefully listed. Although the author mentioned Sodom in his litany, he did not feel compelled to include buggery or sodomy among the sins generated by the theater. In the same period, presentments made against the new playhouse in Bristol failed to list homosexuality as one of the vices encouraged by plays or playgoers. Another early eighteenth-century author, John Dennis, explained that while sodomy was rampant and ever-increasing in England, the theater was not to blame. Stage plays encouraged heterosexual rather than homosexual practices, he argued.[32]

In assessing English attitudes toward sodomy during the Restoration and after, it is obvious that the preponderant mass of material was generated by the upper classes, members of status levels ranging from wealthy merchants up to and including members of the court. It was these people who kept diaries, frequented the bawdy performances of Restoration comedies, read Rochester's crudely explicit verse, and gossiped about the promiscuity of their king, his duchesses, actresses, and concubines. But these people were only a small segment of society. The mass of Englishmen had no connection with the court, were not influenced by continental manners, had never heard of Rochester's poetry or play, and were probably unaware of the shifting sexual alliances in Whitehall Palace.

Despite the difficulties in discerning attitudes of those below the wealthy and the nobility, considerable evidence survives to illuminate the manners, moral standards, and opinions of members of England's middling classes. Probably the most articulate commentator on the nation's social life, at least in London, was Samuel Pepys. As a high official in the Navy, Pepys was close to the court and in public reflected the attitudes of the highest social strata. At the same time, he was also a man risen from a lower social station by dint of ability and constant application to his tasks, and while outwardly he accepted the licentiousness of the royal court, his shorthand diary was filled with expressions of opinion that characterized the middle levels of English society from which he had risen. Pepys regularly wrote with disparagement in the private pages of his diary of the sin and promiscuity he observed among his betters. He commented approvingly of a man he saw making public penance in church for engaging in sexual misconduct, and although he himself frequently indulged in illicit sexual encounters, he was racked with guilt over his indiscretions.[33] He agonized at the thought that any word of his infidelities might reach his wife, and he was driven almost to distraction at one point when he suspected he might be wearing a set of cuckhold's horns like those he had fastened on several others. To make certain that no prying spouse or snooping servant girl would discover his sexual encounters, he took the precaution of recording them in his diary using shorthand in languages other than English, evidently persuaded that foreign words recorded in secret writing would prevent anyone from learning his deeds.

While Pepys did not approve of fornication or adultery, at least in principle, he was no more hostile to sodomy than any other manner of proscribed sexual activity. In a short discussion of political opposition to the clerical hierarchy he repeated the story of the Bishop of Rochester who was accused of "being given to boys and of his putting his hand into a gentleman (who now comes to bear evidence against him) his codpiece while they were at table together."[34] The account was narrated without horror, revulsion, or loathing. Pepys closed the discussion by musing on whether it was possible that similar accusations might be leveled against other ranking clerics. Neither did the allegations have any effect on the Bishop's career. Although he was personally distressed by the circulation of this story and another in which he was said to have engaged a nobleman in sexual contact, he was later made Archbishop of York. At another point in his diary, Pepys included an account of the trial of Sir Charles Sedley, accused of "coming in open day into the Balcone and showed his nakedness—acting all the postures of lust and buggery that could be imagined . . . a thousand people standing underneath to see and hear him." Sedley also abused scripture, preached a heretical sermon, offered an aphrodisiac for sale, and then took "a glass of wine and washed his prick in it and then drank it off; and then took another and drank the King's health."[35] Pepys was no more agitated over the acting out of a posture of buggery than any other part of the performance, and although he wrote that the judges who heard the case were exceedingly perturbed over the display conducted from the balcony of "Oxford Kates," he noted that the bench was equally displeased with the actions of Lord Buckhurst, one of Sedley's associates and companions in frolic who evidently encouraged the public display.[36]

Pepys did comment that his two closest associates, Sir Joseph Mennes and William Batten, had both told him buggery was becoming as common in England as it was in Italy and that London pages were known frequently "to complain of their masters for it." His reaction to the information was perplexity rather than outrage or indignation. He only mused, "But blessed be God, I do not to this day know what is the meaning of this sin, nor which is the agent nor which the patient."[37] Neither was he struck with horror when a family maid informed him that one of his servants, a lad he regarded highly, was "a rogue . . . and strange things he hath been found guilty of, not fit to name." Pepys only wrote that he was "vexed" by such conduct, hardly a severe condemnation from a man who recorded the gamut of powerful human emotions in his diary.[38]

If the reaction of Samuel Pepys to incidents of sodomy was irritation and confusion, the response of his acquaintance, John Evelyn, offers even more convincing evidence that homosexuality was not considered an aberration of monstrous proportions. Evelyn, unlike Pepys, was deeply religious, serious in the extreme, depressed by the moral standards of the Restoration, and not one to vacillate on matters of good and evil. He was a man with considerable capacity for indignation, yet on the matter of sodomy his diary records only sorrow for the accused. He avoided writing the terms buggery or sodomy, preferring to style the offense "a Vice . . . which need not be nam'd," but he added that the accused Lord Stafford, "was not a man belov'd, Especialy of his owne family," and had surely repented his sin.[39]

Judicial authorities in seventeenth-century England did not consider sex crimes minor matters. Men were regularly executed for rape, an act regarded with the same seriousness as other capital crimes of murder, burglary, horse stealing, clipping and coining. So serious was the offense, that on one occasion, capital punishment was exacted despite the fact the victim was a Quaker. Another rapist was made to pay for his crime even after death. His body was anatomized after execution in 1718. Men who molested young girls were treated in a similar fashion. The beadle of Christ's Hospital was convicted of "ravishing" a child of twelve, and although there is no record of his particular punishment, the bringing of an official to account for such an act is indicative of its seriousness. The usual punishment for the offense was death. One John West was fined 20 marks and forced to provide bond for five years good behavior only for toying and tickling the private parts of ten-year-old Mary Bowden. Nor were minor sex offenses ignored in the age of Charles II. A lady "remarkable for her fine Face, Shape, and Air, was taken in a very lewd Posture with a Hackney-Coachman, in the Hay-Market" and the authorities who witnessed the scene were angered rather than amused. She was arrested and jailed for her conduct. An Italian named Bernardi was committed to the Gatehouse after being discovered with two cartloads of obscene cards, books and pictures in his possession. The final disposition of the case has not survived, but documents preserved indicate the precise nature of the offense and a substantial degree of outrage on the part of officials. Among other activities, the accused caused to be painted "fasciculum pictarum cartarum *anglice* packe of cards per eundum fasciculum pictarum cartarum representans diversas. . . . obscenas posturas et figuras." A cause for greater alarm than pornography or scurrilous printed matter was the news in London that a sadist was on the loose in 1681. "Whipping Tom" severely spanked the hindquarters of several female Londoners before he and another man were finally apprehended. Unfortunately there is no record of their trial, but while at large the pair induced considerably anxiety and vocal demands that they be brought to account.[40]

The Restoration attitude toward sodomy is nowhere more apparent than in the punishments meted out by English quarter sessions courts. Much of the record of criminal penalties during the period was preserved by Narcissus Luttrell in his monumental *Brief Historical Relation of State Affairs from 1678 to 1714.* Laconic by nature, any expression of outrage against acts of sodomy would not normally come from Luttrell no matter what his opinion on the subject might have been, but in the roster of crimes and punishments kept with precision over four decades he commonly listed offenses from the most serious in descending order to the most minor. His notice for March 4, 1697 is a typical entry. "The sessions for London and Middlesex began at the Old Baily on the 24th of last month, . . . where several criminals were tryed; 13 received sentence of death, 20 were burnt in the hand, 6 ordered to be whipt, 6 ordered into his majesties service, and 8 fined, and some of them to stand in the pillory."[41] Over the years, the sequence of punishment hardly varied although the pillory was often more commonly used then branding.[42] There was a short period when the authorities experimented with branding on the face rather than on the hand, but this was discontinued because it rendered offenders unemployable, thereby increasing recidivism.[43] The only observable trend in the imposition of punishment was a desire to make sentencing to the pillory more opprobrius by including fines as part of the sentences. Murder, treason, highway robbery, piracy, burglary, counterfeiting, clipping small amounts from gold or silver coins, and rape were the crimes that most often gained death sentences for their perpetrators. Burning on the cheek or hand was the usual penalty for minor felonies such as shoplifting; persons convicted of petty larceny were customarily whipped. Combinations of fines and time in the pillory were usual for a host of misdemeanors ranging from the publication of libellous writings, perjury, subornation, theft of less than ten pence, and speaking against the government, to causing a commotion like that which occurred when "Bish the trooper . . . rode thro' the citty sayeing king William was dead."[44] He was fined 100 marks and ordered to stand three times in the pillory. Multiple appearances in the pillory were often pronounced for a single crime, and sometimes a convicted criminal was forced to stand pilloried at several different locations on different days to allow large numbers of citizens to learn of the crime, witness the penalty, and profit by the example of justice done. The fines accompanying sentences to the pillory varied in amount. They were not particularly severe for minor offenses, but in cases where the criminal was a person of means or when there were political ramifications to the crime, the levy could be very large. A parson at Northampton was once convicted of saying that William and Mary were not lawful rulers of England, denouncing Parliament, and praying for the exiled King James II, his queen, and their son. He was fined £200, spent a time in the pillory, and was commanded to produce sureties for a year's good behavior. At the same time one Nathaniel Reading was convicted of subornation, having stifled evidence in the Popish Plot. The highly charged atmosphere surrounding the whole matter meant Reading was to receive a comparatively severe sentence. He was fined £1,000, sentenced to a year in jail, and committed to stand one hour in the palace yard pillory at Westminister.[45]

The least severe of all punishments available to English judges, sentencing to the pillory, was that most often prescribed for men convicted of sodomy even though the crime according to law could be punished by hanging. Executions for sodomy in Restoration England may not have occurred, and even those who stood in the pillory were sentenced most often for attempted sodomy rather than for committing the act. This may have been part due to the ease of obtaining convictions for attempted sodomy, at least when compared to the difficulties in procuring sufficient witnesses for a guilty verdict in a regular sodomy case. But whatever the reason, the lack of prosecutions and the reduced charges indicate there was no cadre of zealous officials warring against homosexual acts in the England of the latter Stuarts. Newspaper accounts contain more notices of arrests for sodomy than for convictions, indicating only limited enthusiasm for bringing such cases to trial. A 1717 article gives ample evidence that insufficient interest, discreet payments, and the difficulty of obtaining convictions all contributed to the relatively small number of prosecutions. Reporting the arrest of a cleric for committing sodomy with an apprentice and another young man, *Applebee's Original Weekly Journal* noted the case was "buried in Oblivion" either because of the effects of money or the lack of evidence.[46] The only case where the journal seemed to think the perpetrators of a similar crime would "meet with their Deserts" involved a linen draper and an Irishman who were apprehended in the act, indicating the presence of a non-participating witness who could provide proof for the court. In another incident involving the same subject, *Applebee's* reported on a man lodging the night at an ale house who was awakened by a person slipping into his bed and attempting to commit sodomy with him. The intended victim grabbed his pistols and fired them into the air. The house was awakened by the shots, and the accused buggerer was captured and taken to jail. The newspaper account of the incident was not an irate denunciation of homosexual practices. It was written in a tone of mild amusement, expressing more surprise at what happened than alarm over the nature of the event. The writer of the article did not castigate the offender in any way, although he could not avoid mentioning the "Impudence of [the] Fellow." [47]

The one occasion during the Restoration period when sodomy was forced into the public cognizance was in connection with a political dispute, the uproar created by the Popish Plot. The details of the Plot did not involve homosexual manifestations, but the political and religious character of Restoration England were sufficient to produce panic on a national scale at the revelation of an alleged Catholic attempt to assassinate the king, install a Popish successor, and return Britain to the Roman fold. To understand properly the environment in which the Plot was concocted and sold to the nation, it must be remembered that the years 1678 to 1681 were a time of extreme political instability. The king had, within that short span of years, called and dissolved two Parliaments, the third and fourth of his reign. In each of these Parliaments, Commons had passed an exclusion bill prohibiting succession by the Duke of York, the Catholic younger brother of Charles II, but it still appeared to many that the Duke would ultimately inherit the throne despite the clear wishes of Parliament and the citizenry. This, coupled with an increased fear of "poppery" and the certainty that the Jesuits were the world's premier intriguers, made England ready to believe the existence of the Popish Plot when Titus Oates and his cohorts told their tale of proposed assassination and usurpation. Men of all stations were everywhere compelled to take sides on matters of state which had previously been beyond their realm of interest or concern, and the initial prejudice against a popish successor was transformed into an ideology that served as the basis for the beginning of the Whig party and the subsequent evolution of English party politics. No class of Englishman was immune to the infectious hysteria engendered by the charges. From the London mobs, famous for the passion with which they regularly burned effigies of the Pope, to the gentry who feared a loss of their lands if the papists were to gain control, men driven by hatred and trembling with fear became less discerning in what they would accept as truth.

Jesuits, papists, and accused papists were marched to the gallows, convicted on the flimsiest of evidence of murder, treason, and a host of additional crimes. The Catholic Lords, Arundel, Powis, Belasyse, Stafford, and Danby, were committed to the Tower, and the panic sweeping the nation demanded that even those only peripherally linked to the plot be punished with utmost severity. A sentence in the pillory without additional measures was inadequate for anyone associated with such nefarious schemes. John Giles, convicted of assaulting a magistrate known to be harsh on Catholics, was sentenced to stand in the pillory in Lincoln's Inn Fields, at the Maypole in the Strand, and in Holborn near Grey's Inn. In addition, during the time in the pillory, he was to wear a sign signifying his crime, pay a £500 fine, continue in prison until it was paid, and provide bond for good behavior for life. The sentence itself was only part of the punishment. Those sentencing Giles knew well that in the climate of anti-Catholic hysteria he would be lucky to be taken from the pillory alive after the abuse he would sustain from the mob.[48]

Another to suffer greviously as a result of the wave of anti-Catholicism sweeping the land was a Mrs. Cellier who had the misfortune of being the woman friend of Thomas Dangerfield, an associate of Titus Oates. Dangerfield claimed to have discovered a presbyterian plot, the evidence having been found under a meal tub belonging to Mrs. Cellier. The discoveries, which implicated both Lord Halifax and the Earl of Essex, appeared to be a Catholic counter-move, but Dangerfield was playing the role of *agent provocateur*. He soon accused several leading Catholics of arranging the plot to counter anti-

Catholic moves. Cellier, evidently involved in the first half of the plot but unaware of the second half, was handled severely for her anti-protestantism. She was sentenced to stand in the pillory at three places, the Maypole in the Strand, Covent Garden, and at Charing Cross. The documents found under the tub were to be burned before her by the common hangman, and she was fined £1,000, sentenced to remain in prison until it was paid, and required to give security for good behavior during her lifetime.[49]

The level of excitement generated by the Popish Plot could not be sustained indefinitely among the populace, and despite the increasing crescendo produced by charges of murder, treason, perjury, subornation, heresy, anti- and pro-Catholicism, and almost every other imaginable civil or political offense, enthusiasm for the anti-Catholic persecutions and for the discoveries of plotters began to diminish. To counter declining interest, another crime was added to the previous allegations. The charge of sodomy was introduced into the panoply of accusations, and men on both sides of the dispute were named as sodomites. Titus Oates, the Duke of Buckingham, Lord Stafford, and others were denounced for engaging in proscribed sexual practices, but of the many crimes included in the charges and countercharges, sodomy never became a major matter. Numerous pamphlets were written on the accusations, but when Oates went to press to clear himself of the charges leveled against him, his rebuttal to the accusations of sexual misconduct was only a small part of the defense. It was the result of political excesses that destroyed Oates, not rumors of his personal conduct, and when Stafford was executed, he died for allegedly plotting to kill the king, not because he had been charged with sodomy.[50]

The accusations of sodomy were recognized as specious by many who accepted without question the equally specious charges of murder and treason made by the plotters, and most often it was the accusers rather than the accused sodomites who suffered.[51] In the plot hatched by Thomas Dangerfield, a Captain Thomas Blood and several associates were charged with falsely accusing the Duke of Buckingham of engaging in anal intercourse. They alleged he forceably assaulted one Sarah Harwood, entering "both her Privities, as far as he could go, stop'd her Breath . . . then sent her away;" and later arranged to have her murdered. Buckingham easily cleared himself of the charge of sodomy with Miss Harwood and several others, and at least two of his accusers, Philip le Marr and Frances Loveland, his mother, were convicted of *scandalum magnatum* and fined the awesome sum of £30,000.[52] In the anonymous pamphlet detailing the charges made against the strongly Protestant Duke, there were accusations of various crimes. Murder, conspiracy, perjury, rape, bribery, subornation, treason, and sodomy were all included, but of these sodomy was the least significant of the lot. It received little attention from the author or authors of the pamphlet, none of whom were horrified by buggery or even particularly upset by it. It was one of the many crimes mentioned, but they were much more concerned with murder, bribery, perjury, and general duplicity than with the actual act supposedly committed upon the body of Sarah Harwood.

With the end of the uproar over the Popish Plot, accusations of sodomy disappeared from English politics, and it was only for a brief moment in 1699 that homosexuality again became a subject of considerable popular concern when the existence of a large network of homosexuals became public knowledge. The details of the business were not made clear in the resulting exposé. Much of the activity seemed to be centered at Windsor, but even this is uncertain. The only facts of the case that have survived are that a Captain Rigby, the organizer of the ring, was convicted of attempted sodomy and sentenced to stand three times in the pillory, fined £1,000, confined to prison for a year after the payment of the fine, and forced to provide sureties of good behavior for seven years. The punishment only for attempting sodomy rather than committing it was unusually severe, indicating there were other circumstances that have not survived in the historical record.[53] The number of men involved may have created sufficient alarm to force a harsh sentence for a minor crime, but it is also possible that more than fear at the discovery of widespread homosexuality was responsible. In 1699, rumors of the close relationship between William III and Arnold Joose van Kepple, first Earl of Albemarle were being circulated widely, especially by Jacobites anxious to establish the fact of the king's residence at the "chateau de derrière," as it was styled by one wag.[54] William ignored these rumors just as he had always ignored the tales of his purported homosexuality. He did issue a proclamation for preventing and punishing profaneness particularly "in such who are Imployed near Our Royal Person," but it was similar to a proclamation issued two years earlier in 1697. In any case, specific crimes were not enumerated in either document, and it is only from the king's timing that any inference can be made about the extent of the homosexual ring. William III issued his proclamation the very week that the unfortunate Rigby stood in the pillory.[55]

The enormity of the crimes committed by Rigby and his associates did inspire one righteous Englishman to publish a new edition of the 1631 trial of Lord Audley to provide a ready example of the depravity all men should avoid. In the preface to the 1699 account of Audley's trial, the patron of the edition complained of the rampancy of sex crime generally, citing the frequency of rape, child molestation and the "Sin being now Translated from the Sadomitical Original, or from the Turkish and Italian Copies into English." In his denunciation of the enumerated practices, the author was only slightly more exercised over buggery than heterosexual vices. The best clue to his personality is found in his denunciation of non-sexual offenses. Evidently a fastidious individual, the patron denounced not only rape, pederasty, and sodomy, but complained of men "that ne'er could reach above the Rank of a Dung-hill raker," attempting to seduce ladies of "the Best Quality," and he added later that "You all know that Ri-by's other Heinous Crimes was Accompanied with Horrid Blasphemy."[56] The tiny tempest created by the discovery of a homosexual network lasted only briefly before sodomy again became simply another crime. Perhaps the only horror that remained was not of sodomy but of perjured accusations of the crime. In 1707, 25 years after the Popish Plot and eight years after Rigby stood in the pillory, two men were whipped from Temple Bar to Charing Cross, a long distance to travel under the lash, for making a false charge of sodomy.[57]

The popular interest in homosexual activity encouraged by the Popish Plot and the Rigby case did not produce a wave of revulsion or hostility toward sodomy. This is nowhere more apparent than in the work of John Bunyan, one of the most notable Puritan authors of the Restoration and a man deeply conscious of moral transgression. In

his writings he provided what was probably an accurate indication of
the view of sodomy held by many ordinary Englishmen in the latter
half of the seventeenth century. Bunyan was the son of a Bedford
tinsmith, but unlike Samuel Pepys, who rose from humble beginnings to attain wealth and power, he remained a member of the
meaner segment of society all his life. Bunyan was trained in his
father's trade, joined the Parliamentary army as a common soldier at
the age of seventeen, and was repeatedly imprisoned for his religious
views. The concluding years of his life were spent as an itinerant
preacher. He died in 1688. As a religious dissenter, Bunyan was especially sensitive to obvious breaches of divine commandment. Murder, theft, adultery, sacrilege, and blasphemy were all well-known to
him and to his contemporary preaching tinkers, blacksmiths, and
tradesmen. They were ordinary men, although a cut above the London mob, and they preached to ordinary people, sharing, and min-
gling perceptions with their audiences. Bunyan spoke simply in an
allegorical style that appealed to his hearers and aided them to understand his message. His *Pilgrim's Progress* was instantly popular when
published in 1678, and Part II, which appeared in 1684, was received
with similar enthusiasm by a public that knew much of Matthew,
Mark, Luke, and John but nothing of Killigrew, Wycherly, or Ravenscroft. They read the work of this "Mechanick Preacher" by the
tens of thousands, and this was so because he believed and wrote
what they believed and hoped desperately to hear in a time when
all seemed doomed for the dissenters' cause. In the second section of
the work, Bunyan commented in his unpretentious way on the wide
audience he had gained.

> Fright not thyself, my book, for such bugbears
> Are nothing else but ground for groundless fears.
> My pilgrim's book has travelled sea and land,
> Yet could I never come to understand
> That it was slighted or turned out-of-door
> By any kingdom, were they rich or poor.
> . . . . . .
>
> Yet more. So comely doth my pilgrim walk
> That of him thousands daily sing and talk.
> If you draw nearer home, it will appear
> My pilgrim knows no ground of shame or fear;

City and country will him entertain,
With welcome, pilgrim. Yea, they can't refrain
From smiling if my pilgrim be but by
Or shows his head in any company.[58]

Bunyan's pilgrim encountered every conceivable evil, from the "Slough of Despond" through "Vanity Fair" and on to "Doubting Castle" during his progress toward the "Celestial City." Sin, irresolution, pride, sophistication, pleasure, and even popery tempted Christian to abandon his quest and wallow in earthly delight. In examining the whole catalog of evils, however, the sin of Sodom looms neither particularly large or particularly repugnant either to Bunyan or to his pilgrim. There is no emphasis on sexual misconduct anywhere in the work. All crimes of physical passion are usually combined together in allegorical figures. Mr. Love-lust and Mr. Live-loose appear as jurymen in the trial of Faithful, Christian's companion on the journey to paradise. Both vote to condemn the accused, Mr. Love-lust commenting, "I could never endure him," and Mr. Live-loose adding that the presence of Faithful would be unbearable for "he would always be condemning my way."[59] The men of Sodom "were sinners exceedingly," Bunyan admitted, but when Christian and Hopeful reached Sodom on the road to salvation, their concern was much more with the fate of Lot's wife than with the cause of divine judgment on the city. Christian mentioned briefly God's visiting a pleasant city with destruction because its inhabitants sinned "despite of such examples that are set continually before them to caution them to the contrary," and this comment, rather than any specific acts of defiance, was what concerned Hopeful. "Doubtless thou hast said the truth," he told Christian, "but what a mercy is it, that neither thou, but especially I, am not made myself, this [defiant] example. This ministereth occasion to us thank God, to fear before him, and always to remember Lot's wife."[60]

The same theme was expressed again by Bunyan when Christiana, the wife of Christian, reached the same spot on her journey to salvation. Standing at the pillar of salt that stood near Sodom, she marveled only "that men of that knowledge and ripeness of wit . . . should be so blinded as to turn aside here."[61]

By the time of Bunyan's death, broadsides and short pamphlets were becoming some of the most widely read forms of literature produced for ordinary Englishmen. Crimes of violence and treasonous plots were common subjects of the penny sheets, but on the rare occasions when they dealt specifically with sodomy it was clear they regarded it as a minor offense within the panoply of evil deeds. A *Full and True Account of a Dreadful Fire that Lately Broke Out in the Pope's Breeches,* a six-page effort obviously directed to a mass audience, was an anti-clerical manifesto rather than an attack on anal intercourse, but the treatment of sodomy in the poem indicated that the "crime which no Christian dare to name" indeed could be named and discussed, at least in a humorous vein. The ballad tells the story of an English female visiting Rome who happened to catch the Pope's fancy. Raging with passion, his Holiness summoned her to his chamber. The seduction proceeded apace until the Pope, a devotee of sodomitical practice with his fellow clerics rather than a practitioner of heterosexual love, inadvertently revealed the nature of his past sexual experience. In the words of the woman about to be debauched:

> With that, O Holy Sir, cry'd She
> I doubt you've pitch'd too low your key:
> I'll pitch it for ye, if you please,
> And then you may unlock at Ease.
> Then strait She did it with a Touch,
> His Holiness too thank'd her much,
> And withal this excuse did make,
> In the behalf of his Mistake.

The Pope said he rarely used his key to open the "fore-gate," but then revealed it was more likely he had never used it for that purpose. Describing his entry, he cried out in amazement:

> The Key goes in most wondrous easy,
> What is the Key-hole broke, or Greasy?
> Hah! it turns round not very hard,
> I fear your Lock has ne'er a Ward.

The facility with which he could achieve vaginal penetration was only the first surprise for the prelate. Three days after his English

lover had departed, the papal "Pintle Smith" had to be summoned
to cure the malady His Holiness had contracted. The experience was
beneficial for the Pope, teaching him the folly of carnal conversation
with women.

> As soon as e're the Pope grew well,
> He curst poor T- - -s by Book and Bell,
> and vow'd to keep, in spight of Whores,
> His key for to unlock back Doors.[62]

A penman writing for the same market but having fun at the English clergy's expense, humorously denounced those who scoffed at
God's ministers, labeling them worse than Sodomites. To remind
such villains of the draconian nature of the punishments that awaited
them he added:

> Forty two Children were destroyed all,
> That only did God's Prophet Bald-head call.[63]

Another purveyor of broadside doggerel used sodomy in an attack on
a member of his own versifying brotherhood. Asserting the subject of
his lines was better suited to buggery than poetry, he advised him to:

> Forsake thy Muse, Jack; take a School; 'tis better
> To Flogg Boys Arses, then pay Scores with Meeter.
> As once you in a merry Frollick told one,
> A young Bum-fiddle's better than an old one.[64]

The occasional use of sodomy in a humorous fashion by broadside
authors did not indicate they or their readers regarded all sex offenses
lightly. During the same period anal intercourse produced chuckles
for readers who paid their pennies, other broadsides lauded a man
who beat his wife with a cane for infidelity and told of Sir John
Johnston's execution at Tyburn for rape and possibly child molestation. In other literature written for the lower levels of English society
heterosexual offenses were treated with a notable lack of lighthearted-
edness. In a book of moral fables intended for a wide audience of
ordinary folk, readers learned that the place where a Major Weir
committed incest "remained always bare without Grass," and in
another account of Italian heterosexual indiscretions, the English au-

thor described in detail the sad fates of the sinners. Breasts torn off with red-hot pincers, lovers broken on the wheel, burnings alive, strangling, and death were only some of the punishments meted out. The cases included in the book did not take place in England, but the author made it clear in his exemplary accounts aimed at unsophisticated readers that similar events if similarly punished in England might aid in advancing God's cause.[65]

Another incident in the early years of the reign of George I provides an additional example of lower-class attitudes toward sodomy. On a July day in 1719, William Holdbrook was pilloried at Bloomsbury market for attempting to bugger Thomas Pendrill. *Applebee's* reported that "the Mob had certainly Murdered him could they have got him in their Power; for a Hackney Coach was tore to pieces that took him up to carry him to Newgate."[66] If the story was accurate it indicates at first perusal that the mob was seriously offended by Holdbrook's deed. This, however, need not have been the case. The mobs that congregated in London were a fierce and volatile lot, prone to violence on public holidays and popular anniversaries, or as the result of genuine or imagined grievances, and on occasions when no particular cause was discernible. They could assemble in numbers ranging from a few hundred for a minor matter to almost a quarter of a million for a pope-burning ceremony on the anniversary of Elizabeth's accession. The trained bands of London and surrounding municipalities were kept ready to restrain the mob's worst excesses, and there was often uncertainty over whether the civil authorities would be able to prevent widespread destruction.[67] One of the most popular amusements for the rabble was witnessing the administration of justice, and public hangings, floggings, or the like always attracted a crowd. The audience would hoot, jeer, and heap denunciations on the criminals undergoing punishment, and although viewing men confined to the pillory was hardly as spectacular as a hanging or an occasional drawing and quartering, those who passed by an occupied pillory often stopped to offer jibes, throw stones, or injure the hapless miscreant in cruel or brutal fashion. Persons confined to the pillory could sometimes escape abuse and physical danger if they had sufficient friends to protect them as they served their sentence. Benjamin

Harris stood in the pillory near the old Exchange for printing a sedi-
tious libel, but "he and his party hollowed and whooped, and would
permitt nothing to be thrown at him."[68] This type of protection was
usually provided to those sentenced on political charges, since it was
most likely that they would have ideologically committed associates
to defend them. In the case of a man convicted of sodomy it was not
likely a host of friends would be present to protect him as he stood
defenseless. Even then, in the account of William Holdbrook's stay
in the pillory reported in *Applebee's*, there is every indication that the
tormentors were more entertained than enraged by the would-be
sodomite. According to the story, he was pelted "in a most miserable
Manner, with rotten Eggs and Cucumbers," hardly projectiles that
would be chosen by a mob determined to maim or kill. Supporting
evidence is offered by Randolph Trumbach, whose analysis of increasingly hostile English reactions to homosexuality in the eighteenth century is one of the most comprehensive available. He points
out that in an earlier era Stuart kings were able to shield homosexual
behavior, and it was only King William III, a monarch with a pre-
carious hold on the throne during the first years he ruled, who had
to be circumspect in this matter. More importantly, Trumbach explains, it was not until the 1720s that the Society for the Reformation
of Manners made a public outcry against what was by then a large,
conspicuous, and well-organized homosexual subculture in London.[69]

The lack of animosity toward sodomites is also evidenced by the
fragmentary record in one of the rare quarter sessions proceedings
against an individual accused of homosexual acts. The only surviving
documents of the case are depositions sworn by men either involved
with the accused George Dowdeny or who had rejected his advances
at one time or another. The precise reasons for bringing Dowdeny to
public account in 1622 are not clear, but his penchant for buggery
was of long standing, according to testimony. One male deponent
recalled that he was raped by the defendant fourteen years earlier.
Two of the three depositions mention excessively enthusiastic importuning by the accused during the months before the case was brought
to court, indicating his homosexual preferences may have become

too frequent and conspicuous to ignore. There is also an indication that one of his objects of seduction was a lad. Throughout the testimony, there was little expression of anger or revulsion at any of Dowdeny's homosexual acts or attempts. The only moment of stark terror recoverable from the written record comes from the statement of Walter Wiseman. Recalling an incident from the preceding year, Wiseman told how the previous Christmastime Dowdeny made preparations to engage in bestiality with the mare of one William Checkenten. On being appraised of the intention, Wiseman was seized with fear that even discussion of the topic was sufficient to send them both to the gallows, and he immediately fled from the stable where the event was about to take place. The final disposition of the case has not survived, but the available testimony makes it apparent that even for ordinary Englishmen, it required more than simple sodomy to create legal difficulties. Dowdeny was probably a nuisance with his attempted seductions, a pederast, had an eye for a well-turned equine ankle, or any combination of the three. The sworn depositions indicate that of all his offenses, bestiality was considered far more serious than his attempted or actual buggery, masturbations, and occasional exhibitionism.[70]

The same lack of hostility toward homosexuality exhibited by Englishmen from the middle and lower levels of society can be found in the actions taken by English colonists against accused sodomites. In North America, there were no residents from the upper classes and the nobility. Except for a member of the gentry like John Winthrop here and there, colonials were generally the products of families engaged in farming or skilled trades. They lacked wealth, had little formal education, and exhibited none of the sophistication or urbanity common among even prosperous tradesmen in London and in large port towns. When forced to deal with homosexuality, there was none of the humor or bravado found among the courtiers and their associates; there was instead a reluctance to act and when action was taken it was accompanied with utmost compassion. In Windsor, Connecticut, where heterosexual activities contrary to local standards of morality were severely punished, a homosexual was brought to trial in 1677, but only when a formal complaint was made. Nicholas

Sension was charged with sodomizing one Nathaniel Pond. Trial testimony revealed Sension's penchant for sexual relations with young men had been common knowledge in Windsor for years. His first known attempt to obtain a male partner for a homosexual act took place over three decades earlier, and in the intervening years no formal actions had been taken against him despite his repeated importuning. Exactly why charges were preferred in 1677 is not certain, but it is possible that the man who made the complaint, one of Sension's former servants, was merely taking an opportunity to create problems for his ex-master. Nathaniel Pond, Sension's alleged partner, had been killed in King Philip's War and so could not testify. A more likely reason for the trial, however, was that the accused's solicitations were becoming so frequent they could not be ignored. Whatever the cause of Sension's being brought to court, he was tried, convicted, and given an especially light penalty. He was forced only to put up his estate as bond for good behavior. The biblical proscriptions against homosexual acts had not created fear or loathing among the citizens of Puritan Windsor. They ignored the foible of their townsman as long as possible, and when they were forced to take cognizance of his behavior, they did it in a gentle manner, seeking to aid him in avoiding future temptation rather than to punish him for past offenses.[71]

The ordinary Englishmen of Plymouth Colony, like the inhabitants of Windsor, were not particularly horrified by sex crimes of either heterosexual or homosexual types. Severe punishments were specified in their laws for sexual transgressions, but they were not inflicted on the guilty parties. Fornication and adultery were most frequently punished by fines or whippings. Sodomy was similarly punished with the lash and occasional banishment. One offender was branded on the shoulder, but even in cases involving recidivism, the death penalty was never imposed.[72] The only man executed for sodomy in New England during the middle years of the seventeenth century was one Plain of Guilford, in the exceedingly conservative New Haven colony, but even in this single case there was reluctance to send a man to his death for homosexual offenses. The governor of the colony wrote asking for the advice of the governor and magistrates of Massachusetts Bay, explaining that the accused had:

committed sodomy with two persons in England, and that he had corrupted a great part of the youth of Guilford by masturbations, which he had committed, and provoked others to the like above a hundred times.[73]

The Bay Colony magistrates and elders who considered the case recommended execution, and Plain died for his crime. In his journal, John Winthrop, the Massachusetts governor, indicated more was involved in deciding on the penalty than sodomy or masturbation. He noted that in addition to his sexual practices, Plain "did insinuate seeds of atheism, questioning whether there were a God, etc. . . . And indeed it was horrendum facinus, and he a monster in human shape, exceeding all human rules and examples that ever had been heard of, and it tended to the frustrating of the ordinance of marriage and the hindering the generation of mankind."[74]

The only other case of death being prescribed for sodomy in English North America occurred in Virginia in late 1624. Richard Cornish, a sea captain, died for committing buggery with William Cowse, his indentured servant. There were some in the colony who thought Cornish had been wrongfully executed, and local government officials were evidently sensitive to charges of judicial murder. Edward Newell, who objected to the injustice of the sentence, was pilloried, his ears were sliced off, he was required to serve the colony for a year, and rendered forever incapable of becoming a freeman in Virginia. The only clue to the nature of the underlying reasons for the execution came in a brief notation concerning the disposition of Cornish's property. William Cowse, the servant who pressed charges, was awarded to a Captain Hamer for the completion of his term of indenture and the remainder of Cornish's property went to a colonist named George Menefre.[75]

Surviving records, whether legal, literary, or in other forms, are not indices of the prevalence of any sexual practice. This is particularly true of homosexual activity, where the possibility of severe penalties made it prudent for practitioners to attract as little notice as

possible. Wealth and rank also served to shield some measure of
homosexual conduct from public scrutiny, although at the same time
both served to attract attention to known incidents and magnify them
out of proportion. Complicating any attempt to assess homosexual
frequency was the number of cases where accusations were pure fab-
rication, concocted for political or economic purposes. Yet while the
frequency of homosexual behavior is exceedingly difficult to quantify,
attitudes toward it are easier to discern. Despite the draconian proscriptions against sodomy in seventeenth-century England, the legal
reality was very different. Fines, abbreviated stays in the pillory, and
often exoneration were the fates of those accused. Still, sodomy had
its uses in situations where men were otherwise invulnerable to the
machinations of their enemies. Accusations of sexual irregularity were
occasionally employed against political foes for ridicule, to punish
other crimes, or perhaps to obtain property. Where severe penalities
were imposed or when public figures were accused of buggery, motives other than the desire to extirpate proscribed sex practices were
consistently present.

The tolerance of implied homosexual contact in Restoration comedy, the wide readership among the upper classes of foreign works
such as those by Aretino where buggery was highly praised in a manner laden with humor and bravado, the mild response of the courts
to sodomy, and the lighthearted attitudes of newspapers and the popular press indicated that Englishmen in the era of the restored Stuarts
were not inclined to classify sodomy as their descendents would for
the next two and one-half centuries as an act to which the only response was abject horror and profound revulsion. This was true not
only of the sophisticated upper classes but for a large segment of
English society. Whether wealthy or poor, conforming Anglican or
religious dissenter, royalist or parliament man, sodomy was simply
another crime, another work of the devil with little inherent capacity
to evoke passionate detestation. This is not to imply that sodomy was
an acceptable style of conduct. Surely no one regarded being pilloried on such a charge as a desirable experience. Titus Oates felt the
necessity to vindicate himself from accusations of sodomy at a time
when he was near the apex of his power, and in the loftiest reaches

of English society, the Duke of Buckingham took pains to clear his name even though he was accused only of heterosexual sodomy.

The level of relative toleration had its effect on seventeenth-century Englishmen. It is generally accepted that biological needs are modifiable by cultural determinants. Where homosexual acts are admired or even approved, they tend to be more prevalent than where there are severe strictures against them, and there is no reason to suppose England of three centuries past was an exception.[76] Yet the lack of extreme proscriptions against buggery must not be given more weight than it can sustain. The developmental routes by which individuals became adult homosexuals or engaged in homosexual contact are varied and the patterns that result in commitment to homosexual or homosexually directed behavior are psychodynamic and situational as well as cultural in nature. The final existence of homosexual preference or orientation depends on the extent to which a complex series of imperfectly evaluated and often misinterpreted factors reinforce one another to produce a pattern of values and responses. The effectiveness of these factors depends not only upon the matrix of their interrelationship but also on how effectively competing alternatives and overlapping but dissimilar matrices are neutralized.[77] Attitudes in the England of Charles II, as a single feature of society, would have been wholly insufficient to provide a base for the formulation of a functioning and resilient sodomitical pirate society three thousand miles away in the West Indies had it not been for a complex of interrelated social, economic, and psychological conditions. These made it possible for homosexual conduct to become virtually a normal pattern of behavior among large numbers of Englishmen and for many of these same men to transport their sexual practices to a Caribbean shipboard milieu where they became so well integrated into the total social equation that heterosexual contact became a genuinely exotic manner of sexual expression.

TWO

TO TRAIN UP
A BUCCANEER

Seventeenth-century Englishmen on all status levels were remarkably indulgent with homosexuality, at least when judged by the attitutes of their Victorian and twentieth-century counterparts. Their lack of antagonism toward men who gained sexual gratification from other men is especially important in theoretical terms, for it carries with it the implication that society in the Stuart era fostered the development of homosexuality and encouraged the commission of homosexual acts. Attempting to assess the contribution of the social milieu to variant forms of sexual expression is a complex undertaking even in the present. The shortage of various types of source materials for English society three hundred years past only amplifies the problems. The scarcity of data is due in part to the familiar problems of gathering information on homosexuality, but it is also a result of the difficulties plaguing research endeavors on Caribbean piracy. Not only was the corpse of the last potential interviewee dipped in tar and chained to a gibbet between flood marks at Wapping Stairs when George II was King of England, but the usual literary remnants particular to subjects of historical investigation were never extant for the cadre of illiterate and inarticulate sea rovers. Not that pirates, if they had been prone to record their actions and introspections in letters, diaries, and journals, would have revealed either the essence or the periphery of their sexual selves. Literary examinations of sexuality were produced only rarely in their age, and the absence of substantial quantities of documentation for pirate actions does not inhibit research into their intimate lives to any greater degree than would have been the case if more material were available. Still, despite the lack of familiar historical source materials and the total absence of the type of psychological data that has formed the base for much modern research on homosexuality, there remains cause for cheer. The very paucity of information on individuals vitiates many of the conceptual and theoretical problems that have vexed investigators and turned so many of them in directions that produce little but valueless articles. The passage of time and the absence of truly revealing personal records only channels research away from the preferences or general orientation of individual pirates and instead directs it toward the entire pattern of buccaneer homosexual behavior.

The emphasis on collective conduct rather than on the psychological configurations or biological composition of men long dead has the advantage of simplifying the semantic structure of the study by restricting the many taxonomic and etiological digressions that have characterized earlier work on homosexuality. Difficulties created by recent formulations are also obviated by the very nature of society in the Stuart era. Researchers who discern some level of predisposition for homosexuality acquired in early childhood or through biological mechanisms can find ample evidence that those males so inclined would locate social situations to sanction and support their proclivities in seventeenth-century England. Others advocating a learning theory of homosexual etiology or postulating origins in a socially scripted context will discover that among the classes spawning the buccaneers that infested the Caribbean from 1650 to 1720 there were life patterns perfectly adjusted for the imprinting of either homosexuality or preference for homosexual behavior, if indeed they can be imprinted at all.

A vital element of the theoretical construct necessary to interpret the conjugation of homosexual behavior patterns and piracy that became part of the life pattern for so many men was the correlation between income and family size. The relationship between the two and its effect on society is apparent in the compilation of census data made by Gregory King in 1690.[1] His demographic table describing the nation in 1688 divides the population into two expansive categories, the producers of wealth and the consumers of wealth. The producers, according to King's definition, were the nobility, the gentry, public office holders, merchants and traders, lawyers and clerics, freeholders, farmers, persons in the liberal arts and sciences, tradesmen, artisans, and military officers. The consuming classes, including all other persons, were subdivided into a laboring group composed of workers, outservants, soldiers, seamen, cottagers, and paupers. Beneath them came the bottom strata of society, the vagrants, gypsies, thieves, and beggars. Members of the consuming classes outnumbered the producing classes by a majority of slightly less than two to one, which is not surprising given the way King made his division.

The table contains a vast quantity of information on the structure of Restoration society and alters several widely held suppositions about seventeenth-century England. The first is that English men and women often lived in extended family groups including grandparents, uncles, aunts, and cousins three hundred years ago. This was often the case among the very wealthy segments of the population but almost never among the poorer classes. As a general rule, no more than one married couple made up a family unit. A greater number of adults would have enlarged the group beyond the limits imposed by economic necessity. Couples did not reside together no matter whether they were parents and children, brothers and sisters, employers and servants, or associated only for convenience. When a son married he left the family, if that was still his place of residence, to begin a household of his own. If he was not able to establish his own household he did not marry nor could his intended wife marry him and bring him into her family.[2] Another assumption refuted by the table was the commonly held belief that the lower classes banded together in larger existential families (children living with parents in a family unit) than the well-to-do. The largest households listed in the table belonged to the most prosperous men in the land, the Temporal Lords whose families on the average contained 40 persons. Not all members of noble households were relatives of the Lords. The large numbers represented extended families and perhaps some of the closest retainers. These families were few, comprising less than 200 of the nation's 1,350,000 households, but the size, the limited number of families, and the fact that they were presided over by noblemen was indicative of the correlation between status, wealth, and family size. The relationship was constant on all levels of society. Knights had ten family members on the average, gentlemen presided over households of eight persons, and so on down to the poorer members of the producing classes—the lesser clergymen, small freeholders, farmers, artisans, and military officers, none of whom averaged over five and one-half persons per family. Among the consumers of the nation's wealth, the average family belonging to the category of laborers consisted of approximately three persons. Thus the 900,000 families who labored for their sustenance accounted for only 2,700,000 of the country's five and one-half million residents.

Since approximately the same level of fertility prevailed among all classes and the rate of infant and child mortality was not sufficient to limit family size to only one or two children, the problem of offspring in greater numbers than could be supported by the family unit was solved among the lower classes by expelling children from the family group as soon as possible. The usual age when children were ejected from the nuclear family was ten or 12 years, but it was often as low as five or six.

The fate of children of the lower classes over eight or nine years old and no longer dwelling with their families is easy enough to determine. A portion of them died of the usual childhood diseases. Passing successfully from age nine to 15 was far from certain in seventeenth-century England even when the years of highest mortality had been passed, and although any accurate estimate of children dying in the half decade before they became fully mature is impossible to make, there were surely many who never reached adulthood. Other children lived to maturity within the confines of their natal households, but in these cases it is likely either that parents produced only one or two children or that a sufficient number of younger siblings died or were otherwise removed from the family so that the eldest offspring remained home until they reached marriageable age in their twenties. Many other youngsters were apprenticed to tradesmen or were employed as agricultural laborers. Although John Locke maintained, in 1697, that children of the poor must begin some useful work at the age of three, the usual age for a boy to be apprenticed to a trade or to begin learning the rudiments of farming was at about seven or eight. Apprenticeships were arranged for boys in almost any skill or occupation practiced in England, and girls, too, were sometimes apprenticed to learn the "keeping [of] a linen-shop," becoming "a child's coat maker," "washing point and gause," or to acquire other occupations considered appropriate to their sex. Another way to rid a household of older children was to place them as servants in the homes of the producing classes. Both male and female children could be transferred to another economic unit by this means. In Stuart England approximately one-third of all families had at least one servant, indicating that it was not only the wealthy who employed domestic labor. When men and women servants married, they did not remain as married servants but left their masters and established their own households. Servitude was most often a temporary stage, a place in the social structure for those who could no longer remain at home but were not yet able to establish their own households.[3]

Employment as servants, apprentices, or as agricultural laborers did not use up the available supply of young and able-bodied lads in seventeenth-century England and neither did these occupations fully engage those working with them. The many servants who were employed in agricultural labor, as well as regular agricultural laborers, worked only seasonally. The remainder of the year they were often required to shift for themselves. Apprentices, presumably those most shielded from seasonal economic considerations and the vicissitudes of commerce, faced many similar difficulties that destabilized their existence. Although their conditions of engagement were contractually assured, usually exchanging board, lodging, and instruction in a trade in return for their services for a specified number of years, apprentices were sometimes poorly used and the terms of their contract often not fulfilled by either principal.[4]

Servants dissatisfied with their lot also fled from their masters and often joined with absconding or abandoned apprentices, pauper lads, vagrant or beggar boys, and an assortment of unclassified youths to form the bands of children who were a feature of England's roads, towns, and cities in the Stuart era. None of the attempts to restrict or eliminate the number of homeless children were effective at any time in the seventeenth century. The fate of wanderers varied considerably, depending on age, location, strength, skill, and luck. Some found employment, escaped apprentices were occasionally returned to masters, a number of them sickened and died, not a few turned to crime and ended on the gallows, and others met fates as diverse as can be imagined. For some, however, the only available means of survival was to join the bands of vagrants and beggars that wandered England's roads and congregated in the towns. Once a youth enlisted in a wandering group he not only increased the possibility he would one day turn to piracy but also increased the likelihood that in short order he would be engaged in homosexual conduct.

The vagabond brotherhoods that provided refuge for large numbers of runaway lads gave nurture and acculturation for the recruits during particularly formative periods in their lives, and it was the unique set of social circumstances characteristic of the wanderers' communities that dictated the sexual practices of the members. The life patterns of these youths after becoming vagabonds diverged sharply from those of their age-mates apprenticed, retained as servants, or employed in agricultural labor. The distinctions in many respects are simply those existing between persons engaged in socially sanctioned gainful employment and those living at economically marginal levels at or beyond the fringes of acceptability. But the styles of life followed by members of such contrapositive groups went far beyond the many divergences that easily come to mind. Most important of the less visible distinctions are those relating to sexual practices. While boys and young men involved in the usual forms of employment common to their class origins existed in a society that was largely heterosexual, despite considerable toleration for other types of sexual expression, the life of the wandering youth was passed in a predominantly male and primarily homosexual milieu.[5]

There is no way to estimate accurately what proportion of young Englishmen from the lower levels of society lived in heterosexually and homosexually directed environments after they departed from the residence of their nuclear families. Gregory King placed the number of vagrants at 30,000, but his estimate cannot be verified. These people left no records on the tax rolls, in the registries of parishes, or in any other regular and systematically kept set of documents. The only account of their existence is in the tales told of them by their more settled fellow countrymen, who feared them greatly. Chroniclers of the rootless segment of society made it clear that begging was a common occupation in sixteenth- and seventeenth-century England. Practitioners of the art were to be found everywhere, waiting at the doors of houses, outside churches, in market places, and at sides of roads and streets. In Tudor times honest citizens often expressed alarm that so many restless men and women inhabited the land, and over the years Parliamentary enactments designed to reduce their numbers became increasingly savage. Despite the obvious alarm in descriptive sources, there is little data available for quantification. The only survivals in the records are occasional death notices of poor sick beggar lads, the discovery and burial of nameless persons found dead by the side of a road, or brief entries describing beggars being chased out of a parish so they would not become charges on the rates.[6]

The Statute of Artificers, the Settlement Laws, and several other early measures designed to alleviate the problems created by a class of wanderers often exacerbated the difficulties, and even though additional attempts were made to curb vagrancy and attendant crimes during the Restoration, the general mobility in the seventeenth century precluded success. Almost every parish in the land experienced the trouble and expense of eliminating vagrants. In the North Riding of Yorkshire the problem became so severe that literally hundreds of pounds were expended annually to pay constables and other officers for clearing the area of wanderers, and the efforts seemed to have little success. The towns and villages of the coast were even more susceptible to difficulties created by vagrants than were areas in the north. Although most wanderers did not go far from their home parishes or towns, there was a general south-easterly direction to the travel of the homeless. This only ended when they reached coastal towns were they could become lost in the population or, in the case of some men and boys, they continued their travels by signing aboard merchant vessels or being forced aboard one of the King's ships in time of war.[7] During their wanderings, the only sexual outlet available for these men was found among each other and with the large number of boys, the orphans, those abandoned by parents, runaway apprentices and servants, and others driven from their homes who joined with the vagrants as the only means of survival. The attempts by those who wrote of the beggar bands to depict them as a dark and odious army that posed a threat to the very survival of the nation were obviously exaggerated, but with the knowledge that vagrant groups were largely male and that the few women among them were the property of the leaders or physically stronger members, the assertion that sodomy, like adultery or incest, was one of the true tests for admission to the fellowship was probably true.[8]

The individual psychological response to engaging in homosexual acts may have varied considerably among members of wandering groups, although for modern scholarly advocates of homosexuality as learned or acquired behavior, the distance between the parameters of psychological reaction would be considerably reduced. Yet whatever the size of the gap between homosexuals and those committing homosexual acts because of a lack of access to women or as a result of economic or social imperatives, Stuart England was a nation where sex acts between adult members of the same sex were not rigidly proscribed, and the vagrant bands had either no females or access to females was limited by physical and pecuniary considerations. It is certain under such circumstances that homosexual acts were part of the sex experience of vagrants, and although there is no quantitative data on orgasms per wanderer per week, month, or year, the lack of negative conditioning and the paucity of women surely increased the number of homosexual acts over what would have been the case in a homophobic heterosexual population of comparable size. And while the lack of proscription and the situational demands directing beggars' actions may not have created homosexual preferences, availability of opportunity for homosexual contacts and the absence of chances for sexual relations with females probably increased the frequency of homosexual acts sufficiently to transform buggery or sodomy from exotica into the realm of ordinary behavior for large numbers of wanderers.

Advocates of acquired homosexuality, whether of theoretical persuasions similar to Irving Bieber, Harry Stack Sullivan, or others, can find much to cheer them in vagabond society. The greater portion of vagrants had begun their wanderings as part of the gaggles of children present with the bands in greater proportions than they were found in rural villages. Writing in 1608, Thomas Harmon and Thomas Dekker observed that the companies of beggars roaming the countryside were accompanied by "great flockes of Chyldren," and available evidence bears out their judgment. In one group surveyed, two-thirds of the members were under 25 years of age, and in a similar platoon of 20, only four members were over 25, four were between the ages of 16 and 25, and the remaining twelve were under 15.[9] These lads soon learned that homosexuality was not a surrogate method of obtaining sexual gratification. It was an ordinary, frequent, and acceptable way of engaging in sexual contact, and wandering juveniles who joined the vagrants were raised in an environment with little or no opportunity to acquire heterosexual socialization. They were acculturated quickly to the customs and mores of their companions, this occurring at a stage in their maturation processes when it could be theorized they were particularly responsive to the absorption of social and sexual patterns of behavior. Accepting or rejecting homosexual contact on preferential grounds was made additionally difficult or impossible by more pressing social considerations. The new member of a vagabond group was linked with his associates for reasons more compelling than the satisfaction of sexual desires. The members offered the essential socialization without which few human beings can survive, and to reject the group's sexual orientation would be to reject the group and possibly jeopardize even physical existence.

Vagrants' sense of communality, an indicator of the intensity of their mutual identification, was sufficiently strong to appear frequently as the most conspicuous feature of wandering bands, at least for members of respectable society who recorded their depravity. The aspects of human association that go to form a genuine subculture were everywhere visible and always frightening to Englishmen who observed the regiment of blackguards that congregated in their towns or walked the roads. The wanderers spoke a derivative English built around nouns and idiomatic phrases that rendered their talk unintelligible to any but themselves. They maintained a façade of loyalty to one another that made them seem formidable to outsiders, they held within them a hostility to the rest of humanity that was understood within and beyond their ranks, and they were bound firmly by the most durable of considerations, self-interest and the human desire to survive. The benefits belonging to a band conferred were many, the sexual practices required for acculturation may have been no more difficult to adopt than any other practices necessary for admission, and there was little in the background of the youthful recruits that militated against acceptance of homosexuality. If homosexuality can be acquired after the first years of life, as can homosexual patterns of behavior, then beggar bands were suitable places to do so. With all social and psychological pressures from a single direction, vagrant lads could have slipped easily into patterns of preference as they had adopted the conduct patterns they had no opportunity to reject.

Among England's apprentice classes which, like vagrant bands, nurtured some of the youths who ultimately became buccaneers, coordinate conditions also existed which led to the encouragement of homosexual acts or possibly even to homosexual preferences. For apprentices, sexual contact between members of the same sex was probably much easier to avoid for those who chose to do so than would have been the case within wandering male groups, but there was nevertheless much in the situation of apprentices which encouraged homosexual practices. Although apprentices lived and worked in proximity to large numbers of women, some of whom surely visited their favors on yearning lads or sold them to those with the purchase price, it is equally certain that all apprentices or even large numbers of them lacked the charm, purse, or inclination to satisfy their physical desires heterosexually. A portion of these became involved in homosexual liasons as a matter of preference, others as a response to sexual deprivation. The socialization demanded by apprentice groups, like that required by wanderers or beggars, may have conditioned some young men to accept homosexual practices and ultimately to prefer them. If in fact such preferences can be socially induced, London was the perfect place for inducement. There homosexuality was more easily tolerated than in other sections of the country and apprentices were sufficiently numerous to exert a profound socializing effect on each other.[10]

The long journey from apprentice to buccaneer was begun over any of several possible routes. Apprentices frequently signed aboard merchant vessels to escape masters, and a certain number of them became sailors aboard ships of the Royal Navy either as volunteers, or, more likely, as pressed men. Whatever route apprentices took from servitude, whether voluntarily as runaways or against their will as pressed men, many found that on land or at sea it was likely they would be inexorably bound in an environment where homosexual preferences or the commission of homosexual acts were common, opportunities for heterosexual contacts were few or entirely absent, and there was little alternative to remaining where they were. Youths who had not yet evolved a sex-partner preference or those already partially or fully conditioned homosexuals experienced no difficulty. Those disposed toward heterosexuality either conformed against their wills, modified their preferences willingly, or faced the consequences.

There is no estimating how many buccaneers once served as apprentices or wandered the roads as vagrants, but the primary source of hands to man buccaneering vessels was the vast pool of sailors who learned seamanship as boys or young men aboard the ships of England's merchant or naval fleets. For those who went to sea aboard ships of the Royal Navy, the institutional structure within which they lived made involvements in homosexual acts a very likely prospect. English warships in the seventeenth-century were what sociologist Erving Goffman would characterize as impermeable institutions. At sea they were totally isolated from external control; the personnel remained constant, men rarely being added and departing only when as cadavers they were pitched over the rail. The length of time spent at sea for sailors aboard men-of-war was often considerable. Voyages

of one, two, and three years were not unusual, and during the tours
of duty it would not be uncommon for many of the men never to set
foot on shore. The total absence of women from their environment
meant that sexual conduct with members of the same sex was, except
for solitary masturbation, all that was available to the Navy's men
and to most of it officers. Under these circumstances, situational
homosexual behavior was obviously a feature of life at sea for some
just as it is a feature of any isolated and enduring male group, but it
was only one facet of shipboard sexual activity.[11] Most of the men
who sailed aboard the Navy's ships were volunteers, and it is likely
enough that the all-male atmosphere was the very feature of Royal
Navy life that brought a portion of each ship's crew into His Majesty's
service. For these men, the homosexuality they practiced was clearly
a preference rather than an expedient. This is evident from the situation that prevailed between wars when fear of impressment subsided
and maritime employment for men with seafaring skills was often
available on ships that plied coastal waters. Service aboard these ships
allowed frequent access to female sexual partners, as did other types
of alternative waterfront employment favored by sailors not serving
afloat. Yet many men, a proportion of whom were married and the
heads of families, regularly volunteered for service aboard naval vessels in time of peace.

Economic factors played a part in inducing men to go to sea, but
their importance can be exaggerated in assessing the motives of sailors
in selecting particular types of ships. Maritime commerce underwent
its period of most rapid expansion during the Restoration, not in the
Elizabethan age as had once been supposed. Shipping grew from
200,000 tons in 1660 to 340,000 in 1686, and stood at 323,000 in
1702. Bristol shipped 509 cargoes to other English ports in 1685 alone,
and five years later, Gloucester was shipping almost as many in the
coastal trade. Tonnage for vessels engaged in foreign trade grew at a
more rapid rate than domestic tonnage. In the period between 1660
and 1686, carrying capacity grew from approximately 100,000 tons
to 190,000 tons. By 1701 it was over one-quarter million tons.[12]
Construction requirements for English commercial vessels made the
need for seamen even more acute than would have been the case had

the expansion of carrying capacity been the only factor in creating additional employment for sailors. The practice of building merchant ships easily convertible to men-of-war meant that flyboats, doggers, whalers, herring busses, pinks, and similarly specialized vessels, all of which were easily and economically handled by small numbers of men, were uncommon in English ports. The result was an English merchant fleet that required crews three times larger than Dutch vessels of similar carrying capacity.[13]

Gregory King estimated that the number of common seamen in the nation during 1688 was approximately 50,000, and information on the shipping industry indicates his figure is only slightly underestimated even though it represents one percent of the population. The size of English merchant vessels varied considerably during the latter half of the seventeenth century, ranging from the many ships under 50 tons up to large traders in the 300-ton range. The number of sailors required per ton of burthen varied from ship to ship—the largest vessels required only one man per 25 tons, but on smaller craft the number of tons per seamen decreased substantially. A tabulation of the average number of tons per man of ships entering London from foreign ports in 1686 indicates that each sailor was responsible for about eight tons displacement. The rate of eight tons per man was probably a general average for vessels in foreign trade coming into London in the 1680s, but the average was surely lower in the smaller coastal ports where a greater proportion of craft of limited size were involved in commerce. Although it is impossible to make an exact calculation of the average tonnage per man in the whole of the merchant fleet, if the figure were the same as that of international trading vessels docking at London—it was in fact considerably lower—then the nation's commercial fleet of 340,000 tons would employ 42,500 available seamen. Navy figures for the period indicate over 10,0000 were employed on the king's ships during the same period. There is latitude for variation in the figures, but it is apparent that no matter how they are adjusted, there was not a regular or continuous surplus of seamen in England during the rapid maritime expansion the English commercial fleet underwent in the Restoration era.[14]

The fluctuations in wage rates paid to seamen provide further evidence that when Gregory King compiled his table in 1688, there was not a surplus of sailors unable to find work either at sea or on land. Table 1, listing seamens' compensation averages from the beginning of the Protectorate in 1652 to the reign of Queen Anne, shows that sailors earned good money in times of peace, indicating there was no surplus, and also that when war broke out the shortage of men was acute.[15]

The limited supply of sailors meant economic necessity was only a minor factor or perhaps played almost no part in inducing men to sign aboard naval vessels. Neither is there much doubt that if crewmen sailing warships had been hostile to homosexual practices they might with only a minimum of difficulty have found shipboard employment of another variety. Some of these seafarers who married and participated in sexual activity with women while ashore may, in fact, have been engaging in situational heterosexual activity, the response of men grown to maturity at sea in an all-male society to the pressures of a sexually integrated landsman's environment. When the

TABLE 1

Seamens' Wage Rates

Years		Shillings Per Month
1652–1654	(First Dutch War)	30–38
1654–1655		23–24
1655–1660	(Spanish War)	30–38
1660–1664		19–20
1664–1667	(Second Dutch War)	35–38
1667–1671	(Great demand for sailors to man timber ships bringing wood from the continent for the rebuilding of London after the great fire)	27–30
1672–1674	(Third Dutch War)	35–40
1674–1678	(England carries goods for the wars on the continent)	27–28
1679–1688		24–25
1689–1697	(War of the League of Augsburg)	45–55
1698–1702		24–25

SOURCE: Ralph Davis: *The Rise of the English Shipping Industry in the Seventeenth and Eighteenth Centuries* (London: Macmillan, 1962), pp. 135–137.

opportunity to sail came, they may have signed aboard warships with a good measure of relief rather than reluctance.

In merchant service there were two types of employment the prospective sailor or youth going off to sea for the first time might be forced into or select. The coastal trade was the maritime situation most easily available to Englishmen. Britain has more usable coastline per square mile of land area than any of the other major countries of Europe, and almost all of the island's ports were adequate for coastal trading with the small, shallow-draft, sailing vessels in use during the seventeenth century. In 1615, one writer estimated that two-thirds of all English seamen were employed in the coastal trade and as fishermen. That estimate was probably accurate at least until mid-century. By the time William and Mary became joint sovereigns, the coastal trade probably employed a number of mariners equal to the trans-oceanic carriers, the other common type of seafaring employment. The availability of both coastal and oceanic commercial vessels meant that men eager to sail in merchant service had two alternatives. Sailors desiring short voyages, considerable time at home, and a heterosexual environment could choose in most cases a coastal trader or collier, vessels on which it was easiest to obtain employment, for it was well-known their captains were especially receptive to inexperienced seamen or landsmen wanting to go to sea. The sailor could, with a bit more difficulty, gain a berth on an ocean-going merchantman departing for destinations as much as 10,000 miles distant. Aboard these ships there would be no home in the traditional sense, no family, and no women.[16]

The selection of an ocean carrier for employment by as many as half the seafaring population carries particular importance for piracy. It was these men, not the coastal mariners, who thousands of miles from their birthplaces and half a world away from the ports of their departure, made decisions to become buccaneers. They were men who had earlier chosen all-male environments when in most cases they could have chosen the coastal trade. They had rejected at least once what was in all likelihood an opportunity for employment in a heterosexual milieu for a lengthy commitment at sea, isolated from everything but what was aboard their ship and with only their fellow sailors to fulfill their social requirements. There may have been less opportunity for a clear choice to be made in cases of boys sent to sea. Economic considerations or adult convenience rather than personal preference may have been the major determinants in prescribing whether a lad sailed in the coastal or oceanic trade.

There are any number of reasons beyond economic needs and sexual preference to induce men to go to sea or to direct their choice of coastal or ocean-going vessels. The search for adventure may have lured a city lad aboard an East Indiaman loading at Thames-side, while the desire for a journey to London for whatever reason may have induced a farmer or countryman to sign aboard a collier bound for the capital. The decision to sail on a particular ship may have been made with little or no attention to solvency or sex by the rare seventeenth-century Englishman who succumbed to the lure of the sea, the rejected suitor, feeble-minded fellows driven by a desire to avoid the ridicule of the populace, or for the man with a need to flee by the most expeditious means. Those who signed aboard vessels destined for the Caribbean or the eastern seas, whatever their reasons or sexual preferences, found themselves in situations where the only manner of sexual fulfillment was with members of the same sex. Homosexuals may have congratulated themselves on having blundered into good fortune. Those with no preference could adapt easily. Heterosexuals had a choice between sodomy or abstinence, but their choice was influenced not only by their having grown to adolescence or adulthood in a society that did not rigorously condemn homosexual conduct but also by the fact that many of the men aboard were homosexuals; those in positions of authority by virtue of their long seafaring experience were surely aware of the sexual situation aboard ship when they took employment.

The series of circumstances that took vagrants, wanderers, or apprentices from England across the Atlantic to the Caribbean and then gave them the opportunity to become pirates varied widely, but for most of them, one of the vital factors actuating the serried events that brought them to piracy was need of the Royal Navy for sailors in times of war. From the days of the Commonwealth in mid-century to the reign of George I, England was involved in periodic warfare. Although in times of peace naval manning presented only small problems, during the three Anglo-Dutch conflicts, the War of the League of Augsburg, and the War of Spanish Succession, the increased demand for ships and sailors was never adequately met. Landsmen and merchant sailors avoided naval service whenever possible because of the poor conditions, brutal treatment, harsh discipline, and danger of serving aboard fighting ships.[17] So desperate for men was the Navy that whenever war broke out, ship captains thought little about the quality or proficiency of the crews who manned their vessels. According to English law, almost any man with sea experience might be requisitioned for naval service in time of need. Merchant ships bound for home were stopped on the high seas and portions of their crews impressed into the Navy; on land, towns and counties along the coast were scoured for men to sail the King's ships.

The usual method for acquiring forced sailors was to send an armed contingent ashore with instructions to seize all seafaring men except crewmembers of colliers, fishing boats, transports, and those who manned the Archbishop of Canterbury's barge, all of whom were exempted by law from naval service. In practice, press gangs were never particular about who they acquired. Any man or boy who could be caught was usually deemed to have sea experience, and farmers, maltsters, vagrants, wanderers, beggars, unwary apprentices, large numbers of juveniles, as well as men of sixty or seventy years of age often found themselves sailors aboard the Navy's men-of-war. Occasionally the press was resisted. Thirteen bargemen once killed two press-masters who boarded their craft at Lambeth. The defendants were acquitted when it was determined by the court that the warrant carried by the officials was illegal. Such incidents did not halt the practice of impressing men, for even with instant conscription there was never a sufficient number of sailors.[18]

Table 2 provides some indication of the increase in size of the Navy during ten years of conflict, although the numbers are somewhat inflated.[19] It does not indicate the experience, the state of training, or readiness of each sailor, nor does it provide information on

TABLE 2

*Number of Men Theoretically Borne at Sea
Each Year*

Year	Men	Year	Men
1688	12,714	1693	43,827
1689	22,332	1694	47,710
1690	31,971	1695	48,514
1691	35,317	1696	47,677
1692	40,274	1697	44,743

SOURCE: John Ehrman, *The Navy in the War of William III, 1689–1697* (Cambridge: Cambridge University Press, 1953), p. 110.

their employment experience, but the quantum increase furnishes ample evidence that large numbers of non-seafarers were pressed into service when needed.

During the Third Anglo-Dutch War, the situation became so serious that sixth-rate ships had to be dismanned to provide seamen to sail larger vessels. This measure was also inadequate, and press gangs were sent out in increased numbers to roam the streets looking for potential sailors. When the press was out, however, beggars, vagrants, and the unemployed were sufficiently well organized so that word could be spread rapidly. Samuel Pepys noticed on a morning peregrination in July, 1666 that "it is a pretty thing to observe, that both there and everywhere else a man shall see so many women nowadays of mean sort in the streets, but no men; men being so afeared of the press."[20] The comment about the meaner sort of men being absent from the streets indicated which classes made up the coffles obtained by the press gangs. Pepys and others of his social level could go abroad without fear of conscription, but beggars, vagrants, and boys were to beware. In the early weeks of July, the very time Pepys strolled through the city of London, approximately 3,000 impressed men were sent from the Tower to the fleet; some of them were mere children, a portion of them were in rags, and others were obviously sick with the plague. After the Four Days Battle in June, 1666, one observer commented that many of the bodies floating in the water were dressed in the same Sunday clothes they wore when they had been captured by the press gangs outside their church doors.[21]

Transition from beggar boy, vagrant, or apprentice to sailor was easy enough. Often it was made much against the will of the youths when after wandering into or through a port town, they fell victim to the Navy's press gangs in time of war. But if the pressed vagabonds returned alive from their stint of service for the King, they returned with the rudiments of a trade. This did not mean that they chose to exercise the newly acquired skill. Once a man served as a sailor it surely did not preclude his return to the road and the reverse is also true. Depending on the time of year and the state of international relations, the same man might be found reeving the sails of a man-of-war, robbing on the highway, begging in the streets of London, wandering West Country roads, engaging in any one of a hundred swindles, or setting the braces on an East Indiaman. During times of peace there was always an increased chance for men with seafaring experience to sail aboard a merchant ship. When the periodic warfare of the late seventeenth century flared anew, and as wage rates rose correspondingly, the vagrants with some maritime skills not only had an easier time signing aboard merchant ships but sailing on a commercial vessel carried with it the bonus of making men safer from press gangs and compulsory Naval service. Once sailors boarded merchant vessels and shipped for the West Indies, no matter what their motives in joining the crews, their chances of having an opportunity to join the buccaneers increased substantially.

The influx of men into the Royal Navy as a result of the needs of war and the large numbers of newcomers into the merchant marine attracted by the higher wages and the easy availability of berths—made even more easily available by the impressment of merchant seamen—exerted a measure of change on the seafaring population. Certainly some segment of those adults impressed or attracted to seafaring occupations by the increased economic opportunity they offered after 1689 were neither homosexual nor homosexually inclined. Once on board their first Navy vessel they may have resisted sexual contacts with their shipmates. There is no way of estimating or even hazarding a guess at their rate of success in avoiding homosexual contact. Others must surely have succumbed to the prevailing sexual practices, and for this reason the proportion of situational homosexual acts must have risen in both the Navy and the commercial fleet. At the same time, however, almost all of those forced into the Navy or attracted to the merchant service had grown to early adulthood in the Restoration asmosphere of toleration for homosexual practices, and a proportion of them attained maturity as wanderers, beggars, vagrants, or apprentices where homosexual contact was much more a part of ordinary life than among the general population. Men impressed into the Navy, of course, had no choice in the matter of their type of service, but for those who became merchant seamen, the same alternatives were available to those choosing commercial seafaring in earlier years. Both the coastal trade and vessels sailing in international trade were shorthanded in times of war, and the man or boy with the opportunity to select the type of ship on which he would sail could have, in many cases, picked a coaster with its short voyages and ample time ashore or he could have opted for the longer voyages to the East or West Indies and years at sea with only shipmates for companions.

Men and boys with homosexual orientations obviously found the sexual aspects of maritime employment cordial and others adopted homosexual practices if not homosexuality once they found themselves deprived of female partners and in a milieu where sodomy was accepted practice. When these men returned to land, a portion of them also found that the sailor's life ashore offered only limited access to heterosexual engagements. This was due in large measure to the seasonal character of maritime employment. In the Navy, larger ships on patrol in northern waters or along Europe's coasts did not stay at sea past September nor did they venture out before the beginning of April. The vacillation in the number of sailors needed throughout the year was considerable. Figures in Table 3 for 1689 and 1690, the first two years of a major war, indicate that the size of the wartime Navy doubled in the summer months, leaving large numbers of seamen to shift for themselves ashore during the period from January to April. The same seasonal patterns were found among coastal shippers. The coal trade and the smaller vessels that sailed

TABLE 3

Royal Navy Utilization of Seamen,
1689–1690

January–April, 1689	16,362 men
May–September, 1689	24,164 men
October, 1689–February, 1690	21,740 men
March–October, 1690	33,573 men

SOURCE: John Ehrman, *The Navy in the War of William III, 1689–1697* (Cambridge: Cambridge University Press, 1953) p. 110.

from port to port in English waters were laid up in winter, and even the international routes in year-round use were not as active in winter as in summer. In off-months large numbers of temporarily unemployed sailors filled Portsmouth, Chatham, Deptford, Plymouth, and other naval ports, and the same situation prevailed in the hundreds of major and minor seafaring towns dotting the English coast from Berwick around the south and west coasts to the north of Wales. The situation at Hull, a bustling port during the shipping season was typical of other coastal towns. The coming of winter meant:

The streets are crowded with boys, intended for the sea-service, who spend their time in open violation of decency, good order and morality; there are often fifteen hundred seamen and boys, who arrive from the whale fishery, and often double that number of unemployed sailors, are left at leisure to exercise their dissolute manners on the inoffensive passenger in the public street.[22]

All sailors were not unemployed and roistering throughout the winter months. Some found work in any one of a hundred trades or occupations. Porters, ostlers, construction laborers, and tapsters were only a few of the many jobs for which a sailor without a landsman's skills would be adequate. But these occupations and others like them could only absorb a limited quantity of paid-off seafarers, and for those mariners who remained out of work, many of them without adequate funds to see them through the winter, the months from October to April were trying times. Those married could at least supplement their sexual activity with contacts involving females, but for others experiencing the short-term economic doldrums, marriage was out of the question and their financial situation meant women for hire could be had only on occasion if at all. Still, for homosexuals among the men, the problems of obtaining female sexual partners were irrelevant. Practitioners of situational homosexual activity, at least those in need and unable to seduce or purchase women, could always rely on fellow sailors. If they were not preferred partners, they were at least familiar and available.

The origins and backgrounds of men who became pirates in the Caribbean during the Restoration era and the decades immediately following were comparable. The romantic notion of scions from great families being deprived of inheritances by evil brothers and scheming uncles, and then running off to recoup lost fortunes as commanders of pirate ships, has little basis in fact. The infants who would one day reach maturity and ultimately sail as Caribbean pirates were most likely to be born to couples who belonged to Gregory King's consuming classes. They were the children of cottagers, paupers, and agricultural laborers, or their fathers might have been soldiers or sailors. They were forced into economic self-sufficiency usually by the age of thirteen, working for their keep as servants or laborers. If fortunate they may have been apprenticed to a master of one of the less prestigious and less lucrative trades. Another frequent pattern for their lives was to have been ejected from home with little training and no opportunity to acquire a marketable skill. For those in this circumstance there was some chance to find work, but there was also the opportunity to turn to petty crime, starve, or join with other lads in similar situations—runaways, fleeing apprentices, and the like—to become a member of one of the bands wandering the English roads and drifting into the nation's towns and villages. It is impossible to make even a rough estimate of the proportions of boys and young men who entered the ranks of vagrants and those who did not. The many who followed socially acceptable paths were far more numerous. If they were not or if there was even a rough equality in the numbers who went in the two directions, England would literally have been overwhelmed with beggars and thieves. But such was not the case. While in some urban areas and along the roads leading to them it might have seemed on occasion that the world was filled to overflowing with rascals, the mass of England's five million residents were not members of the wandering underground.

The preponderant majority of apprentices, servants, or agricultural laborers lived and worked in a heterosexual milieu. Relations between persons of opposite sexes dominated their observations on every hand and served as the basis for the development of their social and sexual orientation. Although homosexual activity was surely present, probably with some frequency in major towns where there were large numbers of apprentices and limited opportunities for fraternization with females, there is no doubt that theirs was a heterosexually dominant environment.

For the children from the lowest classes of English society, the classes that produced the men who would terrorize the Caribbean in the closing years of the Stuart era, the situation was vastly different. The variety of opportunities available for children of cottagers, paupers, laborers, and the like were severely restricted when compared to the alternatives that could be chosen by their social superiors. Still, many became apprentices, worked as agricultural laborers, or were employed as servants, and in these positions they underwent exposure to social conditions similar, if somewhat reduced in circumstance, to the offspring from the status levels immediately above them. Both groups of young people lived, worked, and were conditioned in a world where heterosexuality was the ordinary mode of sexual expression. Those youths from the lowest levels of English society who were unable to gain employment in these areas in many cases went to sea or became vagrants, gypsies, thieves, and beggars. The feature that distinguished the adolescent experience of young men gone to sea or into various types of vagrancy and illegal occupations from the experience of other English youth of the same general social levels is that the training period was not only shorter, and perhaps more demanding in some respects, but that in the years between the ages of ten and 14 or 16 when they had become adult sailors or criminals, they lived in environments populated either largely or entirely by males. Young men at sea were members of a society composed entirely of men, and although there were female vagrants, vagabonds, and beggars, they were a small minority of the wanderers of England's roads. Even though the proportion of females to males in the vagrant classes may have been as high as one to three, the women were not available for distributive sexual purposes. In practice, most groups of wanderers were composed of from two to six men and contained no females.[23]

While the skills and techniques particular to each type of employment engaged in by wanderers, beggars, sailors, robbers, and the like varied from occupation to occupation, the feature common to all these activities was that they were conducted within a milieu where women were present either in reduced numbers or totally absent. Runaway apprentices could testify that access to women for sexual purposes was often very restricted. The willing master's daughter was not there for each lusty apprenticed lad, although some found them, to be sure. The most frequent company for the apprentice was found among others like him, and although the city of London contained sufficient number of prostitutes to service a substantial number of apprentices and a large segment of the population as well, those women were professionals, vendors of sexual favors to those who could pay. For apprentices in the lower classes engaged in learning menial trades, sex for hire was not easily obtained. Among the bands of vagrants, those men who exercised power among their colleagues often monopolized the females, even those who preferred to travel in all-female groups. For the majority of wanderers, women were not easily available.

If it was difficult for apprentices and vagabonds to arrange heterosexual intercourse, it was virtually impossible for men of the merchant service who engaged in international trade to develop heterosexual contacts while at sea. These were men accustomed to long voyages lasting two, three, and sometimes four years. On the rare occasions where women were carried aboard their ships, they traveled as passengers and were not available to provide sexual services for crew members. This same situation prevailed in the Royal Navy, where men were confined to shipboard sometimes for years at a time. This was not an age of roistering sailors on shore leave from visiting men-of-war. All of that was to come later. No English captain in the seventeenth century granted leave ashore to his sailors during times of war. His men were frequently conscripts and once their feet touched land they would be gone and his ship would be stranded in a foreign port with no hands to sail her. When warships anchored in the West Indies the pressed crewmembers were watched closely to prevent their escape, and those who were sent ashore for supplies or any other duties were closely supervised by officers or senior sailors.

Knowledgeable English seamen insistent on exclusive heterosexuality could avoid the long and dangerous voyages to the East or West Indies or to India. They would instead sail in the fishing fleets, aboard a coastal trader, or serve as a crew member aboard any one of a thousand colliers that plied up and down the coast. But these sailors were not the men who became pirates. Men who sailed aboard vessels flying the piratical flag did not make their decision to become freebooters while in Hull, Exeter, or the Channel Ports. They most often decided when their own ship, an East India merchant vessel or a West Indiaman, was taken by a buccaneer craft. Others who signed aboard pirate craft usually did so after jumping ship half a world away from the villages of their birth. They were men who eschewed service in the seafaring trades closer to home and for the most part had rejected situations where heterosexual contact was more easily available. Often they had grown to manhood among the predominantly male shipboard environment where homosexuality or homosexual acts were accepted practice. Some may have once served in the Navy where heterosexual deprivation was complete, and all had chosen to sail on lengthy voyages, among members of a totally male society where other men were the only sexual contacts available. Though economic considerations or non-sexual factors may have played some part in the decision of many to sign aboard ships making ready for lengthy voyages, rather than those sailing shorter trade routes, the men who went to sea for years on end were not a cross-section of potential crew members. They were sailors who knowingly elected to live in an environment devoid of females for an extended period of time, and when those of them who became pirates boarded their first buccaneering vessel, they found a sexual situation similar to that they had abandoned when they left the merchant service. Later, as they plied Caribbean waters and visited island ports, they discovered that English society in the West Indies did not differ in sexual orientation from that in which they lived aboard ship.

THREE

THE CARIBBEE ISLES

Life patterns for many males of the consuming classes in seven-teenth-century England were well-suited to developing toleration for homosexuality and for encouraging homosexual practices. In the West Indies similar conditions guided the formation of sexual patterns for a substantial segment of the population, but the effect of the patterns for inducing all-male sexuality was greatly amplified by complex interactions of societal, geographic, and demographic considerations. At the same time, the cultural constrictions preventing homosexuality from expanding into a generally utilized mode of sexual expression in England were absent. Legal prohibitions, condemnation by organized religion, the dominance of heterosexual institutions, and opportunity to engage in heterosexual contacts with wives, prostitutes, female acquaintances, or Indian or slave women were all unavailable for pirates, sailors, hunters, servants, and other non-Spanish residents of the Caribbean.[1]

The origins of this unique segment of English society reach back into the sixteenth century when Spain founded her American empire on Indian gold and silver. Elizabethan adventurers soon discovered vast treasure could be had by raiding Spanish settlements and capturing heavily laden ships. Drake, Hawkins, Frobisher, and other English sea dogs returned home rich from New World plundering, and reports of their successes encouraged others to follow their lead. The size of Spain's imperial holdings, the distances from settlement to settlement, and the difficulty of protecting mainland towns and scattered island outposts all made the work of the English easy, and as their activities became widely known, they were joined in the labor of decreasing Spanish prosperity by the Dutch, who had no qualms about despoiling the imperial properties of the nation that once exercised dominion over them. The French had discovered even earlier than the English that profits from commercial activity with the Portuguese in Brazil were small compared with what could be had by transferring operations to the West Indies and raiding the Spanish. Gallic Protestants from La Rochelle and Dieppe were plundering the Spanish Main and Caribbean island towns on a regular basis by the mid-sixteenth century, but after Drake and Hawkins, even Catholic Frenchmen could not ignore the chance for easy wealth. By 1600, there was hardly a Spanish settlement in the Western Hemisphere that had not been sacked at least once.[2]

These sixteenth-century raiders operated in an irregular fashion. They were based in ports on the European side of the Atlantic, their fleets were small, they had no logistical support in the New World, and although many of their voyages produced sizable profits, they were unable to plunder on a sustained and systematic basis. The men who signed on as members of the expeditions did so with the knowledge that though the voyages would be long, if good fortune was with them they could return rich to the ports from which they sailed. There was no thought among them of remaining permanently in the New World as colonists or adopting the trade of corsair as a lifetime occupation. These early raiders were only occasional brigands, and while they demonstrated the vulnerability of Spain in the Western Hemisphere, it was for the rovers of the next century to discover the techniques of continually and systematically extracting Spanish wealth.

The first men to plunder Spain in what would become the greatest age of Caribbean piracy mounted their initial attacks from the islands of Hispaniola and Tortuga. Hispaniola had been claimed for Ferdinand and Isabella by Christopher Columbus in 1492, and at the end of the sixteenth century it boasted a number of Spanish settlements. The island's great size, over 350 miles long and approximately

150 miles at its widest point, meant it was well-suited to large-scale farming, but the settlers were never successful in their efforts to make it an agricultural colony. Most residents preferred to congregate in the towns founded near the coast and take full commercial advantage of the island's many excellent harbors. Nearby Tortuga, only 25 miles in length, was a turtle-like promontory of rock rising abruptly from the sea a few miles north-west of the Hispaniolan coast. Its northern shore had no harbors or beaches except the few gaps that separated steeply rising crags, and only a small harbor on the south side made any settlement possible. It was on these two islands that the first piratical crews were gathered, and it was from their protected coves and inlets that fugitive Europeans in the West Indies first sailed in large numbers to plunder Spain's shipping and raid her coastal settlements.

The origins of these marauding bands date from the first decades of the seventeenth century when the Spanish abandoned their efforts to establish agricultural settlements over all of Hispaniola and allowed much of the island's land to revert to its original heavily forested state. The only evidence that remained to indicate Spaniards had ever been in the areas they abandoned were the large herds of wild cattle and swine, descendents of the livestock the colonists had once attempted to raise on their island farms. With the abandonment of efforts to subdue the interior, only two groups remained to inhabit Hispaniola. A residual population of Spaniards was found in the area surrounding what is now the city of Santo Domingo and in the north was an assortment of men, runaway slaves, a few aborigines who had escaped extermination, and a diverse agglomeration of Europeans: survivors of shipwrecks, castaways, and a complement of fugitives and deserters. The Europeans lived as nomads, tracking the abundant livestock and establishing no permanent habitations. They acquired powder, shot, guns, knives, and other items they could not provide for themselves, by trading hides and smoked meat to passing ships. Vessels of England, Holland, and France engaged in a regular exchange with the hunters, and by 1630 a segment of their commerce was formalized with the founding of a trading post on Tortuga. The Spanish were distressed by the establishment of a permanent settlement on a speck of land they had long claimed, and in 1635 they mounted an attack. Most of the residents of the island were killed in the massacre that followed the Spanish victory, but those few who escaped made their way to Hispaniola and reestablished themselves as traders. The authorities were no more willing to tolerate illicit enterprise on Hispaniola than on Tortuga, and in 1640, mobile lancer squadrons—"cinquantaines"—were sent to destroy Hispaniolan commerce, killing what hunters they could and starving the rest into submission by exterminating the herds that provided their livelihood. The Spanish policy achieved a limited degree of success, but in the end, their measures created more difficulties for their imperial designs in the Caribbean than they had ever envisioned when they moved to reassert dominion over all of Hispaniola.

The price of destroying the wandering bands of men was high for the Spanish in terms of money and blood, but these immediate expenditures were only a fraction of the treasure the Hispaniolan policy would ultimately cost. The difficulties created by the pursuing soldiers and the steadily reduced amount of game turned many of the hunters to the sea for their livelihood, and when they traded the island's forests for the decks of small, fast, maneuverable ships, they brought with them a uniquely juxtaposed set of qualifications for plundering. The skill they had gained as riflemen during years of stalking wild cattle and swine was added to the previous seafaring experience of many of their company and then combined with a burning hatred of Spain that was first kindled by the Reformation and then stoked into flame by their fierce resistance to the cinquantaines. Until 1640, Hispaniolan hunters plundered the Spanish in a sporadic fashion, sailing from their island sanctuaries in open craft the Dutch called "flyboats." The French who still traded on the island coast named the men after their vessels, styling them "flibustiers," a term the languid-tongued English pronounced as "freebooter." Not content merely to Anglicize a single Gallicism, Englishmen in the Caribbean carried their penchant for linguistic corruption even further. They took the word *"boucan,"* used by the hunters to identify the small racks on which they smoked their meat, the fire pit beneath the rack, the meat itself, and the process of smoking as well, and with a proper degree of mispronunciation, designated the hunters "buccaneers."

In the years when the hunters first turned to piracy, and the words "buccaneer" and "pirate" became interchangeable, they created only minor difficulties for Spanish shipping. They raided isolated settlements and turtling camps, captured only smaller vessels, but failed to take rich prizes. Yet as the European population of the Caribbean increased, the size of the colonial settlements grew, and commerce expanded proportionately, castaways, victims of shipwrecks, deserters, servants fleeing their masters, and fugitives also increased in number. For many such men, joining the buccaneers was an acceptable alternative to the lives they had abandoned. The anti-Spanish character of the enterprise precluded participation by Spaniards, but seafarers of every other nation that sent ships to the Caribbean joined the pirate crews. Many of the earliest sea-going buccaneers were Dutch, but as the number of English in the Caribbean increased, the census of English pirates rose proportionately, and by 1660 the plundering of Spain in the New World was an industry dominated by men from London, Wales, and the West Country. The French also continued their depredations, evincing no more scruple over looting their co-religionists in the seventeenth century than they had shown in the latter decades of the sixteenth. The anti-Catholic sentiment normal to English and Dutch vessels meant French buccaneers usually sailed aboard ships manned entirely by Frenchmen, but this in no way diminished the fury of their attacks or their enthusiasm for booty.

At the same time English sea rovers were plundering Spain, others of their countrymen in the first decades of the seventeenth century were attempting to conquer and colonize in the Caribbean. Numerous attempts were made to plant settlements on the coasts of South and Central America and on a score of islands. Most of the early efforts were unsuccessful for a combination of economic and tactical reasons, and before 1650, the English had reined in their expansive efforts to establish footholds all over the West Indies and on the Spanish Main. They concentrated instead on colonizing five islands: Barbados, St. Christopher, Nevis, Antigua, and Montserrat. The largest of these, Barbados, was windward of the Spanish settlements, far off at the easternmost edge of the Caribbean. The other four were also distant from the ports that might host Spanish predators; all were located in the Leeward Islands, north of Barbados and a thousand miles or more from centers of Spanish strength in Cuba, Central America, or on the South American continent. The five islands selected by the English were all obviously fertile, but the terrain was covered with hard-to-clear jungle and was often mountainous. No precious metals were to be found, dye-bearing plants did not flourish, and no herds of wild cattle or pigs roamed their interiors. The apparent limited potential of the islands, their isolation from Spanish settlements, and a windward location that made them easier to reach from Europe than by sailing east from Maracaibo, Cartagena, Porto Bello, or Havana, gave the English settlers a measure of security they were denied in more central Caribbean locations and undoubtedly assured the survival of their settlements.

The first permanent English colony was established at St. Christopher in 1624, but it was a tenuous effort that survived only because the colonists were able to combine with the French already resident on the island, destroy the Indians, and repel a Spanish invasion in 1629. Even then, peace did not prevail. The French and English fought intermittently for control over the next 80 years and constant turmoil on the island caused many settlers to leave St. Christopher and migrate to other islands. Nevis, the next of the Leewards to be settled, was a mountain top protruding from the sea. It offered less arable land and more difficult terrain than St. Christopher, but it provided at least a measure of security for the settlers. Englishmen abandoning St. Christopher also established colonies on rugged Montserrat in 1632 and on Antigua, which had ample farm land and a good harbor but was deficient in water supply. If any of these farmers had hoped to become prosperous in the Leewards during the first decades of settlement, they were surely disappointed. Before 1650, Nevis, St. Christopher, Montserrat, and Antigua supported subsistence tobacco farming and little else. The largest English Caribbean establishment in the first half of the seventeenth century was on the island of Barbados. The English began the task of converting the island's 150 square miles of jungle-covered, fertile soil into farms in the 1620s, and as was the case in the Leewards and the continental colonies of Virginia and Maryland, the planters labored as peasant tobacco farmers.

English institutions were transported across the Atlantic by the settlers and they took root easily in the New World. The common law proved its durability in frontier settlements, as did English political ideology, English customs, and the national church, but the feature that most distinguished early-day Barbados settlements and the Leeward colonies as well from similar efforts on the North American continent and from rural agricultural communities in the mother country was the peculiar demographic structure of the island's European population. The society that grew in the English Caribbean was composed almost entirely of males, and the few women present were, as a result of the social, economic, and legal structure of island society, unavailable as sexual partners for members of the brigand crews.

Any population survey of English West Indian islands in the seventeenth century is a dangerous undertaking. Records for the period are fragmentary or nonexistent, but from information available on shipping registers and tax rolls, and from the descriptions of travelers and residents, it is possible to get a fairly accurate picture of the distribution of sexes for various decades. On this one aspect of early island society, all sources agree. The number of women on the islands in the years when tobacco cultivation was the major economic activity were statistically insignificant. The origin of this demographic anomaly is not difficult to discover. Colonies in the earlier years of exploration were not planned as permanent places of residence for large populations. They were seen as commercial enterprises, founded to produce wealth—large amounts in relatively short periods of time— and as such there was no need to settle them as complete communities. The economics of founding the earliest colonies in the West Indies and on the mainland at Virginia required the establishment of all-male villages. Space aboard ship was at a premium, the cost of transporting colonists was high, the dangers were considerable, and expending capital on the transport of women, who would surely not be producers of profit in the New World, could hardly be countenanced.

The character of Jamestown altered over the first two decades of settlement and the colony changed from the creature of the Virginia Company's Board of Governors into a self-contained American commonwealth due to the desperate attempts of the shareholders to induce migration from England to their fief in America. Offers of vast acreage were made to anyone who would travel to the colony, additional land was provided for family and servants brought over, and at one point shipments of females were actually sent to Virginia to make conditions in the frontier settlement more bearable and to encourage immigration.[3] Later continental colonies, Plymouth in 1620 and Massachusetts Bay and Maryland a decade later, were different in concept and purpose from Virginia or from establishments on West Indian islands, and demographic patterns of the migrants reflected the differences by exhibiting a rough sexual equality in their populations. A similar balance between males and females was not present in the seventeenth-century English Caribbean. Although few records that go back beyond 1700 survive for the Leeward Islands and there is almost no information on the settlements for the years before 1650, what scraps of information that have not been lost reveal that plots of land were small, tobacco was the main crop on the four islands, and the female population during these earliest years was almost nonexistent.[4] Like the first arrivals at Jamestown in 1607 and the initial settlers of St. Christopher, the earliest settlers on Barbados, the 74 English who arrived with Captain John Powell in the ship *Peter*, included no women.[5] A later tabulation of Barbados residents made in 1635 shows 94 percent were male, none were under ten years old, and there were virtually no married couples among the group.[6] Richard Ligon visited the island a decade later, and his observations confirm the male nature of its society. In the three years he resided on Barbados, from 1647 and 1650, he chronicled the details of almost every facet of life in the settlement, but except for an account of a planter who attempted to obtain a female servant in trade for a sow by a cash-barter agreement in which the price of the woman was determined by matching her weight against that of the pig, he hardly mentioned women. Ligon was not a misogynist by any definition. Although he did explain that the weight of the obese servant woman— and thus the cash required to consummate the bargain—was sufficient to persuade the planter to return home with his sow and abandon his design of acquiring a female for his plantation, Ligon was an astute admirer of the feminine form. He had an eye for a firm breast, a fetching smile, or a well-shaped thigh, and while visiting St. Jago in the Cape Verde Islands on his voyage across the sea, he tested the limits of his descriptive powers cataloging the grace and loveliness of several women he encountered on his few days ashore.[7]

Perhaps some explanation of his failure to mention white women was an exquisitely tuned sense of feminine perfection that could not be excited sufficiently by any of the more ordinary females who resided on the island. Discussing the pleasures available locally he complained that on Barbados the sense of feeling was little gratified by touching the skins of women. "They are so sweaty and clammy, as the hand cannot passe over, without being glued and cemented in the passage or motion; and by that means, little pleasure is given to, or received by the agent or the patient."[8] If his evaluation was generally shared by other males of his acquaintance it might go far toward providing an understanding of his comment on planter sociability. "So frank, so loving, and so good natur'd were these Gentlemen one to another; and to express their affections yet higher, they had particular names one to another, as, Neighbour, Friend, Brother, Sister: So that I perceived nothing wanting, that might make up a firm and lasting friendship amongst them."[9] It would be too easy to read extraneous meaning into both statements. The likely explanation for Ligon's writing nothing of white women was that there were few of them on the island and their participation in most activities was insignificant. Ligon regularly discussed female slaves, noting that planters made conscious decisions to purchase them in quantities equal to the male slaves they held. This was necessary, he explained, for the males would complain excessively if wives were not available to them. Some deserving blacks were even permitted two and three wives. He does not mention if this was also the case with Amerind

slaves, but their number was always so small on Barbados that no
matter what the ratio of men to women among them, it would have
no extraordinary demographic effect on the island's labor force.[10]

There are no exact figures for the number of white females on the
island either as servants or free, but some indication of the ratio between males and females is available. Ligon noted that when he arrived on the island an epidemic was raging, killing ten men for every
woman that died. The disparity in numbers between male and female might have been the result of the dissolute habits of the planters, as Ligon suggested, but it is more probable that it reflected the
sexual imbalance of the population. This is not controverted by the
existence of a standing committee on the island to punish adultery
and fornication. The committee was "rarely put in execution," indicating either a paucity of women or high standards of morality among
the planters; there is ample evidence to refute the latter.[11]

Ligon also took the opportunity to advise his readers on the correct
procedure to be followed in setting themselves up as sugar planters.
He explained in detail the exact steps to be followed. He specified
the amount of capital needed, the items to be carried to the West
Indies for sale to the residents, the manner of gaining enough cash
to establish a plantation, the procedures for planting, tending, and
processing sugar cane, and the number of workers needed to get the
job done. One hundred slaves would be required, 50 males and 50
females to provide the bulk of the labor force. White servants would
be needed on the proposed plantation. Thirty would be a sufficient
number, he said, and among them there were to be skilled carpen-
ters, joiners, masons, smiths, and coopers. There were also to be
women, although Ligon did not mention any specific skills that might
be required of them. Of the 30 servants, ten were to be female according to his plan, indicating white male servants had much less
need of the opposite sex than the slaves. The women would be divided into two groups; four would serve in the plantation house and
the remaining half-dozen were to "weed, and do the common work
abroad yearly." What the common work included he did not say, but
the employment of ten white women on the plantation to engage in
light field labor and in household chores was Ligon's idea of what a

plantation should be, rather than a reflection of what he had observed in his three-year sojourn on Barbados. In his discussions of women engaged in light agricultural labor, he mentions only black women; the servants he observed carrying out household chores in the homes of planters were in every case male slaves. The same sex distribution for laborers was prescribed by another observer for setting up a cocoa walk. Richard Blome specified "3 Negro men, and as many Negro women" would be needed, but only "4 White Servants" and an overseer were necessary. Blacks had to be acquired in equal numbers, he explained, but he made no mention of any reason for obtaining white females.[12]

The disparity of women in the islands was made even more acute by the political situation in the mother country. After gaining control of England during the civil wars of the 1640s, Puritans attempted to expand their brand of Protestant extremism into the Caribbean by establishing a colony on Providence Island to glorify God and to line their pocketbooks all in a single endeavor. They were not successful in attaining either goal. The proximity of their settlement to Spanish strongholds on the mainland prevented it from prospering according to plan, the commercially oriented Puritans who formed the early contingents of colonists departed, and the island was left to men similar to those who roamed the Hispaniolan forests. Despite the debacle on Providence Island, the Puritan-dominated government was determined to expand their style of Christian militancy into the West Indies. Under the direction of their Lord Protector, Oliver Cromwell, they evolved the "Western Design," a plan to enlarge English holdings in the Caribbean by taking islands from Spain one after another. Much to Cromwell's disappointment, the "Design" was foiled. Efforts to capture Hispaniola were repelled, and the only success came when an expedition under the command of Admiral Sir William Penn and General Robert Venables was able to wrest Jamaica from the Spanish in 1655. The results of the scheme in terms of territorial aggrandizement were less for the Puritans than had been hoped, but the influx of soldiers and sailors added to the rapidly increasing male population in the Caribbean. The numbers of men in the islands were further augmented with colonists from two other groups. Those unhappy with the defeat of the Royalists and the beheading of Charles I, at least a portion of them, preferred migration to the fetid and disease-ridden tropics rather than life under the Puritans. To these disaffected English were added large numbers of war prisoners, captives taken in the civil wars and during a protracted rebellion in Ireland. Shipping them to America seemed to the government an ideal solution to the problems of two hemispheres. England would be rid of potential troublemakers and America could put them to work. More prisoners were probably shipped to the Caribbean after having been captured in the Irish uprising than had been forced across the Atlantic by all the civil strife in the mother country, and like other groups in the English Indies the shiploads of war-induced migrants, disgruntled losers, Royalist captives, and Irish prisoners of war were composed almost entirely of men.

The heavily male character of the cargoes of Irish sent to the West Indies caused a degree of consternation among government leaders, and for a time there was some sentiment to equalize the sexual balance by shipping large numbers of Irish females to Barbados and the Leewards on the premise that an adequate number of women would stabilize island society. In September, 1655, Henry Cromwell wrote to Secretary of State John Thurlow: [13]

Concerninge the younge women, although we must use force in takinge them up, yet it beinge so much for their own goode, and likely to be of soe great advantage to the publique, it is not in the least doubted, that you may have such number of them as you shall thinke fitt to make use uppon this account.

Interest in sending the women could not be sustained without broadening the proposal to include males, and within two weeks the younger Cromwell also recommended sending some 1,500 to 2,000 boys of 12 to 14 years since, he argued, Ireland could easily spare them. The Council of State duly voted to ship 1,000 girls and a like number of boys under the age of fourteen to the West Indies. Some further preparations were made to implement the scheme, but there is no evidence it ever reached fruition. More likely it was abandoned in favor of sending only adult males who were already available instead of expending time and effort capturing over a thousand girls. Moreover, it is unlikely that if 1,000 youthful females were actually shipped to the Caribbean, they would have disappeared without a trace.[14]

After the Irish insurrection was crushed in 1656, the Caribbean also provided a convenient place to send soldiers of the victorious but potentially troublesome Puritan army.[15] The volume of immigrants to the West Indies from Ireland, the willing as well as the recalcitrant, became so great that the government was forced to contract for their shipment. Sir John Clotworthy received permission to carry 500 "natural Irishmen" to America, a Bristol shipper named Richard Netheway was to carry 100 Irish Tories to Virginia, and a group of Bristol merchants were empowered to carry 400 Irish Tories to "the Caribbee Islands" the following year. Later a sweeping order was issued for the transportation of vagrants to the West Indies. Wanderers taken in Limerick and Cork were to be transported by Captain John Norris, and all persons in the jails of Clonmel, Waterford, Wexford, Kilkenny, and Carlow were to be sent by John Mylam, a merchant. One Colonel Stubbers was given permission to transport 60 women from Connaught to the West Indies in June, 1654, but there is no way of determining with precision the proportion of women among the Irish shipped to the Caribbean in any year.[16] The only thing known certainly is that the number was never large. The greatest single shipment sent from Ireland during these years was 1,200 males, and those Tories sent against their will were soldiers or men whose political sympathies were known to the authorities and were regarded as unacceptable. Even if the numbers of vagrants rounded up and sent off included women, as it surely did, there is no reason to suppose that vagrant groups in Ireland included any greater proportion of women than did similar groups in England.[17]

Irish rebels and an assortment of Royalists were not the only victims of forced emigration during the Cromwellian period and after the restoration of Charles II. From time to time small groups of Quakers were shipped over, as were occasional Scottish Covenanters who could not be reconciled to the Restoration religious settlement. Over 1,000 of these deeply committed advocates of Protestant reformation from north of the Tweed may have been sent to the colonies.

Another contingent of prisoners of war or rebels sent to the colonies in the latter portion of the seventeenth century were the vanquished supporters of the Duke of Monmouth. After their failure to wrest the throne from James II, they presented particular difficulties for the authorities. Many were men of power and influence, at least on the local level, and if allowed to escape punishment could be troublesome. A measure of the problem was solved by the gallows, but the total number was too large to be dispatched conveniently in such fashion. The ideal solution was transportation, and 500 of the Duke's supporters were sent to the West Indies where, under the terms of royal order, they were compelled to be indentured servants for ten years even if they were able to purchase their freedom.[18]

While importation of prisoners of war, rebels, and a number of religious dissenters contributed to the largely male demographic character of the islands, equally important in reinforcing the peculiar sex distribution in the West Indies was the continual state of war that prevailed in the Caribbean during the latter half of the seventeenth and into the early decades of the eighteenth century. Throughout these years, the English were engaged in a series of wars against the Dutch and against France, but in the interludes between there was no peace in the Caribbean. The jointly occupied island of St. Christopher was in frequent turmoil as English and French attempted to gain control from one another. The French at one point drove the English from Antigua and Montserrat, and the Dutch island of St. Eustatius in a single decade changed hands almost ten times. With each invasion and counter-invasion, considerable property damage resulted. Slaves were carried off, crops destroyed, buildings and equipment stolen or burned, and settlers killed and deported. Even when colonists from England, Holland, and France were not fighting each other, there was always the threat of a Spanish attack to destabilize the situation or in later years the fear of slave insurrection. The danger of invasion increased the need for males to serve not only as field hands but to protect the islanders from their chattels. As early as 1642, the Governor of St. Christopher estimated there were 1,600 fighting men on the island, and only 13 years later over 800 unattached males left St. Christopher to join the expedition against Jamaica.[19] Planters frequently petitioned England to send more military strength, explaining that the French outnumbered them, their own resources were limited, and the only way to make the area safe was by the presence of troops from England and a substantial naval force. During the first years of the Restoration, the Council on Foreign Plantations resolved that 400 foot and 150 mounted troops be sent to Jamaica for the island's protection, and to secure further the English settlements it was recommended that two ships be constantly plying the coasts. The number of men sent varied widely from year to year, making estimates difficult, but the troops ran into the thousands during especially unsettled periods. Many of the regulars sent to the islands did not return home with their units. A good share of them were buried in the West Indies, the victims of disease, ill-treatment, and the unhealthy tropical climate, but those who lived and stayed on to plant, farm, or eke out a marginal existence in some other way further skewed the distribution of the sexes and contributed toward male preponderance on the islands. Even when large numbers of regulars were present, islanders continued to fret. The colonial assembly of Jamaica was sufficiently concerned in 1673 to require all men between the ages of 12 and 60 to join one of the local companies of horse or foot. Masters were ordered to see that their eligible servants were members of the units, and a £5 fine or corporal punishment was mandated for those who illegally avoided their militia duties. The legislation dealing with the militia did not reassure the government, and they remained uneasy about the islanders' abilities to protect themselves. In the closing years of William III's reign the Council of Trade and Plantations recommended to the Lords Justices that all men between the ages of 14 and 60 be required to serve.[20]

The number of militiamen on Jamaica at any given time is not easily ascertained. Although figures sent to London indicate that almost every adult male was enrolled, there appears to have been a good deal of fraud involved in militia service, and strength on paper was not necessarily an indication of the number of battle-ready men on hand to defend the island. The need for more and more males to make the island safe forced the planters to strive hard to increase the number of white male inhabitants, and although there is considerable doubt about how successful they were in attracting immigrants in this most sought-after category, those that did come further increased the proportion of men in the population. The same situation prevailed in Barbados and elsewhere, where the dangers of foreign invasion and slave insurrection were as acute as on Jamaica. A report in April 1676 gave the militia strength for St. Christopher at 1,000 men, Nevis had 1,550 men to bear arms but only 1,000 weapons, Antigua claimed a militia of 1,100, and Montserrat had 1,500 or 1,600 men under arms. A census taken only two years later reported the white male population for the same islands at 695 for St. Christopher, 1,534 on Nevis, Antigua with 1,236, and Montserrat with 1,148.[21]

The influx from Ireland and the residual population of former soldiers and sailors did not alleviate the shortage of workers in the West Indies, and planters sought to obtain men to labor in their cane fields from another source: the convicts that jammed many of England's jails. Sending convicts to the colonies began in earnest during the Protectorate, and when Charles II became king he continued the practice after receiving a petition from a group of Jamaican colonists asking that transportation not be halted. Records indicate at least 4,500 convicts were sent to the colonies between 1661 and 1700. They were shipped to the mainland colonies as well as to the Caribbean, but after 1697, the majority of those transported went to the West Indies.[22] Christopher Jeaffreson, a Leeward Island gentleman, was one of those who sought to obtain convicts for the West Indies. He originally journeyed to London in the 1680s to procure servants for the islands, but he found little enthusiasm among the lower classes for traveling to the Caribbean, and it was only in desperation, after failing to recruit any quantity of servants, that he sought out the convicts. Jeaffreson presented a petition to the authorities for permission to transport 300 criminals and his request was granted.[23] He then went to secure his cargo from the prison officers, little anticipating the difficulties that awaited him. When he arrived at the Old Bailey, he found to his dismay that he would not be given the opportunity to select convicts but was required to take those chosen for him by the jailors. The feature of this arrangement that particularly distressed Jeaffreson was that when the prison officials used the word "men" in reference to their charges, they used the term in its generic sense rather than as it was more commonly employed as a denominator of sex. The men in Jeaffreson's group included a good many women. Jeaffreson was looking for field hands, not females, and he learned immediately that he was at a disadvantage in trying to secure them because, he claimed, the Jamaica agents in London would take women and children along with the men, and the authorities naturally preferred to deal with them. He wrote a series of complaining letters explaining the situation to Thomas Hill, the Deputy Governor of St. Christopher, and at the same time continued his efforts. At one point he descended on the prison keepers immediately after the exposure of the Rye House Plot and the apprehension of the conspirators. He reasoned that those arrested were largely male and thus chances of securing a cargo of convicts with a high proportion of men was substantially increased. He was not successful in this particular foray, but neither was he daunted. He memorialized public officials, conferred with members of the Lords' Commissioners for Foreign Plantations, harrangued the jailors, and engaged in an assortment of political machinations.[24]

Jeaffreson's persistence was rewarded, and over a period of time he managed to send most if not all of his allotted 300 convicts to the Indies. Unfortunately, since the prisoners were sent in small batches, there is no record of all who endured forced emigration as members of the contingents he shipped. In the three groups for which Jeaffreson mentioned the sex distribution in his correspondence, the males outnumbered the females by a margin of over three to one. A roster of convicts he included in a 1684 letter to Governor Hill listed 23 men and five women on their way to serve in the islands. The next year he wrote of two other shipments; the first contained 30 men and eleven women, the second 29 men and nine women. In the letter informing officials on St. Christopher that the cargo of 29 men and nine women was being sent, Jeaffreson made it clear he had not reconciled himself to being forced to send females to the West Indies, and lamented the fact that after all his labor, securing convicts was still a very frustrating business.[25] He complained to Governor Hill at one point of the covert payments he was forced to make to jail officials, explaining that he had to pay the fees for 39 prisoners:

but finding one of the women to be sicke and infirme I resolved to leave her behind, which the keepers were very angry at; and I could not prevail with them to retourne me the £1 11s. payd for her; which I chose rather to lose than to hazard the loss of five pounds more upon a sickly woman.[26]

It seems likely from the surviving evidence that the number of male convicts sent to the West Indies by Jeaffreson outnumbered the female convicts by at least a three to one majority, indicating he had done a poor job of securing males. Women sentenced for crimes serious enough to warrant transportation to the colonies represented only 15 to 20 percent of such offenders, and the same is true for crimes in which the death sentence was pronounced. In capital cases, however, the sentence was often changed to transportation to the colonies, and thus those females actually shipped to America were probably even less in proportion to the number of men, for women often would "plead their bellies" (i.e., claim to be pregnant) and thereby escape death or being sent to the New World. In a number of cases reported from the early eighteenth century, the ratio of offenders sentenced to death was six males for each female, but in every case the women testified they were pregnant, and in so doing gained a chance to cheat the hangman and avoid forced emigration to the Caribbean.[27]

Despite Christopher Jeaffreson's assertions to the contrary, the ratio of women to men in the shipments sent to Jamaica was probably no higher than in groups sent to the Leewards. The Jamaicans also made it clear they were at least as unenthusiastic about accepting women convicts as were other islanders. On December 28, 1696, a group of merchants informed the Board of Trade they were unwilling to accept a consignment of 80 criminals "because most of them were women, and because persons of bad character were not wanted in Jamaica." During the summer of the following year, Newgate prison filled with female convicts, but none could be persuaded to take them. Inquiries were made among colonial agents to try and transport at least 50, and while the Leeward Island representative agreed to take some of them, the Jamaicans would accept the women only if 150 men were also sent. The decision was made to send the women to the Leewards, but it is not certain they were ever sent although men continued to be transported to the West Indies during the months the women awaited shipment. Like other West Indian colonists, the Barbadians were opposed to allowing female convicts to be sent to their island. They were willing to accept convicted criminals, but the colony's agents in London advised the Council for Trade and Plantations to send female convicts to Virginia or Carolina where, they said, white women worked in the fields.[28]

The administrative complications, fees, frustration and bribes required to secure convicts for transportation gave encouragement to a much more insidious type of forced migration, kidnapping. The illegal nature of snatching persons from the streets and roads of England for shipment to America meant that few records survive that might indicate the number who found themselves in a new life as the direct result of force, but the absence of both expense and administrative difficulties made kidnapping profitable and convenient. The usual method of obtaining cargoes was to ply intended victims with alcohol or, if children, to lure them into the kidnapper's clutches with sweets. By the fifth decade of the seventeenth century, kidnapping for the colonies had become sufficiently widespread so that regular depots were established in lower class sections of London, especially in St. Katherines near the Tower and the docks. Victims were brought to any one of several houses where they might be kept prisoner as long as a month before a ship captain could be located to take them away.

Kidnapping was so common that Christopher Jeaffreson, at one point during his difficulties acquiring a shipment of convicts, considered the possibility of "spiriting" persons off to the Indies. He rejected the practice not because he found it morally opprobrious but because by the time he hit upon the idea, "the Lord Chief Justice hath so severely handled the kidnabbers, and so encouraged all informers against them, that it [was] very difficult to procure any."[29] The wrath of the authorities, he complained, had caused a £500 fine to be levied against a slopseller convicted of involvement in kidnapping, and several other men accused of similar dealings were placed in disrepute. The result was that merchants informed on kidnappers and reaped the rewards while at least some ship captains, fearful of being reported to the authorities and severely fined or disgraced, refused to carry persons taken against their will.[30]

London was not the only place where kidnappers plied their trade in Cromwellian and Restoration England. The city of Bristol received so many complaints about kidnapping that on September 29, 1654, they ordered "that all boys, maids, and others thenceforth transported as servants should before shipment have their indentures of service enrolled in the Tolzey Book."[31] The ordinance was to be enforced by a fine of £20 for violations, and copies of the ordinance were to be posted in conspicuous places so that none could plead ignorance of the law. In July, 1662, the town corporation petitioned the King for power to ascertain the identity of passengers on all ships bound for the colonies to prevent the "spiriting away" of unwary persons and to prevent the escape of rogues and apprentices. There is also a notice in the Corporation minute book containing information that children were daily being enticed from their parents and servants from their masters by merchants and captains trading to Virginia and to the West Indies. Kidnapping in Bristol was too profitable to be suppressed by fines, and the magistrates exhibited their tacit approval of the industry when, the following year, they sentenced two men convicted of manstealing each to stand one hour in pillories for three consecutive market days with notice of their offense placarded to their breasts. They were careful to ensure the safety of the men from the citizenry in this case; officers were present to make sure the miscreants were kept safe from stones and missiles hurled by passers-by. Other kidnappers were similarly punished, and the leniency shown them by the magistracy was hardly calculated to deter the traffic in unwilling human beings.[32]

West Indian merchants and planters were anxious to increase their labor force, and many of these unwilling migrants were surely welcomed by the local residents, in need of servants and agricultural workers as they were. But persons sent to the Caribbean against their wills also created serious difficulties for the islanders. Many victims of the kidnappers were "idle, lazie, [and] simple" people who would "rather beg than work." Others, angered over their forced migration, were understandably hostile. A group of leading Jamaica merchants petitioned Charles II in 1682 for a law making it more difficult to kidnap Englishmen. They asked that servants under the age of 21 be bound for service in the colonies only with the consent of an offical higher than a magistrate, thereby eliminating the abuses of corrupt officials on the lower administrative levels. They also asked that in cases of those under 14, the parents be required to sign the necessary documents to bind the children for shipment.

The West Indian population of convicts, vagabonds, deserters, and deportees was a source of recruits for Caribbean pirate vessels in the seventeenth and eighteenth centuries, but there was still another group from which pirates were able to gain crewmembers: Englishmen living in the Indies who had come voluntarily to engage in occupations not directly connected with seafaring. Large numbers of the English who sailed for the Caribben in the years after the civil wars made the migration freely because they hoped to improve their economic situation. These were not the desperately poor, the cottagers or the wandering beggars of England. They were people whose situation was such that they had aspirations of at least attaining greater prosperity than they enjoyed in the homeland. Yet while they hoped to better themselves economically, at the time they elected to migrate they were unable to afford the voyage across the Atlantic. To pay their passage, they sailed as indentured servants; they sold themselves into servitude for a number of years, most commonly five, to cover the cost of transportation to the New World. Some idea of the type of people who became indentured servants can be gleaned from surviving records. In 1654, the Bristol Council required the names of all servants bound for overseas to be enrolled as city apprentices. The entries were carefully kept until 1685, and in that time approximately 10,000 names were entered. That the opportunities offered in the New World were well-known throughout England is substantiated from the list. Most who sailed from Bristol, as might be expected, came from the surrounding areas. The West Country, Somerset,

Gloucestershire, and Wiltshire provided almost 85 percent of the migrants, but the remainder came from Wales and from every other county in England except Rutland.[33]

Over one-third of the indentured servants made their living from the land before deciding to migrate. Approximately 36 percent listed their occupations as yeomen or farmers, with a majority preferring to style themselves yeomen. Artisans and tradesmen made up another 22 percent, while unskilled laborers, the most economically distressed segment of the migrants, composed only ten percent of those who sailed. There were a few professionals and gentlemen, who had presumably fallen on evil days, but they numbered only one person out of every hundred voyagers. There is also the possibility that eight percent of the indentured servants on the list may have been minors. The Bristol data is confirmed by another similar list from London for the period from 1683 to 1684 which contains the names of 750 persons who sailed from the city for the New World. Skilled workers were the largest number of indentured servants, outnumbering farmers by a majority of two to one. Again it appears that approximately eight percent of the London migrants were children, and, more significant for the development of the West Indies, on both the Bristol and the London lists of indentured servants, males outnumbered females by a margin of three to one.[34]

The need for indentured servants was nowhere more evident than on the island of Barbados. From its earliest years of settlement the Barbadians had tried a number of schemes to induce Englishmen to come to the island, but none of them, including the payment of bounties, was successful. It was not until the development of a regular system of indentured servitude that some progress was made in bringing laborers to the undermanned plantations. This began in 1636 when the ship Abraham sailed to Ireland to take aboard approximately 100 servants for shipment to Barbados. When the vessel arrived, the captain learned that the agent in charge of recruiting was able to induce only 41 men and 20 women between the ages of 17 and 35 to go to the island. The large number of women did not please the agent, but he explained in a letter to his employer that the reasons so many women were included was because he could not persuade enough men to go. Even then, the sex ratio forced on the reluctant agent underwent change. Three persons whose sex cannot be determined left the group even before they sailed, reducing the number to 58. Later three women were discovered to be pregnant and put ashore and another was also put ashore when it was learned she had the "frentche dizeas."[35] Before departure two additional servants were evidently procured, for 56 of the contingent were presented for sale and sold in the West Indies. At most only 18 of these could have been women, meaning a ratio of over two males for each female, but depending on the sex of the three who disappeared and the two late additions, the ratio may have been over three to one.

Even then, the distribution of the sexes in the Abraham's cargo was more equally balanced than on the island where there were as yet practically no women. It was not until the 1650s, when large numbers of servants began arriving on Barbados, that the number of females began to increase.[36] But as was the case with migrant groups to all the islands, the sex distribution of the indentured servants remained heavily skewed toward the males. Reflecting some concern over the problem, and at the same time trying to rid themselves of a local difficulty, London authorities in 1656 actually sent soldiers into brothels and other places frequented by loose women, rounding them up for shipment to Barbados. The exact count of prostitutes persuaded to travel to the Caribbean in this fashion is not certain, but estimates range from 400 to 1,200.[37] Whatever the number actually sent, it was insufficient to redress the island's sexual imbalance. The shortage of women was so severe that one observer noted in 1655, "A Baud brought over puts on a demour comportment, a whore if hansume makes a wife for some rich planter."[38] How many soiled doves became the wives of landowners is uncertain, but it is known that households in Bridgetown, on Barbados, contained fewer wives and children than households in Bristol Rhode Island during the same period. One island observer claimed to know of 20 women on Barbados who had married as many as five or six times, each of them wedding anew at the deaths of their husbands. Female servants were so much in demand for sexual purposes that the legislature had to provide severe penalties for males who married serving women with-

out first obtaining consent from the masters of their brides. Such
men were required to labor double the time remaining on their wives'
term of service to compensate the injured master. Free men impregnating indentured women were required to serve the womens' masters for a period of three years or provide a substitute for the same
length of time and the women were forced to perform an additional
two years of work. A servant impregnating another servant was forced
to yield up double the female's remaining term of service when he
completed the requirements of his own indenture.

After 1650 sugar replaced tobacco as the agricultural mainstay of
Barbados, and the increased specialization and capitalization required
for the new crop meant small holdings were gradually reduced in
number. Most large landowners were sufficiently prosperous by the
closing decades of the century to return to England, leaving overseers
to manage their estates. Small plantations almost disappeared from
the island, and slavery took over almost entirely from white labor.
The total white population of the island declined, and although the
proportion of women among the whites increased, the number of
white females remained small; the demand for women among the
resident whites was never met, and prices remained high for white
females. A list of people filing notice of their intention to leave Barbados in 1679 contained 593 names; 22 who planned to depart were
married couples, 59 were single women, and 512 were single men.
This ten to one ratio is similar to the proportion of men to women
who died in the epidemic years before, and it is identical with the
ratio found on a 1680 list of landowning Barbadians where womens'
names appear along with the names of 1,225 male freeholders. None
of these pieces of information indicates a sex ratio of ten to one among
the general population on the island, but they do provide strong evidence that the number of men far exceeded the number of women.
The actual figures of 1673 were 9,274 white men and approximately
3,800 white women. In 1690, Dalby Thomas estimated a sugar plantation could be operated with 50 blacks and seven English to super-
vise them, but with the diminishing white population and the increase in the importation of slaves, planters and their agents wasted
little time trying to persuade women to travel to the island. They

needed European males to secure the plantations in the event of slave rebellion, and although planters were required by law to maintain one white servant for every ten slaves, they were rarely able to meet the statutory provision.[39]

An unequal sex distribution similar to that on Barbados also prevailed in the Leewards, and in like manner, the disparity was partially redressed over the years as landholdings were consolidated, slaves replaced indentured servants in the fields, and the white population decreased. Yet the shortage of women in the islands was severe, and masters complained regularly that their female servants were being seduced or lured away by lonely males. The lack of available females became so disruptive on Nevis that the legislature in 1675 enacted a statute entitled "Women Servants Inveagled." It specified that any man, servant or free, who should keep company with female servants, distract them from their duties, or entice them with promises of marriage and freedom would be punished unless they did so only with the permission of the masters. The situation did not immediately improve, and five years later the legislature found it necessary to reenact the same statute. On Nevis, Antigua, St. Christopher, and Montserrat in 1678, the total number of men exceeded the number of women by a proportion of two to one, but for servants the disparity was probably even higher. A census taken 40 years later, when the proportion of males and females had become approximately equal on most English West Indian islands, revealed that the same tendencies operating on the demography of free white residents were not necessarily operative with servants, among whom the males continued to outnumber the females by over two to one.[40]

Englishmen came later to Jamaica than to the other islands, but after its seizure from the Spanish in 1655, they proceeded to develop it in much the same manner as Barbados and the Leewards. As in the other settlements, men were present in substantially larger numbers than women during the early period of colonization. In the first years of the Restoration, a stream of almost entirely male migrants came from the mother country, in many cases from its jails, and even when His Majesty's settlers were transferred from Surinam to Jamaica, the transplanted male colonists outnumbered their women by a margin of two to one. Island authorities and colonial agents encouraged only male migration to provide labor for the fields and men to bear arms in case of attack. Indentured servants, convicts, prisoners of war, and deserters came to Jamaica, as did men from the other islands who hoped to find on this largest of all English West Indian possessions the land and wealth they were unable to obtain on Barbados, St. Christopher, Nevis, Antigua, or Montserrat. The local assembly provided bounties of land to migrants, and at one point offered exemption from port charges to any master bringing over 50 white male servants to the island. In 1661, the ratio of white men to white women on Jamaica was approximately six to one. The following year, the gap had diminished somewhat. The *Journals of the House of Assembly in Jamaica* reveal that in 1662, the number of white males on the island outnumbered females by only four to one. Ten years later, as the labor force of the island was transformed from white workers to black slaves, the proportion of males to females dropped to two to one and this distribution remained until at least 1676. In this same period of ten years, however, the total white population of the island only doubled, while the number of blacks increased twenty-fold. The exact ratios and the population figures for the first decades of English domination of Jamaica vary slightly from source to source, but no matter which tabulation is accepted as genuine, the same over-all picture emerges of a population composed initially of males, followed by a gradual increase in the female population altering the ratio between the sexes from six to one to four to one and then two to one.[41]

Of particular importance for buccaneering was the main city of Jamaica, Port Royal, which served for a time as the veritable capital of English sea rovers in the Caribbean. Widely reputed to be the most corrupt and debauched town in all His Majesty's dominions, the evils of Port Royal were probably no greater than in the waterfront areas of London, Bristol, or other seaports. But if Port Royal was no more wicked than other comparable towns, it was without doubt the most sophisticated place in the English Caribbean. The many ships that entered its harbor brought a wide variety of European manufactured goods and foodstuffs. The only dietary staple characteristic of the mother country that was not present in quantity in the markets of Port Royal was good quality bread. Codfish from the Newfoundland Banks, herring from England, and Irish salmon were easily available, and wealthy merchants could satisfy their taste for delicacies with locally baked cheesecakes, custards, and tarts. There were taverns for men from every social level and occupational category in Port Royal, and Englishmen could slake their thirst at The Blue Anchor, The Three Tunns, the Sign of the Mermaid, The Ship, or scores of like establishments, often bearing names similar to their counterparts in the homeland. One complaining visitor to the city claimed there were ten tippling houses for every hundred inhabitants, and while such a statement is somewhat exaggerated, his assertion that those lower-class drinking places "may be fittly called brothel houses" is probably accurate. Some of the taverns were actually owned by women and others surely sheltered ladies who plied their trade on the premises. Yet despite this, there is only one establishment that can be identified as a house of ill fame. The 1680 census mentioned a John Starr, whose property held 21 white women and two black women. The paucity of females and the tendency of males to marry them quickly upon arrival or upon the expiration of their indentures makes it unlikely there were more establishments of similar character.

Port Royal followed the typical demographic pattern of West Indian settlements. It was at first overwhelmingly male, but numerical equality between men and women evolved rapidly in an urban situation where there was less need for gangs of convicts, indentured servants, prisoners of war, and young men spirited away for agricultural labor. In 1660 there were approximately 400 free men and half that number of free women. A dozen years later the figures stood at 714 to 529, and by 1680 the numbers were approximately equal. The lists of persons killed in the 1692 earthquake that destroyed most of Port Royal contain roughly equal numbers of men and women. The white population of the town ranged between 1,500 to 2,000 persons in the decade before the quake, but the sex distribution figures as well as the population totals give a misleading impression of the composition of the city. Port Royal accommodated, in addition to its resident population, a large number of seafarers, most of whom engaged in piracy or privateering. Even before Governor Thomas Modyford in 1664 began his policy of encouraging pirates to seek safety in Jamaica, there were 22 full-time privateering craft using Port Royal's facilities, and each may have carried an average crew of 60 men. During the two-year period from January 1, 1688 to January 1, 1690, a total of 208 ships of from three to 180 tons docked at Port Royal; their aggregate displacement reached almost 7,000 tons. Added to this figure were the Campeachy logwood ships based in the port and accounting for over 400 sailors and cutters. There is no way to calculate what might be a median number or modal seafaring population in Port Royal at any given day or month. Pirates, honest sailors, and woodcutters were often at sea, returning only after successful forays to expend their wages or booty or seeking a safe harbor during the months when Caribbean navigation was particularly dangerous. The number of buccaneers in town fluctuated greatly from day to day or week to week, but despite the vacillation in the quantity of ships in the harbor and the men ashore, Port Royal was organized to accommodate a large, transient, seafaring population, many of whom were pirates. A 1670 estimate of Jamaica-based seafarers placed the number at 2,500 "lusty able men," and it is likely that a substantial number of them engaged in illegal activities when design or chance gave them the opportunity to plunder. The town contained sailors' lodging houses and grog shops to serve them and the other seafaring men who came ashore, and there were, of course, prostitutes for those who wanted them. Yet nowhere in the surviving evidence of the demographic character of the city is there any evidence of a large contingent of unattached women to serve the hundreds of mariners always in port.[42]

As sugar replaced tobacco as the primary cash crop of the English Caribbean colonies, the demographic character of the islands changed in response to the new agricultural imperatives dictated by the cane. The sexual balance between numbers of white men and white women gradually moved toward equality as the need for labor was satisfied by the importation of slaves; had other factors remained constant, Caribbean pirates might have been found putting into island ports where ordinary sexually balanced English societies were established. In fact, however, by the time the population approached equal numbers of men and women on islands with long-established settlements, or, more accurately, by the time populations reached two to one sex ratios, the pirates had departed. There is no indication that the increase in the proportion of women was in any way responsible for driving pirates away from Jamaica, Barbados, or the Leewards. By the mid-1670s, planters were coming to understand that prosperity would be obtained and stability insured by maintaining peaceful commercial relations with their neighbors, the French, Spanish, and Dutch, but pirates were an unsettling factor in the new economic equation. In times of war, of course, there was no alternative to raiding and disruption, but when Europe was at peace, the colonial ruling classes realized that the prosperity buccaneers brought to the islands and the protection they afforded were meager compared to what could be achieved if tranquility could be established in the Caribbean.

One step in the direction of encouraging prosperity was to halt the past practices of encouraging buccaneering and providing ports, markets, and protection for pirates. The Assembly in Jamaica approved a new anti-piracy law in 1678, and in the next few years at least some captured pirates were sentenced to death by the island's courts. Most of the men condemned for buccaneering ultimately escaped the gallows through legal maneuvering and various other means, but it was clear that piracy was no longer to be tolerated by Jamaicans. The new hostility made it more difficult for pirates to have their prizes condemned, they were never sure of their reception at Port Royal, and they learned quickly that the old practices of tolerance and encouragement were gone. The same transformation of opinion took place in Barbados where, by the end of the century, the local legislature voted to authorize the sending of their own expeditions to suppress piracy. After the Treaty of Ryswick in 1697, the home government joined enthusiastically in the attempt to destroy Caribbean freebooting. New laws were debated and passed, forcing colonial governors to move more actively against pirates; Royal Navy patrols in the Caribbean were increased.[43]

As operations became more difficult in Jamaica, the Leewards, and further to the south, pirates were forced to move from their established sanctuaries. Some crossed the Isthmus of Panama while others sailed through the Straits of Magellan or around the Horn to find plunder in the South Sea, as the Pacific was called. Still others went to the Indian Ocean to rob the heathen Muslims, but most simply went northward to the Virgin Islands, the Bahamas, Bermuda, and to the North American colonies, where at least some government officials were anxious to cooperate with the marauders if profits were to be had. Despite the northward shift in their bases, buccaneers continued their depredations almost everywhere in the Caribbean until well into the eighteenth century. But in their newly discovered havens, they found, as others of their kind had discovered 30 years earlier, that on islands still in early stages of economic development they would be welcomed by a community composed largely of men where their all-male society could be transferred from ship to shore without essential modification. To be sure, many pirates harried from their West Indian bases traded at St. Thomas in the Virgin Islands or in many harbors on the coast of North America, but in these well-established settlements, particularly the proprietaries where they received special encouragement, according to some sources, they remained under the control of a heterosexual society. They were bound by its regulations, at least in the public portions of their activities, as would have been the case had they been honest seamen putting in at Bristol, Dartmouth, or London.[44]

It was in the Bahamas and Bermuda where pirates actually established bases, and were able to gain control of the islands, dominating the governors with bribes or the threat of force. Governor Richard Cony of Bermuda complained to the Earl of Sutherland that public pressure forced him to release a pirate captain who landed at the island with over £3,000 in Dutch goods, and there is every indication that the preponderant number of residents were either pirates or ex-pirates. Often the island residents did not need to force officials to aid them. Nicholas Trott, a Bahamian governor, regularly cooperated with buccaneers. He encouraged them to stop at the islands under his administration and was particularly delinquent in bringing accused marauders to trial. Some clue to his conduct in office can be obtained from a letter written by the then-Governor of New York, the Earl of Bellomont, to the Council of Trade and Plantations in 1699. He expressed surprise that Trott had been appointed to office since he was known as a friend to the pirates and had made somewhere near £50,000 in his dealings with them. Edward Randolph complained to the home government that there were seldom less than four pirates on the Council at New Providence, and the Council of Trade and Plantations received notice that a member of the Bermuda Council had once been a fiddler aboard a pirate ship. There seems to be little doubt that buccaneers could work their will on the islands. Governor Elias Haskett complained that residents of the Bahamas regularly imprisoned officials who angered them, and his assertion could have been substantiated by George Larkin, a commissioner sent to try pirates for their crimes. He was jailed for lewd and scandalous practices, indicating freebooters, like their fellow citizens in the mother country, knew the art of achieving political ends by leveling unrelated charged of misconduct at their enemies.[45]

Woodes Rogers, who administered the Bahamas for a time after 1717, reported as had others before him, that the residents preferred pirates to Royal officials, but he explained that such was to be expected from a population of dubious moral character where even those who had never been pirates were poor and lazy. Not only were the Bahamians prodigious drinkers, perhaps even equal to Bermudans, but one English official reported they copulated with little restraint, utilizing each others wives with abandon and their own sisters and daughters when convenient. Every man, he said, considered every woman his property. While the description sounds as if the islands hosted a continuing heterosexual orgy of adultery, rape, fornication, and incest, the small number of women in the Bahamas in the first years of the eighteenth century when the description was written precluded participation by all males on a regular basis. The invasion by the Spanish and French in 1703 killed all males who could be caught, probably several hundred, which did not include the men who were at sea when they struck. Later in the year the only survivors of the raid, some 80 women, were taken off the islands. The Bahamas were deserted for a number of years, but when the English began to return the number of females in the population remained very tiny. There were only 12 families that could be located in 1716 and the following year the number had risen only to 30. One resident of New Providence deposed that there were approximately 50 men on the island ravishing the few females available, but by the time he made his sworn statement the male population of the Bahamas had grown considerably and if 50 men were ravishing women, it indicates there were several hundred pirates as well as an undetermined number of additional male residents uninterested in joining the ravishment.[46]

In the years from 1660 to 1690 when buccaneers plundered freely in the Caribbean, and before a series of political and administrative policies adopted by London drove them northward, the ratio of men to women on almost every English island ranged from a high of approximately five to one to a lower ratio of two to one. This is obviously a situation far different from penitentiaries where men are confined for extended periods of time and deprived entirely of access to females, or so it would appear from the numerical distribution of the sexes. But in fact the ratio of men to women taken alone gives a misleading picture of the frequency potential for heterosexual contact. If European women in the West Indies had been available for distributive sexual purposes, the ratio of men to women, whether three to one or even ten to one, would have been adequate to provide the residents with sufficient opportunity for sexual activity, but this was hardly the case. Women were in short supply, and neither of the two categories of female emigrants to the Indies were suitable for providing general sexual services. The few women who came to the islands without indentures were in almost every case brought by husbands or other relatives. They were comfortably situated, usually members of the small local aristocracies, and hardly the sort of women to be put to work as prostitutes. The females who migrated to the Caribbean as indentured servants, approximately 25 percent of all persons who sold their labor to pay transportation across the Atlantic, were usually purchased on arrival by planters who wanted their services as domestic laborers or for light agricultural work, and the owners of indentures made it clear that fornication with their female servants was not to be allowed. Statutes on Nevis provided punishments for males who "distracted" female servants from their duties. Elsewhere indentured females were forced to serve extra time for pregnancy, hardly an agreeable prospect, and the penalty for marrying secretly was usually fixed at an extra year of service. On Barbados, local authorities were especially vigilant in guarding against males making advances toward their female servants. The manservant who secretly married faced an extra four years of servitude, fines and whipping were the penalties for fornication, and child support could be assessed if the malefactor were a free man.

A portion of these female servants, some of whom were convicts, ultimately married their purchasers, reducing further the single female population of the English West Indies, but marriage and families were clearly reserved for landowners, and most such unions seem to have been contracted in America, for the records of men coming to the Caribbean with wives and children were very few. On Jamaica by 1680, two-thirds of the large planters had managed to secure wives, but further down the social scale, only half of the smaller farmers were married. For men excluded from the landowning classes, the indentured servants, convicts, prisoners of war, vagabonds, or victims of kidnapping, marriage was economically impossible even if there had been adequate numbers of women available. Those women who could marry were soon wed to landowners and the remainder of men had no alternative but to remain single.[47]

A good deal of the numerical imbalance between the sexes in the seventeenth-century West Indies was the result of economic imperatives. Unlike the colonies in North America, which were subject to family migration and settlement or became home to family units soon after their founding, the Caribbean colonies of three centuries ago were not settlements where family life flourished. The climate, tropical diseases, and the appalling death rate made each island a place where men came to make their fortune and then return to England leaving their estates in the hands of overseers who, like their masters, hoped to become men of property and return to a secure and comfortable old age in the mother country. This, and the possibility of making a large fortune in a relatively limited space of time contributed toward keeping the West Indies a man's country. For migrants anxious to build fortunes rather than colonies, there was little purpose in importing women who were unable to engage in the necessary agricultural labor, and once it was discovered that slave labor could be used more effectively than white men who were difficult to acquire in sufficient quantities, then Africans replaced indentured servants and other classes of reluctant workers in the cane fields.

Although the number of males and females was kept in rough balance among the slave population to ensure continuing agricultural productivity, the desire for numerical equality of males and females among the slave population was not so rigid that it prevented masters from copulating with their slaves. The Antigua Assembly once passed a statute against "Carnall Coppullation between Christian and Heathen," but the increasing mulatto population observed in all colonies provided evidence of the ineffectiveness of such prohibitions. The shortage of European females in the Indies undoubtedly contributed to the frequency of interracial sex—there is agreement among travelers who visited both the island and the mainland colonies that miscegenation was more conspicuous in the Indies—but again there are frequent examples of married planters, solid family men and model citizens, openly living with their slave concubines apparently without censure from their associates. Young squires whose economic position would have entitled them to wives often preferred the favors of slave mistresses, as did their fathers. The psychology of the master-slave sexual dyad goes far to explain miscegenation in the West Indian colonies, but heterosexual contact between owner and chattel was economically regulated like any heterosexual activity in the English settlements. It was restricted not just to any white man who could own a slave but to those who could afford the luxury of a female slave, who would produce less labor than a man and whose economic value was further reduced by the loss of work time entailed in pregnancy, the possibility of death in childbirth, and the effort required for her to look after her mulatto infants. As was the case with marriage or even fornication with a white female indentured servant, sexual access to female slaves was denied to that segment of the white population bound to service by indenture or other devices.[48]

This same is true for the small number of free white and mulatto women in the various colonies. Even those women willing to exchange favors at a price were not available to island bondsmen who received no remuneration during their terms of service. At most servants were given a severance payment when they had finished their terms after anywhere from four to ten years, but sex is rarely to be had anywhere on promise of future payment, and it is unlikely West Indian prostitutes were any more likely to grant credit than their modern-day sisters.[49]

The economics of sexual deprivation is sufficient to explain the lack of female availability for male members of the island's lower classes, but there is considerable evidence to indicate that this deprivation was not as difficult to bear as it might first seem. Plantation owners attempted to import black men and women in approximately equivalent numbers because they perceived that black men would not work as efficiently without access to women. There were no such perceptions in the case of white laborers in the West Indies. It might have been that racial attitudes on the part of planters dictated the divergent views of the sexual needs of white and black workers, but more likely the need for women by many whites who came to the West Indies was not particularly acute. Complaints about the lack of women on the islands are difficult if not impossible to find. It is true that if such dissatisfactions existed they would have been manifested most often in letters, memorials, petitions, and similar documents written by members of the island upper classes. Since the wealthy were not deprived of heterosexual outlets, it is understandable that they did not express such frustrations. No landowners speculate on the sexual outlets available to their servants or bondsmen. They were also quick to legislate against heterosexual activity, and in their policies they sought always to increase the number of men sent to the Caribbean while reducing the number of women similarly transported. It cannot be firmly established that the white males in the Indies were misogynists or men with no need for women, but such a feeling persists even when their actions are interpreted with an understanding of the need for laborers. Despite the shortage of females in the Leewards, Christopher Jeaffreson was particularly upset when he learned his overseer, an Ensign Thorne, had taken an Irish woman for a mistress. He complained from London of her Irish origins, described her as fit only to be a servant of servants, and wailed that since her promotion to his overseer's bed he had received reports she behaved as the director of his own West Indian estate.[50] While Jeaffreson's reluctance to accept female convicts can easily be explained and understood in economic terms, his hostility to women in the islands seems something more appropriately elucidated by Freud. The Earl of Carlisle, Governor of Jamaica from 1678 to 1680, gave every indication that the same relaxed attitude toward homosexuality that prevailed in England was also found among the English in the Caribbean. In a letter to officials in London, he noted that five sailors from the *Jersey*, a Royal Navy vessel, were tried in Jamaica for sodomy. One was acquitted, but the remaining men were found guilty and sentenced to death. Three of the four were quickly pardoned by the Governor who explained white men were scarce on the island. The fourth, a Francis Dilly by name, was executed. He, too, would have been pardoned except, according to the letter, he was the ringleader.[51] If the attitudes of Jeaffreson and Carlisle were shared by planters and the poorer white residents of the Indies, it goes far toward explaining why the only serious initiatives for redressing the sexual balance in the islands during the first century of English settlement came not from locals but from officials in the mother country.

Thomas Walduck, a Barbadian colonial, was one of those who commented on homosexual conduct in the Caribbean. He wrote:

> All Sodom's Sins are Centered in thy heart
> Death is thy look and Death in every part
> Oh! Glorious Isle in Vilany Excell
> Sins to the Height—thy fate is Hell.[52]

Walduck's verses were written in 1710 when the sexual imbalance on Barbados had been redressed, and it is possible that the dictates of rhyme and meter combined with alliterative excess may have had some effect on the content of his poetry. Yet his use of Sodom to characterize the moral tenor of what he observed was repeated over and again by those who described conditions in the West Indies. The judgment of Sodom was to befall the islands. The Jews that crucified Christ might here behold themselves matched or outdone in evil and wickedness in this the worst of Sodom. Port Royal was the Sodom of the Universe. All were descriptions given by contemporary commentators. Even more candid than the males who related the state of the English Caribbean was Madam Margaret Heathcote. Writing from Antigua to her cousin, John Winthrop, Jr. in 1655 she said, "And truely, Sir, I am not so much in love with any as to goe much abroad . . . they all be a company of sodomites that live here."[53]

In commenting on sodomy in the West Indies, neither Walduck nor any other contemporary writers discussed reasons for its frequency, but they are easy enough to discern. The inadequate numbers of women was a primary motive for homosexual behavior on the part of some, but it is also likely the shortage of women on Barbados, Jamaica, the Leewards, and later on the islands to the north was a partial result of the restricted demand for their presence. They were inferior to men as field laborers, and for the West Indian residents with preferences for males, they were similarly inferior as sex partners.

FOUR

BUCCANEER SEXUALITY

Prison populations are one of the few groups of men living without women over long periods of time on whom comprehensive and detailed studies have been done. There is an obvious nexus between convicts in modern England or America and West Indian buccaneers in the seventeenth century in that access to women is limited for both groups, but most noticeable after the single sex composition of each population are the many features that distinguish one from the other. Aside from a monumental gulf of three centuries and the vast distinctions between life patterns in periods of time so widely separated, there are the disparate situations in which the convicts under study and Caribbean pirates lived their daily lives and conducted their sexual activities. Prison regimen is regulated from without by men who are heterosexual or who accept heterosexuality, at least outwardly, as the normal human condition. Homosexual contact behind bars exists only within a framework of rigidly applied rules and stipulations imposed from beyond the ranks of inmates. Although homosexual activity is often ignored or at least carefully regulated by supervisory personnel, it must still exist within a social structure determined largely by a dominant order that is antipathetic both to the prisoners and to homosexual contact. Of equal importance in distinguishing pirate society from the prison community is the tendency of heterosexual prisoners, by far the majority of participants in most studies of prison life, to view their exclusively homosexual experiences during incarceration as a temporary activity imposed by unfortunate circumstances. Even prisoners who engaged in occasional homosexual activity before being committed to penal institutions and who expect to continue occasional homosexual activity after release from confinement consider the exclusively homosexual nature of prison life a temporary condition. The transitory character of prisoners' sexual contacts is reinforced by the convicts themselves who rigorously observe many of the heterosexual conventions of the outside world in their homosexual confinement. This is in vivid contrast to the behavior of West Indian pirates, who rejected or ignored heterosexual patterns and rarely took the opportunities to reach Europe or America where they would be able to abandon piracy and engage in heterosexual activities. They were permanent pirates for the most part who had abandoned, rejected, or been denied the opportunity to live lives in the usual heterosexual manner.[1]

In terms of the study of sexual behavior patterns, however, both convicts and buccaneers are unique in that they share the same range of sex-surrogate and sexual options. Solitary masturbation, fantasies, nocturnal sex dreams, and sex contact with members of the same sex are their alternatives. No estimates are currently available on nonsexual or sex-surrogate masturbatory or dream frequencies among prisoners, but the number of inmates engaging in homosexual contacts during incarceration is placed at somewhere between 30 and 45 percent according to several studies. Despite the incidence estimates ranging from less than one-third to almost half of convicts participating in homosexual practices, there is agreement among the authors of the studies that the frequency of contact between those engaging in homosexual acts is low, even among cellmates. In almost no case does it approach either the heterosexual or homosexual frequency rates of the same men before incarceration. The use of a 30 to 45 percent incidence figure for homosexual contact among convicts and the additional information that prisoner contact frequency is unusually low cannot easily be projected backward to long-vanished pirate communities. Even if some features of convict life thought to retard sexual activity were operative for pirates, at the same time buccaneers were freed from many of the constraints that reduce contact frequency and inhibit the incidence of homosexual behavior. Many of the cues normally channeling men into sexual contact of any sort are absent in prison. There is little privacy, at least from other inmates if not the custodial staff, there are few familiar social situations that call for sexual responses (dating, drinking, parties, etc.), a certain amount of sensory monotony might retard sexual arousal, and there is a total absence of women.[2]

While these factors may inhibit the incidence and frequency of homosexual contact in prisons, they might have been less pronounced in their effect on buccaneers. The absence of privacy aboard a pirate ship was at least as acute as that encountered by prisoners, but the passage of three centuries and the widely differing concepts of personal and sexual privacy in the seventeenth and twentieth centuries may in this situation have created a more favorable climate for sex aboard pirate vessels than in prisons. Men from the lower classes in Stuart England were not accustomed to modern standards of privacy. They lived jammed together with their families as children, and later shared close quarters as servants, apprentices, wanderers, or as youths aboard ships. Heterosexual contact was not restricted to the bedroom in this age of single-room dwellings, and homosexual acts, too, were conducted with what seems today, at least to some, as a disconcerting lack of concern with the presence of others.

The monotony endured by convicts was probably as severe for pirates, restricted as they often were to the decks of small ships and surrounded only by an unbroken horizon. How effectively the lack of sensory stimulus reduces sexual activity is highly problematical. Although it is assumed by a number of authorities to dull senses and desires, it might be instead that boredom increases erotic arousal for sheer lack of alternate diversion. But whatever the effect of monotony on sex frequency of either group, buccaneers differed from prisoners in that they were not without social situations that called for sexual response. Successful practitioners of the buccaneer's trade often had occasion for drinking and revelry after successful battles. The capture of prizes, many containing ample store of alcoholic beverages, led to scenes of debauchery that are well-chronicled in the literature of piracy. The benign Caribbean climate may also have led to situations conducive to sexual contact or excess. The warm waters rotted caulking rapidly between planks and encouraged the proliferation of assorted marine organisms that affixed themselves to hulls or bored into the planking. The effects of warm water, heat, and various creatures all combined to increase the need for ship maintenance. When pirates landed at isolated quays or safe harbors and careened their ships, wild revelry often accompanied the work of scraping, caulking, and coating their ship hulls with sulphur and tar.

More important than these factors, however, is the knowledge that sexual activity in prisons increases, sometimes to rather high rates, as the order of custody is lowered. If freedom from social and behavioral constraints increased sexual activity for buccaneers as it apparently does for convicts, then the West Indian sea rovers surely made the most of their liberty. Many were men with abiding hatreds of rules and regulations acquired after terms of service in the merchant and naval services. They gloried in the freedom or license they enjoyed as buccaneers, and, if research on modern convicts does in fact provide clues to pirate behavior, it seems likely enough that their joy in exercising their wills was not confined only to the non-sexual phases of their lives. Life experiences of buccaneers before they sailed under the pirate flag may also have acted to increase incidence and frequency of homosexual acts. Prison experience is not the sole determinant of convict sexual behavior. It is a complex blending of the inmates' preinstitutional experiences and the organizational structure of the institution that determines some portion of the sexual patterns adopted by those incarcerated. The same is undoubtedly true for buccaneers, all of whom grew to adolescence or adulthood in a society where sexual experiences with members of the same sex were not as emphatically proscribed as is the case in the England or America of today. The fear, guilt, and social opprobrium that inhibit the homosexual functioning of at least some heterosexual convicts might have been less forceful or even totally inoperative on the men who became pirates.

At the same time that an assortment of factors acted to increase buccaneer sexual activity, there were also several features of their lives that probably reduced its incidence and frequency. It is generally recognized that high levels of anxiety inhibit sexual functioning, as does inadequate nutrition. In both areas, pirates were in worse condition than convicts. Not only were their diets poorly balanced by modern standards—although frequently they ate as well as their fellow countrymen who remained home in England—but they lived often with an extremely high level of anxiety. The constant anticipation of combat surely exerted a profound influence on them, and although there was at the same time always the threat of capture, trial for piracy, conviction, and death on the gallows, the likelihood of being taken by authorities was so remote it probably constituted no serious impediment to their sexual functioning. Whether privacy, socially determined cues, monotony, or anxiety caused the incidence of homosexual acts among pirates to fall within, above, or below the 30 to 45 percent range cannot be estimated. The single certainty is that the only non-solitary sexual activities available to buccaneers for most of the years they spent in the Caribbean and for almost all of the time they were aboard ship were homosexual.

The effect of socio-environmental factors on the incidence of homosexual acts is especially difficult to estimate since several features of pirate life could effect sexuality in either positive or negative manners. Within the pirate community, there is less need for equivocation in assessing the influence of some aspects of shipboard life. The ratio between men with homosexual preferences and men participating in homosexual conduct in the absence of opportunities for heterosexual engagements or out of dissatisfaction with available solitary or non-sexual alternatives exerted considerable influence on rates of homosexual contact. Precise figures are difficult enough to obtain from prison research studies on the ratio of homosexuals to situational practitioners of homosexuality, but even if more seventeenth-century data were available, the same would be true for pirate crews. The best that can be had from surviving evidence, at least that available on relationships between pirates and females, is some indication that the proportion of homosexuals among pirate crews was higher than among convict populations studied. When buccaneers had the opportunity for engagements with women prisoners, they were rarely taken, and in their relationships with members of the opposite sex, most pirates give every indication they were uncomfortable in the extreme. To be sure, the men with preferences for women took the chance to slake their appetites for females when in ports where they were available, but buccaneer homosexuals rejected the same opportunities. When women were captured or otherwise present aboard ship, by far the greater number of pirates ignored the opportunities to use them sexually.

One writer on piracy asserted that buccaneers regarded women simply as the spoils of war, "and were as profligate with these as with the rest of their plunder."[3] Such an assertion is not a mere oversimplification; it is totally incorrect. The experiences of Caribbean pirates seem more in harmony with homosexuals to whom Gardner Lindzey and his associates administered the Thematic Apperception Test. Their results indicated individuals "characterized by strong homosexual tendencies display consistently negative attitudes toward women [and] a lack of full, rich, and satisfying relations with members of the opposite sex."[4] Investigating patterns of pirate behavior by contrasting them with results of modern studies is an obvious enough methodological procedure. There is an attractive simplicity and directness in examining the one using the structure of the other as a guide, especially with homosexuality, the very object of the investigation, providing the bonds that unite the two. Unfortunately, the passage of 300 years and the features that divide the Caribbean pirates from gay communities in the United States or England, when added to the manifold complications inherent in comparative studies of greatly divergent groups and the radically dissimilar situations of homosexuals in the modern western world from that of the buccaneers, make correlations a tenuous matter. The same cautions must be observed, and awareness that the technique illuminates possibilities rather than proves deductions must always be borne in mind. Only then can the striking similarities between the negative attitudes toward females of both buccaneers and the homosexual subjects of studies by Lindzey, Irving Bieber, Lawrence Ross, Laud Humphreys, Brian Miller, Alan P. Bell, and Martin S. Weinberg be interpreted meaningfully. Alexander Exquemelin, the famous pirate surgeon who

sailed and fought with Henry Morgan, gives testimony to establish
the value of the comparison. He noted contemptuously that "Spaniards are of such a nature they cannot live without women." He then
related the story of one such effete enemy who "took himself an Indian wife to look after him and for him to use for his pleasure (if one
may call this pleasure)." As might be expected, the Spaniard was
cuckolded by the wife. He discovered her engaged with a lion, according to the account, and abandoned her. Exquemelin also related
an incident of disease caused, in part, by debaucheries with women,
and added the tale of an incompetent pirate captain who was "inclined to sit drinking and sporting with a group of Spanish women
he had taken prisoner." While he was occupied in such dissolution,
a treasure galleon, one of the most rich and sought-after prizes, was
lost.[5] Another buccaneer, speaking of women on Barbados in the last
decade of the seventeenth century, noted that local ladies were good
housewives, but also grumbled "some that went over Servants be-
stirred themselves so well that they have gott great fortunes."[6] A
present-day writer, projecting the pirates' dislike of females a bit beyond bounds that can be sustained by evidence, accused the buccaneers of fetishism, asserting the "affection that they might have shown
for wife or child went to their guns, long-barreled beauties from
Nantes or Dieppe, polished to a gloss and stored from the damp in
hide cases."[7] Even the vicissitudes of weather were blamed by at
least one pirate chief on women. Captain William Cowley, in an
account of a voyage wrote "Then haling away S.W. we came abreast
with Cape Horn on the 14th Day of February, where we chusing of
Valentines, and discoursing of the Intrigues of Women, there arose
a prodigious Storm, which did continue till the last Day of the Month
. . . so that we concluded the discoursing of Women at Sea was
very unlucky, and occasioned the Storm."[8]

Evelyn Hooker and D. J. West note this same hostility toward
females in the homosexual sample groups they have worked with,
but Hooker maintains that it is less universal than alleged by Lindzey
and by other researchers who maintain at least that homosexual psychopaths had a decided lack of female friends, especially at the ages
of 16 and 17 and that this was a part of a pattern running back to the

ages of ten or 11 when they had few female playmates. The same research on homosexual psychopaths indicated that all men in the sample whose crimes had been committed against adult males had little success inducing orgasm in females on the occasions when they attempted heterosexual intercourse.[9]

Few pirates were ever married and no specific details survive about the ability of those who were to generate successful coital union with their spouses, but among those known to have had wives, the marriages were uniformly unsuccessful. The failure of Blackbeard as a connubial partner was so well known that it became part of a ballad.[10]

> When the Act of Grace appeared Captain Teach
>   and all his men
> Unto Carolina steered, where they us'd him kindly
>   then;
> There he marry'd to a lady, and give her five hundred
>   pound,
> But to her he prov'd unsteady, for he soon march'd
>   off the ground.

The lyric seems mild enough, indicating Teach departed leaving his bride to the fates that often overtook the wives of seafarers, but the final couplet indicates more was involved than a case of a sailor going off to sea. It begins oddly enough with Blackbeard giving his lady 500 pounds. In an age when dowries came from the wife, he should have received the money rather than paid it. If the woman had been a servant that he purchased, not only would she have been an expensive lass, but the payment would have gone to the owner of her indentures, not to her. The phrase "soon march'd off the ground" is also unusual. If the poet meant Blackbeard sailed away it is likely he would have said so. Mariners "set sail" or "go to sea" or "sail the world around." The phrase used implies not departure but failure, as when soldiers are driven from the field of battle. It is true that "ground" rhymes with "round" in the previous line, and the poetic abilities of the author are obviously limited, but the use of the word "unsteady" indicates the poet paid careful attention to the meanings of words he chose. "Unfaithful" could easily have been substituted without doing violence to the meter, but "unsteady" refers to a defective performance and "unfaithful" does not.

The evidence that survives about Blackbeard's marriage or marriages also indicates difficulties with females. He was rumored to have a wife and child in London and at least a dozen wives scattered about in various ports. Multiple wives were not the norm in the seventeenth century, although they were not unheard of among seafaring men, but the large number ascribed to the buccaneer was unusual. The details of his last marriage in North Carolina, in addition to the payment, also indicate an insecurity in dealing with women. After using his wife sufficiently to satisfy his appetites, it "was his Custom to invite five or six of his brutal Companions to come ashore, and he would force her to prostitute her self to them all, one after another, before his Face."[11] Even with such treatment, Mrs. Teach might have considered herself a lucky woman when compared to females captured by her husband. Determined to enforce his rule of no women at sea, Blackbeard was known to strangle captured women and pitch their bodies overboard.[12] Stede Bonnet, too, found the married state uncomfortable and his shrewish wife is alleged to have been one of the reasons he ran off and became a pirate. Like Blackbeard, his mentor in the buccaneering trade, Bonnet saved only male prisoners. Women were neither needed nor wanted aboard his ship.[13]

Testimony from the Bahamas in the early eighteenth century reveals at least four married pirates operating from the islands, but one witness to connubial relations in New Providence, where the male population was composed largely of pirates and ex-pirates, spoke of only 20 married couples in the entire population, and added that they regularly traded and stole each others' mates, creating great anxiety among all involved in the business.[14] The two pirate marriages for which no negative information is available are those of a Captain Cockram in the Bahamas and the union of Pennsylvania Governor William Markham's daughter to a buccaneer commander. In both cases, however, love and sex were not primary attractions. Cockram selected for his bride the daughter of Harbor Island's richest resident, and Markham was notorious for protecting pirates who sailed into Philadelphia with plundered cargoes.[15]

Like Bahamian pirates, English and Irish seafarers were generally casual about connubial ties in the seventeenth and eighteenth centuries. Woodes Rogers, sent out to eradicate piracy from the Caribbean and not above engaging in a bit of capitalism "on the account" himself, wrote that the members of his crew who boarded his ships in Cork departed from their wives by drinking "their Cans of Flip till the last minute, concluded with a Health to our good Voyage, and their happy Meeting, and then parted unconcern'd." Henry Teonge, a chaplain who sailed aboard several Restoration-era naval vessels, wrote that many of his fellow crewmen sorrowed at leaving their women. But he explained their grief was only temporary and expressed usually while in an inebriated state. The good chaplain, though twice married, made it apparent enough that he did not care for seafarers' consorts. He described them variously as Delilahs, Myrmidons, and whores. At one point he styled his captain's wife a virago.[16] Alexander Selkirk, the Scottish pirate after whom Robinson Crusoe was patterned, had assorted but unspecified difficulties with women, eloping with one, abandoning her, and marrying again. William Davis, a pirate who wed an African woman, was even more casual. He enraged his in-laws and their relations by trading his wife for a bowl of punch when he was hot and thirsty. Another buccaneer, Thomas Howard, had even worse luck with the kinfolk of his native wife. He was a morose, ill-tempered fellow, and treated his spouse so badly her relatives finally killed him.[17]

In their relationships with women, pirates seemed to prefer situations where the females could easily be dominated. Native women, under this circumstance, made excellent sexual partners for men inclined to vary their largely male experiences. They were heathen, dark-skinned, and regarded as moral, spiritual, and racial inferiors by xenophobic English or European pirates. Native sexual customs that differed in substance from those familiar to pirates also contributed toward easing psychological disabilities in dealing with members of the opposite sex. Most commentators noted that native women could be bought easier than raped, Captain William Cowley remarking that in one tribe the men had no qualms about sharing their wives with Europeans but were intensely jealous over advances made by other

tribesmen. Another pirate noted that native females were quite willing to submit to the desires of Englishmen, and William Betagh added
that "any man may lye with the [California Indian] women for a
rusty knife, or a porringer of thick milk."[18] In 1709, Woodes Rogers's crewmen were not only willing to give away a lovely female
slave as a gift, but they were willing to give away the best looking
one of all their captives. We "put our young Padre ashore, and gave
him, as he desir'd, the prettiest young Female Negro we had in the
Prize," explained Rogers, adding, "The young Padre parted with us
extremely pleas'd, and leering under his Hood upon his black Female
Angel, we doubt [not] he will crack a Commandment with her."[19]

Instances of pirates cavorting with native women in the West Indies are infrequent. Most Caribbean natives were exterminated before
the latter decades of the seventeenth century. Even in the West Indies, however, all pirates were not desirous of native or slave females
even when they were available. Captain Cowley and his crew once
allowed five dozen captive women to perish from the cold as they
sailed southward along the coast toward Cape Horn. Surely boys or
young men would not have been treated in such fashion. Cowley
himself disliked native women, once describing a group of them as
"the foulest Creatures that ever I saw they wearing nothing but sheep
skyns over theire shoulders with wool or the women wearing a Leather
Bagg before theire Private Parts."[20]

On the rare occasions when pirates were in ports where there were
prostitutes to be bought with gold doubloons and pieces of eight, at
least some pirates enjoyed dominating such women. In one incident,
a pirate in Jamaica gave a whore 500 pieces of eight just to see her
naked. That was an excessively high price, but there is no way of
understanding the psychodynamics of the exchange.[21] The buccaneer may have wanted to look but not touch (a good indicator of
insecurity), he may have been drunk, or perhaps he was only a big
spender.

The capture of European women often created emotionally difficult situations for pirates. Their position as captors gave them power
to dominate the women and take them by force, but in fact this rarely
happened. White, Christian females, the very sort dimly remem-

bered from England, were far distant in their youths and usually unobtainable even when they were desired. They could not be purchased in the casual manner of prostitutes nor could they be dominated and then discarded without a thought as members of what they considered to be inferior racial stocks. They had to be approached cautiously, in emotional terms, to prevent the possibility of severe psychological damage. One manner of dealing with these women was rape. The literature of piracy contains only a few accounts of women being carried off from plundered towns and debauched. Strains of almost childish reverence for captured females are much more apparent in their treatment of women prisoners. Aboard the *Revenge*, commanded by pirate John Phillips, the crew adopted as one of their regulations an article stating "If at any Time we meet with a prudent Women, that Man that offers to meddle with her, without her Consent, shall suffer present Death," and a member of Bartholomew Roberts's crew, a pirate nicknamed Little David, actually set himself up as guard and protector of a captured woman. One man could not have done this aboard any pirate ship without at least the tacit consent of his comrades, and although Little David raped his charge in short order, it is nonetheless true that there was some effort to preserve her honor that was sanctioned by the crew.[22] There are numerous other examples of men who were no respectors either of property or persons striving to prevent the abuse of captured women. One of the rules posted by William Betagh's crew in 1719 stated that "Every man aboard a prize found drunk, or in any indecent act with a white or black women, to be punished according to the nature of his offense."[23] There were without doubt sound tactical reasons for such a regulation, but had the crew been lusting for women over months or even years, rules of that nature would not have been promulgated by men with little respect for law, custom, or the persons of captives. In another incident, a pirate crew killed all the males on a ship they had taken, but the one female found aboard was not raped or sexually abused in any way. She was simply tossed overboard in the fashion of any other unwanted material. The event took place in the Indian Ocean rather than the Caribbean, but it indicates the perpetrators, who soon transferred their operations to American waters, did not acutely feel the absence of women to satisfy their sexual desires.[24]

The uneasy mixture of fear, dislike, and reverence could sometimes produce a softening of even the most hardened and vicious pirates. Henry Johnson, an exceedingly bloody and cruel buccaneer, once saved a white woman from rape for no apparent reason. In another incident the actions taken by the buccaneers who sacked Cartagena in June, 1697 indicate a similar ambiguity of attitude toward European women. During the time after the capture, while the pirates were occupied torturing the male residents of the city, attempting to extract information on where wealth had been concealed, a pair of buccaneers killed two females. If the women had been murdered in an attempt to torture them into revealing where their wealth was hidden, there is little likelihood any action would be taken, but the women had been killed for another, unspecified reason that so aroused the indignation of the pirates that the murderers were sentenced to be shot.[25] This same emotional dichotomy is nowhere more evident than in Henry Morgan's raids on Porto Bello and Panama City. Morgan's men were sometimes hesitant to take liberties with the women of captured cities or towns and their leader actually insisted that the women of Porto Bello be treated with gallantry. After the capture of St. Catalina, the women were neither raped nor brutalized in any other fashion. They were fed and locked in the church for protection, although it is not clear if they were kept in custody to gain ransom or to keep them out of the way of the more serious business of collecting booty. Whatever the motive for their confinement, it is apparent Morgan and his lawless buccaneers preferred to use the women for economic gain rather than to assuage sexual desires.[26]

In the case of the Spanish beauty taken at Panama, Morgan himself demonstrated a degree of uncertainty in matters of sexual aggrandizement that he never would have exhibited on the field of battle. He treated the captive with exquisite delicacy, providing her with private quarters, a cook, and food from his own table. Despite the grand treatment, he was unable to seduce her. Later he tried starvation and humiliation but neither were they successful. Obviously

Morgan could have raped the woman had he chosen to do so, but to force so rare a woman to submit might have produced extensive trauma for the pirate leader. Not only was the woman uncommonly beautiful, but she was white, Christian, and possessed social status far higher than native women, prostitutes, and the ordinary run of captive females.[27] It was a situation where the dynamic and resourceful buccaneer captain was psychologically bested, defeated completely, and rendered totally unable to work his will. His paralysis was extended to his men, either by implication or by order, and they refrained from wholesale rape. But had his unruly army been bent on rape or any other type of sexual engagements with women, it is unlikely their commander could have controlled them. Yet even Richard Browne, one of Morgan's political enemies, conceded that at least on this occasion, the victorious English did not force their attentions on the Spanish women. This was later confirmed by another pirate, Bartholomew Sharp, although Sharp also insisted some time later that Exquemelin's tales of torture were fraudulent.[28] The same hesitancy to rape women who were neither slaves, Indians, or prostitutes was found among Woodes Rogers's men at the capture of Guiaquil, Peru in 1709. At one house, the pirates found "above a Dozen handsom genteel young Women . . . the Ladies offer'd to dress 'em Victuals and brought 'em a Cask of good Liquor. Some of their largest Gold Chains were conceal'd, and wound about their Middles, Legs, and Thighs, etc. but the Gentlewomen in these hot Countries being very thin clad with Silk and fine Linnen . . . our Men by pressing felt the Chains, etc. with their Hands on the Outside of the Lady's Apparel."[29] So the Spanish women were not forcibly debauched by a fierce band of pirates who were intimidated by women of their own sort, white, European, Christian, and either their equals or superiors in status. When English plunderers in the Pacific captured the Spanish ship, *El Santo Rosario*, Basil Ringrose noted that there was aboard the most beautiful woman he had seen in the South Sea. His account contains no other information about her, although he goes into some detail about the members of the crew taken prisoner.[30] Governor William Beeston of Jamaica, in his account of the French invasion of the island in 1694, provided persuasive testimony that Gallic buccaneers had as much difficulty adjusting to women as their English counterparts. Speaking of the French forces, which included large numbers of pirates, he related that "Some women they suffered the negroes to violate, and dug some out of their graves, so that there were never more inhuman barbarities committed by any Turks or infidels in the world."[31]

If buccaneer contacts with females indicate considerable reticence in dealing with women, there are no similar examples of hesitancy in the relationships between pirates and another class of potential sex partners, the boys who served aboard their ships. It is difficult to gain an idea of the number of male juveniles who sailed with the buccaneers. Seaborne plundering and raiding of coastal villages occasionally resulted in boys as young as ten or 12 years old serving side by side with seasoned buccaneers, but available evidence indicates that most youths captured or pressed into service by pirates were in their middle teens. Lads were not normally listed in the rosters of pirates captured and neither were they customarily brought to trial, but despite the absence of military and judicial records that would provide detailed information on the ratio of boys to adults aboard the ships of Caribbean sea rovers, surviving accounts indicate they were occasionally members of the crews. Some pirate ships carried enough boys to make it necessary to specify their duties in the vessels' regulations and to enumerate the procedure for apportioning their share of the plunder. Information on one captured buccaneering ship revealed it was manned by 25 sailors plus four cabin boys, and pirate commander George Cusak once forceably took four lads from a captured vessel. Jamaica's Lieutenant-Governor Hender Molesworth released two boys captured when the ship commanded by a buccaneer captain named Bannister was taken. The pair pleaded that they served only under compulsion and their plea was accepted.

Whatever their precise number, there was little need to acculturate most youngsters aboard buccaneer ships. Many served earlier as cabin boys, helpers on commercial vessels, or as powder monkeys in the Royal Navy. While at sea, boys lived with adult crewmembers, ate and slept with them, served their needs, accepted their values, and adopted their mode of life. The homosexual proclivities of seafarers were surely familiar to boys who went to sea, just as they were to young men who first wandered the roads of England and then became seafarers but had not acquired a full complement of nautical skills before being captured or joining a buccaneer ship for other reasons. When boys boarded a pirate vessel for the first time as either captives or volunteers, they discovered the sexual orientation of the crew was the same as that of their companions aboard the merchant or naval vessel where they previously served or in the wandering beggar bands where they first encountered the ways of the world.

If the youthful recruits needed little sexual education from pirates, it was imperative that they complete their training in the ways of seamanship. As lads grew older they were increasingly able to undertake the chores of able-bodied sailors, and training in the necessary skills could not be left to chance. The educational requirements aboard pirate ships were met in a different fashion than in merchant service or in the Navy. On vessels with legally authorized and rigidly enforced systems of command and regulation, youthful crewmembers were the responsibility of no single member. Their training was directed and supervised by those in positions of authority, and while in cases of cabin boys and others who provided personal service to officers there may have been understandings or formally recognized agreements that some boys were the charges of specific officers, most powder monkeys and apprentice seamen were simply junior members of the crew. In contrast, boys aboard pirate vessels were almost always under the control of a single individual, and often the supervising adults were deeply attached to their lads.

A number of commanders had youths for their exclusive use, and usually they were assiduous in securing their welfare. Captain Charles Swan's chosen lad was always provided a share when booty was apportioned, and although there is no way of knowing how carefully pirate Captain John Quelch looked after his Negro boy, the price the lad brought at auction in Boston after his master was captured, some £20, indicated he was in good condition. Aboard Kidd's *Adventure Galley* even the ship's physician, Dr. Robert Bradenham, had a little Negro boy of his own. Blackbeard was especially cruel in his treatment of captives and crewmembers alike, but had a Negro boy that he raised with considerable care.[32] Captain Charles Swan, who also made sure his lad received a share of the loot, was equally considerate in the details of child-rearing. He evidently had loved his boy since first setting eyes on him when the child was only seven or eight years old. He was determined to have him, and ultimately resorted to kidnapping when all else failed. The boy was taken aboard Swan's ship and despite the tearful pleas of a parent, the pirate would not return him. He promised the mother only that he would "make much of him," and the captain was as good as his word. He trained the lad carefully, according to surviving testimony, to be witty, brave, and possess considerable dexterity.[33] William Dampier, one of the most notable of early eighteenth-century sea rovers, was also deeply attached to a boy he had acquired from another European seafarer in 1690. To purchase the boy, Dampier was forced to buy the mother as well, but there was little doubt about which of the pair appealed to him. The boy, Jeoly, "was painted [tattooed] all down the Breast, between his Shoulders behind; on his Thighs (mostly) before; and in the Form of several broad Rings, or Bracelets round his Arms and Legs."[34] Ownership of Jeoly had its pleasures but all was not joy for the Captain in the relationship. When the mother died, the boy endured a lengthy period of sorrow, and Dampier was deeply disturbed over the agonies he suffered. Later in England, when he had returned from his sea adventures, Dampier was forced to sell the tattooed lad, but it was a hard decision for him to make and was done only because he was in exceedingly straitened financial circumstances.[35]

Lads sometimes appear in court records as witnesses in the trials of the pirates they once served, and some measure of the devotion of men to their boys can be gained from the testimony. Bartholomew Sharp was one of the many buccaneers who stood in the prisoner's dock and heard the words of his lad used in an attempt to persuade a jury of his guilt. The youth in his case, a 16-year-old Spaniard named Calderone, jumped ship when Sharp and his crew returned to England after privateering in the Caribbean. Calderone complained to his ambassador in London, the ambassador demanded Sharp be brought to trial, and there the boy's account was used against him. Had the captain been determined to ensure his own safety, he could have easily eliminated the possibility of Calderone's testimony by pitching him overboard before returning to England, but he did not. That Sharp had been persuaded of the fidelity of his young charge is easily understood, but if that were true, it only indicates he was willing to hazard his personal safety on the word of a Spaniard, not something a seasoned English sea-rover would likely do unless under the spell of infatuation.[36]

The use of boys as sexual partners was not universally accepted among pirates. Some captains rejected the practice entirely, not because they were particularly repelled by notions of pederasty, but because they evidently believed the boys were a cause of conflict aboard ship. The men who served under Bartholomew Roberts were especially emphatic in this regard. They subscribed to a set of articles that provided "No Boy or Women [was] to be allowed amongst them. If any Man were found seducing any of the latter Sex, and carry'd her to Sea, disguis'd, he was to suffer Death." Significantly, there was no penalty for seducing a lad or smuggling him aboard.[37] Pederasty was simply a violation of the rules not a capital crime.

The percentage of pedophiles among the general buccaneering population cannot even be guessed. It is known that there were among buccaneers some who preferred sexual contacts with boys rather than with their fellow adult crew members, hardly an unusual circumstance for pirates whose early histories, like those of modern-day pedophiles, reveal little opportunity to experience heterosexual relationships, little contact with women, and a very low rate of attempted or successful sexual contacts with females. Neither pirate nor pedophile customarily took full advantage of prostitutes when they were available, and in unfortunate cases where members of either group married, the results were usually exceedingly frustrating and unfortunate.[38]

The most visible characteristic of pirate pedophiles is that in every case those men with preference for boys were not integrated members of their crews. This squares with findings of modern research on pedophiles, where the men interviewed seemed to experience as much difficulty adjusting to adults as to women. Moreover, at least one group of fellators involved with delinquent boys did not appear to participate in any aspect of the informally organized homosexual community in their city. They avoided gay bars, baths, and other institutions frequented by adult homosexuals. When questioned about their preference for boys, they answered in most cases that youths were less demanding, more easily dominated, and less critical of their partner's performance. Generally they suffered from feelings of inferiority, immaturity, and passivity rather than any condition that could be described as neurotic or psychotic. Most of their social contacts as well as their sexual contacts were with children, and they clearly felt that adult sexual contact was beyond their capabilities. With the exception of immaturity and passivity, all of those characteristics commonly associated by modern researchers with pedophilia can be found among buccaneers known to have a proclivity for youthful cohorts. This is particularly true of the one class of pirates who most frequently sought out young companions, the captains. Command isolation is a feature of any ship, and may be necessary for the exercise of authority at sea, but in the seventeenth century the need of the commander to be separate from his crew probably encouraged pedophilia among some captains, whether they commanded merchant and naval vessels or buccaneering craft. The long periods of solitude, the responsibilities of command, the inability to interact socially or sexually with members of the crew, and the presence of a youthful personal servant all contributed toward making pederasty the only available sexual outlet for the commander other than solitary masturbation, dreams, or fantasies. For pirate captains, the likelihood of a preference for youthful partners was probably even greater than for the commanders of ships sailing legally. Although Blackbeard, William Dampier, and Bartholomew Sharp could not be described as passive individuals, Blackbeard was the archetype of the immature personality unable to cope with adults except through the use of his superior physical strength. All three men, Blackbeard, Dampier, Sharp, and other captains who had their favorite boys, probably suffered continually from feelings of inferiority and insecurity similar to those of pedophiles interviewed by researchers. This would have been a normal psychological state for buccaneer leaders who, although they had

undergone the same maturational patterns experienced by their crewmen, were sustained in their command positions only by the consent
of their crews. They were men with deep-seated feelings of inferiority
or hostility toward their social superiors, and all were prohibited from
forming satisfying relationships with their men, for they were compelled to remain distant from them.[39]

A similar situation prevailed among other pirates who were known
to have boys of their own. In almost every case where a boy can be
assigned as the protégé of an adult, he is identified by the occupation
of the mentor. They are "the carpenter's boy," "the cook's boy," or
"the fiddler's lad." None of these uniquely skilled men, or surgeons,
smiths, and others with special training, were regular members of any
ship's company. They were set apart by relatively esoteric knowledge,
extensive training, the ability to perform necessary tasks, and work
schedules and quarters different from ordinary sailors. They rarely
associated with one another, and their boys were needed to ease the
burden of isolation from their fellows aboard the same ship. Regular
crew members, in contrast, had each other for comradely and sexual
socialization. In the surviving records of piracy, there are no lads
identified as the "bosun's boy" or "Tom the Sailor's lad," and neither
are other youths connected in any fashion with individuals who actually sailed the ship, reefed the sails, caulked the seams, or carried
out the tasks that were the lot of the common seaman.

Transgenerational relationships may also have been a solution for
the sexual difficulties of another particular type of buccaneer, those
who found themselves aboard pirate vessels as the result of capture,
ill fortune, or other circumstances, but who were predominantly heterosexual. The only analogous situation on which any volume of
research has been completed is that of heterosexual males confined
to prisons. Although the evidence of their adaptive techniques is fragmentary and conclusions rest to a considerable extent on assumption
and surmise, there is some indication of behavior patterns unique to
such a situation that may also have existed 300 years past. The essential difficulty facing any heterosexual male suddenly a pirate crew
member—at least those considerations remaining after physical survival had been assured—revolve around the difficulties encountered

in integrating with shipboard sexuality. The mechanisms by which this is done, at least in the cases of males whose self-image was that of a domineering and aggressive individual, is not understood, although the need of such men to subordinate other males predominates in all likelihood over affective ties that might evolve over the course of any relationship. In modern societies where research has been conducted on the problem, the presence of females and participation in coitus defines maleness for some, and their frequent requirement for varied sexual partners suggests an ongoing need for masculine validation. In prison, as may have been the case aboard pirate vessels, the necessary validation can be obtained only by creating surrogate heterosexual relationships. Under the circumstances, acquisition of boys may have served as a substitute not only for heterosexual intercourse but for overt homosexual contact as well. What had the appearance of pederasty may have been in some situations the attempt to recreate heterosexual situations with male dominance in the manner of the prison "jocker" reaffirming his masculinity in domination of his "punk." Relationships of this nature, though accompanied by the full panoply of homosexual contact and symptomatology, are probably the result of other than sexual needs, and may often be the resolution of the conflict between dependency and the need to exercise authority. Lads aboard buccaneer ships would be the obvious targets for reaffirming the masculinity of those who had come to doubt their own manhood. The relationships created under conditions similar to these could easily serve as substitutes for the absent heterosexual acts and heterosocial contacts necessary for self-affirmation.

The general techniques employed by prisoners for acquiring "punks" has the benign, concerned, quality found in the relationships between adult buccaneers and their boys. Essential elements in the seductions include some measure of training, considerable protection, and tentative physical contact leading to a complete sexual relationship. The initiations may vary in speed and technique and as in the case of any attempted seduction, success is not always the end result, but despite the dangers of drawing analogies over the centuries, the frequency and ever-present nature of the process in penal institutions studied makes it appear to be a wide-spread product of males living with only themselves. The regularity and ubiquity of the process make it seem likely it is not a recently evolved human response to a relatively unusual human situation.[40]

Whether pedophilia was frequent or rare among pirates, it was a species of homosexual conduct. There is no record of any female juvenile sailing as a marauder crewmember. The similarity in many cases of the relationships between pirates and their lads with patterns of behavior observed among known pedophiles indicates a possible form for the adult-child dyads aboard buccaneer vessels, although it is highly unlikely that every adult involved in superintending a youth was a pedophile. The interest of some might have been fatherly or avuncular; others could have fallen victim to the scoutmaster syndrome (although there are numerous examples of men taking the leadership of scout troops only because of the sexual opportunities available); some might have merely been helpful. The only indications that pedophilia might have been much more common among buccaneers than in random population samples drawn from either the seventeenth or the twentieth centuries comes from the frequent references to men and their boys, the deep concern of many pirates for their charges, the lack of heterosexual alternatives, the likelihood that the ratio of homosexuals to situational practitioners of homosexual acts was high among the crews, and the existence of *matelotage*, an institutionalized linking of a buccaneer and another male—most often a youth—in a relationship with clearly homosexual characteristics.

As practiced by buccaneers on Hispaniola early in the seventeenth-century, *matelotage* was probably no more than a master-servant relationship originating in cases of men selling themselves to other men to satisfy debts or to obtain food. In many cases *matelots* were no more than slaves, overworked, beaten, sexually abused, murdered, or sold by their owners. However, the generally recognized bond it created between men and the understanding that an inviolable attachment existed between the two as long as the master wanted it to remain so gave *matelotage* a sacrosanct aura among buccaneers. As the decades passed and the utility of the institution was appreciated by increasing numbers of pirates, an informally accepted system of mutual obligations became recognized between master and *matelot*. Alexander Exquemelin, who had served as a *matelot* before becoming a surgeon with Morgan's expeditions against the Spanish, commented fondly about his own master who, when drunk in port, would set a butt of wine in the middle of a street and demand all passers-by drink with him or be shot. One of those who drank, and deeply enough to quench his thirst, was surely Exquemelin himself, for by the second half of the century when he arrived in the West Indies, a sharing of all property was a recognized feature of *matelotage*. The common ownership of goods even extended in most cases to inheritance. According to European law, wives or children were entitled to all property of the deceased, but in the Caribbean wives and children were as uncommon as observance of legal niceties, and when a man died all goods went to his partner, whether master or *matelot*. So strong was the practice that after his attack on Maracaibo, the pirate captain L'Olonnais was careful to make certain that the booty was divided not only among the survivors, but that the portions of those killed were distributed to their servants. On occasion, the mutual ownership of property was even formalized by setting down in writing the agreement that all goods belonged to the survivor.[41]

On the rare and unfortunate occasions when pirates took wives, the rights of the *matelot* were eroded only in terms of his claim to survivor's benefits. He remained *matelot*, retained access to his master's property, and demanded and usually obtained the same connubial rights as the husband. When Captain Louis Adhémar Timothée Le Golif made the decision to wed one of the women imported into Tortuga by Governor Bertrand d'Ogeron some time during the decade following 1665, Pulvérin, the captain's *matelot*, was distraught. He first sought solace in drink, but subsequently claimed his right and was admitted to the marriage chamber. Despite his access to all that was his master's, Pulvérin was never reconciled to sharing Le Golif with a female. He concealed his dissatisfaction for a time, and in due course he was able to obtain revenge. On returning early from a raid, the Captain sent Pulvérin ahead to notify the waiting wife of her husband's impending return. As is often the case when ships sail into port too soon, Madame Le Golif was surprised in congress with another man, and the bearer of good tidings became the deliverer of retribution. Pulvérin killed the woman and her lover, then disappeared. Le Golif found another *matelot* named Le Beque, and was especially fond of him, but he never recovered entirely from the loss. His heart remained always with Pulvérin.[42]

The attachment of buccaneers to their *matelots*, boys, and lovers must have occasioned hostility and conflict, although one authority argues that in homosexual relationships jealousy and paranoid delusion do not occur, and that while there are often quarrels and recriminations, they rarely lead to physical damage or murder.[43] A sizeable body of data from modern court records could be assembled that would bring the assertion of pervasive homosexual gentleness into doubt, but the most convincing evidence that homosexual passions are easily as intense as those of heterosexuals comes not from examples of violence but from instances of deepest devotion. The volume of literature on piracy is concerned primarily with maritime depredations, but the few instances that survive to reveal the more human side of the buccaneers demonstrate a willingness on the part of at least some marauders to suffer torture, deprivation, and even death to protect their lovers. One such incident occurred aboard the ship commanded by Bartholomew Roberts when a crewman, having too much to drink, made the grave mistake of insulting the captain. Roberts demonstrated that his reputation for a quick temper and as a formidable adversary in individual combat was well deserved. He drew his sword and killed the fellow on the spot. When the dead sailor's partner, a man named Jones, learned of what had occurred, he sought out the captain and showered him with vituperation. The captain was no more willing to accept insults from Jones than from his mess mate. He again drew his sword and ran the man through. The second thrust was not as well aimed as the first, and Jones was only injured. Ignoring his wound, the enraged sailor grabbed Roberts, threw him over a gun and beat him soundly. Jones was later sentenced to receive two lashes from every man aboard for daring to attack the commander, a deed that no man would have attempted unless severely distressed.[44] In an altercation with the captain aboard another ship, Richard Simpson recorded that the offending seaman was tied to a gangway and repeatedly doused with cold water. His comrade, distraught over the treatment being visited on his friend, secured the fellow's release by agreeing to take his place and receive the last half of the punishment.[45]

An even more compelling example of a pirate's devotion to one of his shipmates was the action of George Rounsivil, who truly tested the limits of one man's love for another. Rounsivil was an experienced buccaneer who had once been captured, tried for his crimes, and sentenced to death. He escaped the judgment of the court, probably in one of the general pardons declared from time to time by English kings, repented his previous actions and worked for a while on land as an honest tradesman. As time passed, Rounsivil either could not resist the lure of the sea or he was persuaded by the pangs of poverty to return to his old occupation. He joined a crew headed by a pirate acquaintance, and sailed off to plunder in the Caribbean. The voyage was not profitable, and it ultimately ended in disaster when the ship was driven by adverse winds onto the rocks situated near Green Key Island. The ship began to break apart under the pounding of wind and water, and Rounsivil with five other men managed to launch the ship's boat and make for shore; as they were going off to safety, Rounsivil's companion shouted from the poop of the sinking vessel for them to come back and save him. The men in the boat refused. "Rounsivil begg'd his companions to put back, and take him in; but they answered, that the rest would be as willing to save themselves as he, and of Consequence, so many would crowd into the Canoe as would sink it, wherefore they would not venture it; upon which he jump'd into the Water, and swam to the Vessel, and there perished with his Friend since he could not save him."[46]

Nor were pirates above the practice of homosexual nepotism when one of a pair of lovers was in a position of authority. Captain William Dampier once elevated his steward to the rank of midshipman, and George Shelvocke, a privateer commander, was accused of undue solicitousness in ensuring the safety of both his cabin boy and his own son.[47] Matthew Stuart, the cabin boy, was a lad of good sense and good education, which may have explained the captain's concern for his well-being, but when he was promoted to first mate over several other more able men even though he was unable to tell "a brace from a bowline," there was dissatisfaction among the crewmen. One sailor complained that the unusual promotion "gave us all a kind of emulation, wondering what rare qualifications Shelvocke could discover in a fellow, who but a few days before rinsed our glasses and filled us our wine."[48] Some time after, Shelvocke and Stuart had a falling out, and the favors once bestowed brought the captain little gratitude. Stuart returned the kindness at a later date by testifying that Shelvocke was involved in diverting funds from the sponsors of the voyage.[49]

As is the case with unions between men and women, the bonds that evolved among pirate couples originated in economic necessity, custom, and in love, but the disruptive tendencies making modern homosexual dyads difficult to sustain did not exist in the Caribbean of three centuries ago. Social opprobrium, ecclesiastical condemnation, and the hostility of the law could not damage relationships established by pairs of buccaneers, and the links that held them together may well have been as strong and compelling, although not as permanent, as those uniting heterosexual couples. As is the case with marriages of male and female, jealousy, promiscuity, alienation of affection, boredom, and another score of considerations operate to separate persons tied to one another, and pirate couples were surely no exception. The absence of ecclesiastical approval, legally binding pronouncements, a home, and children made buccaneers more likely to dissolve their partnerships than heterosexuals. *Matelots* were sold or traded from one hunter or pirate to another, and the *matelot* who was not owned as a servant or whose term of servitude expired was often free to select a new mate if he chose to do so. Pirates who preferred boys rather than adults as sex partners found that their young innocents soon grew older and the physical characteristics and uncritical acceptance of their tutor's affections were soon replaced with the look of a man and the sexual sophistication that diminished their attraction to the pedophile. Both were then freed to locate new comrades, the man having lost his lad and the lad having become a man. Among relationships involving two adults, the vicissitudes of health, combat, and simple ennui often worked in concert to split them apart and send them seeking new partners.

How often men joined with another member of their crew, the average duration of pirate marriages, or what proportion of buccaneers ignored opportunities for close relationships with other men and simply lived lives of unrestricted promiscuity cannot even be guessed. If interpersonal relationships were in the seventeenth century "at best cold and at worst hostile," as Lawrence Stone describes them, with a low level of affective character limiting the capacity of individuals for evolving warm or mutually dependant unions, then under such combinations of circumstances where centrifugal tendencies were apparently sufficient to fragment most types of human bonding, perhaps the only adequate explanation of the relationships existing between pirate pairs was the homoerotic unity often observed among men in times of hardship, crisis, or danger.[50] The strange and distant world of the Caribbean, the fragility of life in the tropics, the constant danger of the buccaneer's trade, and the hardship of life at sea may all have been mitigated for some in the *camaraderie*, friendship, or even love often generated by men for each other under particularly trying circumstances.[51] What evidence survives indicates these factors or others yet unaccounted for were operative, and pairing, or pirate marriages if the term can be used, formed an important part of life for many buccaneers.

Pirate crews varied greatly in size. Depending on an assortment of circumstances, they ranged from half a dozen in number to several hundred on more elaborately organized expeditions. Larger pirate ships that plundered the Caribbean in the closing years of the seventeenth century sometimes carried as many as 250 men, but ordinary buccaneering expeditions in the 1670s or the 1680s were considerably smaller. The suitability of almost every member of a pirate crew as a sex partner for almost every other man means that aboard ship the potential for wide-spread promiscuity existed, but it is not entirely certain whether pirates availed themselves of the opportunities for frequent shifting of partners or for group sexual experiences. Several studies of homosexual patterns in large American cities indicate that promiscuity is fairly common, with many cases being reported of men having hundreds of partners within fairly limited time periods. The social imperatives that substantiate permanence among heterosexual couples—economic necessity, religious beliefs, the presence of family, and peer pressure—are all considerably reduced in the case of homosexuals, but among buccaneers they were entirely absent. The constantly changing composition of any ship's crew due to deaths from natural causes, desertion, those killed in combat, and the frequent arrival of men and boys captured aboard other vessels all may have made relationships of long duration between pirates difficult to perpetuate.[52]

There is no way of speculating on the number of pirates who rejected sexual promiscuity or at least restricted their contacts to a limited number of partners, but there were conspicuous instances of buccaneers who entered into sustained relationships with others of their company, with their boys or with their servants. The unions between buccaneers often involved deep and abiding love and exhibited many of the traits usually associated with compatible heterosexual couples. The intimate association between lonely male adventurers is hardly a surprising phenomenon, at least for readers of nineteenth-century American literature. James Fenimore Cooper's Natty Bumppo abhorred women and lived isolated from them on the frontier where he was safe from their wiles and could expend his love and devotion on Chingachook, his male Indian associate. There is also the narrator's love for Hope in *Two Years Before the Mast*, but most familiar is the relationship between Ishmael and Queequeg in Melville's *Moby Dick*. "I found Queequeg's arm thrown over me in the most loving and affectionate manner. You had almost thought I had been his wife," related Ishmael, ". . . he still hugged me tightly, as though naught but death should part us twain . . . Thus, then, in our heart's honeymoon, lay I and Queequeg—a cosy, loving pair . . . he pressed his forehead against mine, clasped me around the waist, and said that henceforth we were married."[53] In the chaste literary atmosphere of a hundred years ago, relationships between men were interpreted as the innocent male love that is expressed in locker room back-slapping or the fraternity singalong. In the case of Cooper's Natty Bumppo this may have been an accurate assessment, but both Dana and Melville knew their sailors far better than the reading public knew them, and they understood their feelings were not unusual in the world of ships and mariners, where passions were often of an intensity equal to the level of emotions that bind men and woman.[54]

Surveys of modern homosexual groups reveal a wide variety of sexual practices and techniques are commonly employed by members, and it is possible that pirates as well as other seventeenth-century English homosexuals also indulged in a multiplicity of sexual practices.[55] The absence of any indication of oral-genital contact among homosexuals in the Tudor-Stuart centuries could be the result of the same reticence that produced vague and unspecific statutes dealing with sexual matters over the years. English judicial officials and lawmakers were commonly drawn from the easily scandalized upper-middle classes, and men who experience a severe degree of discomposure on the subject of anal intercourse are not likely to write extensively of oral-genital contact, discuss it among themselves, or admit it occurred with sufficient frequency to necessitate legislating specific prohibitions against it.[56]

While pirates may have practiced fellatio on a regular basis without leaving any evidence of doing so, it is equally possible that the variety of their sexual practices was more restricted. Trials of both seafarers and landsmen for homosexual offenses during the age of Caribbean piracy contain references only to anal intercourse and mutual masturbation of the serial and simultaneous types. Although it is difficult to believe pirates were unaware of the possibility of oral-genital contact, on the lower levels of society where they were socialized and acculturated there may have been hostility or even outright prohibitions against fellatio. Studies have revealed profound class distinctions in attitudes relating to alternative forms of sexual expression, with members of economically disadvantaged groups exhibiting considerably less enthusiasm for various modes of non-reproductive sexual practices than the wealthy. The same pattern may have been present in Restoration England where oral-genital practices were employed by the sexually sophisticated aristocracy but may have been eschewed on the levels of society that produced buccaneers.[57] Environmental conditions could also have been responsible for encouraging pirates to engage only in anal intercourse and masturbation, if in fact they did not practice oral-genital contact. Aboard buccaneering vessels, homosexuality was an accepted part of life, in contrast to the homosexuality of American interviewees who provided information on which at least one survey of the variety of sexual experiences was based. The opportunity aboard ship for extended fear-free copulation meant pirates could participate in leisurely anal-genital contacts without the need of the modern American homosexuals to practice a form of sexual contact that enables the participants to disengage quickly and with a minimum of discomfiture in order to avoid detection. The hurried, impersonal, and taut encounters that have conditioned the homosexual experiences of many Americans were entirely foreign to pirates who had no need to include in their sexual practice techniques well-suited to furtive encounters.[58]

The apparent concentration on anal intercourse and masturbation might also be explained in terms of divergent preferences among various groups. Studies of present-day English homosexuals reveal that unlike their American counterparts whose primary method of contact is fellatio, they prefer genital apposition or very close body contact without penetration as a means to achieve ejaculation. The terms "rub off" or "slicklegging" are usually used to describe their practices. The distinct preference of Americans for fellatio may be due in part to the universal practice of infant circumcision in the United States. In countries where the practice is rare, the accumulation of sebacious secretions beneath the foreskin and the resultant odor might render olfactory and penile proximity distasteful and induce uncircumsized Englishmen to restrict themselves to other manners of sexual gratification. It also indicates that similar considerations may have been responsible for the practice of oral-genital sex among the Restoration aristocracy while it was rejected by the lower classes. The use of perfumes, lotions, unguents, and scented potions with purported aphrodisiacal qualities was common among the wealthiest classes in late seventeenth-century England. Pubic depilation was practiced by some aristocratic females, and members of both sexes bathed frequently, at least by the standards of the age. Among cottagers, paupers, laborers, and vagrants, body cosmetics were unknown and soap and water were rarely or never expended on the person. Although the continual accumulation of smegmal matter, desquamated epithelial cells, bodily secretions, fecal and urinary traces, perspiration, bacteria, dust, and dirt in the pubic regions may have rendered the practice of oral-genital contact appealing for some, it is at least as likely that these same accumulations could have made it obnoxious even for those who would normally have experienced sexual stimulation from moderately pungent genital odors. This much is indicated by eighteenth-century attitudes toward the bidet. It was known in England as early as 1752, but never became popular largely because of moral rather than hygenic objections to its adoption, indicating an association of the ideas of oral-genital sex and cleanliness. But whatever the causes of the divergence in present-day trans-Atlantic homosexual practice, whether induced by hygenic considerations or social conditioning, or of yet undetermined origins, it does indicate that a variety of homosexual manifestations are feasible and increases the likelihood that homosexuals three centuries past engaged in patterns of sexual gratification widely different from those employed by present-day groups.[59]

The possible preference of buccaneers for anal intercourse over other types of homosexual acts might well provide a clue to at least one portion of community life aboard ship. In the youthful experiences of a group of adult homosexual convicts interviewed by investigators from the Alfred C. Kinsey Institute for Sex Research at Indiana University, anal-genital contact played only a minor part in their indoctrination into homosexual practice. However, in their early contacts only six percent of those involved participated exclusively as inserters while 37 percent served exclusively as insertees. Anal intercourse requires a clear definition of roles, unlike mutual masturbation or some types of oral-genital relations. One participant must be active while the other remains passive in most circumstances, and as such it is eminently suited to a situation involving a youth and an adult where the adult is the dominant partner in all phases of the relationship, not only those involving sexual activity. Aboard ship or among bands wandering England's roads this type of relationship would naturally be more common than in modern America, where the survey of homosexual convicts was conducted and where youths are segregated into more homogeneous chronological groupings than those found on pirate vessels or among seventeenth-century vagrants. The pattern of sexual experience aboard buccaneering ships may well have been set by the pedophiles. As each man's particular lad grew older and left the tutelage of his adult mentor, those who did not acquire any preference for younger partners simply joined the other crewmen in sexual activities, serving alternately as inserter, insertee, or in both positions as the situation required. Yet while abandoning their exclusively submissive sexual role in an adult-youth dyad, they continued using anal intercourse, the type of sexual expression their early life experiences conditioned them to regard as normal.[60]

FIVE

THE BUCCANEER
COMMUNITY

The coterminal limits of the physical and psychological boundaries of the ship, when combined with its impermeability or insulation from outside influences, created an environment for the seventeenth-century mariner that has been characterized as a total institution. This is a situation where entry or egress is severely restricted, the normally segregated activities of life, eating, sleeping, working, and recreation, are all conducted within the same spatially constricted area, each phase of the participants' lives is lived out in the immediate company of others of the institution's participants, with events being sequenced and directed from a higher authority within the institution for the attainment of a goal or goals recognized as desirable by all participants. The comprehensive effects of personality and interaction between members of any such institution are profound, but aboard buccaneering vessels the added elements of danger, frequent dietary deficiency, occasional drunkenness, the unlikelihood of ever returning to the mother country (a desire which probably affected some), the imminence of death, and the sea itself all combined to increase the "totality" of the surroundings beyond that experienced by the convicts, military men, or asylum inmates who have been studied in institutional settings.[1]

In attempting to discern possible modes of behavior by pairing pirate communities with "total institutions" such as asylums and modern shipboard communities, the same caveat that applies to prison studies and research on modern homosexual activity and pedophilia must be even more firmly propounded. There is considerable divergence, as might be expected, in the experiences of modern mariners separated by so wide an expanse of time from buccaneers, but despite the obvious technological and perceptual variations, social structure aboard ship has changed little in many respects since the age of sail. Data garnered from men now taking their livings from the sea has considerable complementary utility in reconstructing selected features of past maritime relationships, and the correlations sometimes make the structure of buccaneer life appear more clearly from the opaqueness imposed by the passage of time. Again, trepidation and caution are watchwords in dealing with sailors in this fashion. Advances in nautical construction, varying economic expectations, increased safety, alterations in the character of work experience, improvement of physical surroundings and the differences in outlook and attitudes occasioned by the passage of time all separate modern seamen from their seventeenth-century counterparts and prevent results of recent investigations of shipboard life from being applied uniformly and uncritically to relationships among crewmen three hundred years ago. Still, striking parallels in the responses of men to socially similar circumstances are to be found not only in comparisons of seafaring life with that in total institutions but in analyses of shipboard conditions and mariners' responses in both the seventeenth and the twentieth centuries. Sailors' difficulties in the present, in many respects, were also their difficulties in the past. The close proximity of every man to his shipmates, the complexities of evolving interpersonal relationships, and the protracted boredom on many of today's vessels were surely present aboard well-manned pirate ships and naval craft, where the necessary contingent of fighting men was far in excess of those needed for sailing and maneuvering no matter how severe the weather. Occasional difficulties and deprivations, even when the social features of deprivation were chosen rather than only endured, compounded the effect of shipboard features with potential for social disruption.

The necessity to ration food, alcohol, or water aboard buccaneering vessels, like smoking curfews on submarines running submerged for prolonged periods of time, exacerbated morale problems and in combination with other aspects of life aboard ship—the low turnover of pirate crewmen and the restricted amounts of usable space—often created for sailors then and now an atmosphere much like prisons, where similar conditions prevail. In both types of total institution, prisons and ships, various aspects of community produce a high level of anxiety in which antagonistic associations are formed that have directive force in the operation of the community; but in like manner, closeness, boredom, and enduring a common set of woes create situations that are primarily affective as well.[2]

The very features of shipboard life that produce this social paradox are also the features responsible for many of the situations that attract men to seafaring. Within the institutional imperatives, no matter what ratio exists between mutual hostility and interpersonal esteem, there develop stable life patterns that are, and were in the age of buccaneering, meaningful, reasonable, and normal within particular limits. According to interviews in a recent study of seafarers' attitudes, the reasons for chosing a maritime career were all of those that might be expected: the opportunity to travel, the prospect of an exciting and varied life, the chance to meet people, the possibility of advancement, and the community atmosphere aboard ship. The majority of motives given by the interviewees probably had little appeal to lads who first went to sea from English port towns in the seventeenth century, but the last mentioned attraction, the chance to participate in a community of seafarers, may have served as a particularly desirable quality for boys who were ejected early from their parents' homes, forced into vagabondage, placed as apprentices, or were put out as servants or laborers. For young men in such circumstances, whether the choice to go to sea was taken voluntarily, forced by hunger, or made at the urging of an armed press gang, seafaring may have provided the opportunity to retain for a time the adolescent dependence made difficult to perpetuate by the loss of home, parents, and familiar surroundings. Their dependence on the total institutional structure of the ship and officers created for them a home-like situation where social and physical boundaries were easily discerned and food, shelter, recreation, compensation, work, and conduct were all regulated. In a recent study aboard a nuclear submarine, an age-regressive style of juvenile gang behavior developed among the crewmen who divided themselves into units on the basis of technical skills, and similar patterns of behavior have also been observed in projective tests administered to subjects in confinement experiments. How accurately observations of present-day sailors and laboratory behavior studies replicate motives and responses of seafarers from the past is not a question that is easily answered, but the types of behavior observed by researchers in their subject populations are apparent in pirate groups as well. The desperate cohesiveness with which freebooters fought for one another and their awareness of being not only members of their own ship's community but part of a "Brethren of the Coast"—one band even carried their sense of unity to the point of adopting a group name, "The Flying Gang"—indicate that juvenile male bonding, among youths as well as their older companions, was a pervasive feature of buccaneering.[3]

The sailors who opted for lengthy voyages to distant points of England's trading patterns and the pool of men from which the bulk of pirate crews were drawn made their choice of seafaring life styles for a complex of reasons in which each obtained maximum gratification from living and working in an institution with low permeability. The same preference is found among sailors and officers serving on large oil tankers. Loading and off-loading procedures often keep them anchored far from shore. Their contact with persons other than their fellow crew members are at a minimum, and the periods at sea can run into months or even into years for some men who rarely leave their vessels and are considered to be suffering from what mariners call "tankeritis." In both cases, men elect to spend lengthy periods at sea because it offers a secure base for their socialization and provides the masculine security and interpersonal satisfaction unavailable ashore. For the pirate in the Caribbean, the effect of those features that made long voyages more attractive than coastal trading were amplified by serving aboard a buccaneering vessel. Limited permeability at sea was reinforced by the ship-like low permeability of the English

Caribbean towns—with their limited access to women—that the buccaneers visited. There was little likelihood that pirate vessels would ever sail to England or other European ports where the crews would be paid off in the manner of merchant seamen or the sailors from men-of-war and set ashore to live in a landsman's world.

During abbreviated stays in the more complex social milieu of the landsman, if the pattern of present-day mariners is applicable at all to mariners of three centuries ago, buccaneers probably experienced uneasiness in communication and a feeling that the tavernkeepers, prostitutes, and others they came in contact with in various colonial towns did not understand their way of life. A measure of the difficulty on land was undoubtedly due to poorly developed social skills resulting from extended periods aboard ship, but the dissatisfaction was also enlarged by awareness of the extortionate rates charged pirates for goods and services by merchants.[4] Pirate ships were in and out of port often on a more frequent basis than East Indiamen, and any new buccaneers they acquired were either "Brethren of the Coast," experienced merchant seamen, or novices in the business of seafaring. Socialization of the new man created little problem for the buccaneer. Pirates and merchant sailors integrated into their midst without causing more than a ripple, and prisoners, escaped servants, or convicts posed no threat to the experienced buccaneer. He was secured by his highly developed skills and the established shipboard relationships, which precluded the danger of status diminution by recently acquired replacements. By the time new personnel that survived were initiated into the ways of the sea and had mastered sufficient technical knowledge to compete with the older buccaneers, they were fully socialized and acculturated into the shipboard community. Captives who refused to join the pirates presented no difficulty. Their status as prisoners removed them from the social system that provided pirates with their identity and offered each marauder an extra tot of security in being able to exercise easy domination over other human beings.[5]

Additional impetus for rapid and permanent acculturation for men taken aboard pirate vessels was the relatively pleasant life patterns enjoyed by the crew, pleasant at least when compared with those experienced by men in the Navy or sailing aboard less desirable merchant craft. Buccaneer discipline in matters relating to day-to-day life was less rigid and less brutal, although the totality of the institution was not appreciably diminished by such liberalism. The values and normative expectations of sailors turned freebooter retained a high degree of coherence, powerfully sanctioned as they were by the crewmen themselves. A man joining a pirate crew gained freedom from particularly galling aspects of regulation and considerable arbitrariness while at the same time retaining the institutional structure that provided for his social and psychological requirements.

Shipboard Buggery and the Nature of Prosecution

The acculturative security and tightly bonded community structure provided by ships in the seventeenth century is nowhere more apparent than in the surviving records dealing with shipboard buggery. Although the first secular statute condemning homosexual conduct in England dates from the reign of Henry VIII, over a hundred years passed before sexual relations between sailors of the Royal Navy was given official notice by high-ranking officers. It is not known if there was a single incident or series of incidents in the fleet that precipitated Admiralty cognizance of events aboard their vessels, but the propensity of King James I for male lovers may have provided the example that convinced the Navy homosexual behavior was a problem. Significantly, they did not move to restrict or eliminate it until 1627, after James was cold in his grave and Charles I, particularly prudish in matters of sex, was installed on the throne. In that year a regulation was put into effect providing that "If any Person belonging to the Fleet shall commit Buggery or Sodomy, he shall be punished with Death."[6]

Two years later, public interest in the subject was aroused when the Earl of Castlehaven was brought to trial both under the 1533 statute prohibiting homosexual practices and on several other sex-related charges, but even with the scandal created by the Earl and the new regulation requiring death for buggery and sodomy, the Admiralty prosecutions that followed were few in number. Of those actually tried, there is in every case solid evidence that more was involved than homosexual acts. Violations of shipboard community standards or interference from outside the maritime milieu seem to determine the need for prosecutions. Robert Hewitt, brought to trial in the early 1630s, was apparently an excessive practitioner of sodomy as well as a child molester. He was accused of buggering Marmaduke Warnham, Roger Head, and a boy, George Hungerforde, all during a single voyage of the *Royall Mary*. In a similar case brought later in the decade against Robert Stone, a "saylor," there are even clearer indications that the accused was being tried not simply for violating Samuel Organ, a lad aboard his ship, but was in fact a notorious sodomite, regularly crossing the social boundaries that divided sexual and non-sexual relationships aboard ship and in all likelihood seeking partners among those already involved in permanent or semi-permanent arrangements.[7]

If studies of modern seafarers give any clue to the lives of their predecessors, the proximity of one man to another aboard ship amplified the relationships between men, intensifying sexual competitiveness when present because of the limited number of men available as partners and increasing the anxiety level aboard the ship where the institutional "totality" prohibited easy resolution of the problem. Some quantity of the competitive viciousness generated by close quarters and sexual competition may have been involved in the indictment of Richard Kingston some years later where it appears more than proscribed sex acts brought him to the attention of the authorities. Kingston, of Magdalen College, M.A. Oxon, and minister to His Majesty's frigate *Forsight*, was a man of some experience as a seafaring cleric. He had served for 14 months aboard the *Advice* before joining the *Forsight*, and was commended in a deposition by the captain of the *Advice* for doing an excellent job. Under the circumstances it would seem unlikely he would be indicted for sodomy, but ill luck was with Kingston. Although his fellow crewmembers evidently had no complaint about his conduct, an alleged victim of Kingston's lust, a 15-year-old lad named Richard Ellery, reported the event or events when the ship returned to England. The accused minister denied the charge, but he admitted he had whipped the boy

severely on at least one occasion. Whether the whipping was a manifestation of homosexual sadism or punishment for some offense cannot be discerned from the indictment, but Kingston evidently was
not tried for the offense, indicating the accusation well may have
been Ellery's revenge for the flogging.[8]

Like the indictments of Hewitt, Stone, and Kingston, a 1649 incident involving the buggery of 16-year-old John Durrant of Stepney
also had overtones that carried it beyond an act of anal intercourse.
The feature of the case that seemed to irritate the captain who conducted the trial was not that buggery had been committed repeatedly
or that it had been done with the boy's consent. The horror of the
event was that an English lad had allowed himself to be penetrated
by a heathen, Abdul Rhyme, a "Hindostan peon." Numerous witnesses testified to having seen the two frequently involved in buggery
and in mutual masturbation on the quarter deck as well as below.
The truth of the testimony was assured by having nine Christian witnesses swear on the Bible to the veracity of their statements. Corro-
borating statements were also taken from a number of Hindus, but
their word was useful only for supporting what had been attested to
by Christians. It could not sustain a conviction alone, according to
the trial record. In this case, the accused mariners were convicted,
and each was given 40 lashes, the wounds to be rubbed with salt and
water. According to the sentence, there were to be several later ad-
ministrations of ten lashes with more salt and water, and the sodomites were to be limited to a diet of bread and water for an unspecified
period of time.[9]

Harsh as it may seem, the punishment meeted out to Abdul Rhyme
and Durrant was considerably less than the death sentence specified
in the regulations, but again, the rantings of the trial's presiding officer indicate he was more agitated by acts of miscegenation that dis-
rupted the operation of the total institution than buggery, which was
an ordinary part of the vessel's functioning. Indeed the tendency to
regard interracial sex as far more serious than homosexuality was not
a pecularity of this particular captain or a feature of life aboard an
individual ship. In a later satirical pamphlet, using a pirate craft for
what might have been an allegorical treatment of William III and his

associates, a mutineer was discredited not by accusing him of buggery but by inducing a Moor to testify that the accused had once asked to be buggered by him.[10]

In another case for which records survive, Samuel Norman, a ship captain, was accused of pulling down the breeches of his servant and inserting his "Yard or privity into his Backside" on at least three separate occasions. The alleged offenses were committed with more delicacy by Norman than those of Durrant and Rhyme. He closed the door and locked it to prevent observation by the crew, then embarked on a scenario of seduction similar in some respects to that used by prison "jockers" bringing youthful convicts into their homosexual arrangements. He first employed deviousness to induce the cabin boy to provide him with a rubdown. The ship was at anchor and Norman had been ashore horseback riding. He informed the lad after his return that his legs ached from the unfamiliar exercise and removed his breeches so that the pain could be massaged away. The 14-year-old was well aware of the commander's intentions and suggested another, more receptive, lad then aboard ship as a suitable partner, but Captain Norman would not be dissuaded, according to the testimony. When gentleness failed, Norman turned the boy about, bent him over, bared his posterior, and the deed was quickly done. The commander surely assumed that there would be no repercussion from his initial act and those that followed, but again, on the ship's return to England, charges were brought not by the victim or outraged crewmembers, but by a father incensed that his son had been used in such fashion. Norman was never brought to trial. An indictment was denied for reasons that have not survived. Still, the case bears similarities to the others in that it was not simply a matter of a buggered boy complaining but of an outsider requesting action be taken.[11]

The use of sodomy as a political weapon was as convenient for buccaneers as for Englishmen in the homeland. During a 1680 cruise in the South Sea, a severe disagreement, over whether to continue in the Pacific or return through the Straits of Magellan to sail in the vicinity of established English settlements in the Caribbean, severely divided the crew of a Captain Sawkins. By the time the disagreement reached crisis proportions, Sawkins had died, leaving the expedition without a leader. Three men evidently vied to take command: Bartholomew Sharp, John Watling, and Edmund Cook. Sharp first was elected captain, but opposition to him remained strong and he was deposed by the supporters of Watling. Cook, too, assumed he was qualified for the post. He had sailed many years as a privateer, served as commander of a number of vessels at various times, and once led a land force of over 350 pirates in an attack on a Spanish colonial town. At this point, Cook's servant was forced or persuaded to confess "that his Master had oft times Buggered him in England. . . . That the same crime he had also perpetrated in Jamaica; and once in these Seas before Panama." Watling seized what he thought was an advantage, and tried to have Cook imprisoned for sodomy. That would have the obvious effect of removing him as a contender for the captaincy. Watling soon discovered that incarcerating him for a homosexual act was too transparent a pretext, hardly a measure that would persuade seasoned buccaneers of his unfitness for leadership. Moreover, Watling's attempt to confine Cook was further weakened when the servant who made the original accusation refused to reaffirm it as he lay dying of an unspecified malady. The only solution was to discover another odious act committed by Cook, and this was done. A paper was found in the possession of the accused sodomite listing the names of the men with whom he sailed. It was charged by Watling, according to the testimony of privateer Basil Ringrose, that Cook planned to provide the list to Spanish prisoners aboard the ship. It was not entirely clear why Cook would give the list to the Spanish, or even if that was his intention, but when the accusation of buggery failed, another charge was needed to enable Watling to clap the hapless Cook in irons and secure his own command.[12]

A most vital factor concerning the cases is that they are not a random selection but the sum total of all such incidents for which records survive in the century between the Admiralty regulation of 1627 and the freeing of Captain Norman from Newgate Prison in 1723; there is no indication that there were other similar cases for which the records are missing. Taken as a group, they indicate that cases necessarily must involve more than ordinary buggery or sodomy for them to be considered important. They must be disruptive of ship-board totality or involve an outside factor. Robert Hewitt and Robert Stone were apparently excessive buggerers; one case involved a complaining victim of floggings; John Durrant had not only been buggered, but more seriously he had been buggered by a heathen; another case included a complaining parent; Cook was the victim of a power struggle.

In dealing with buggery and sodomy, there appears to be a distinction in the way it was regarded by men from different classes. With Durrant, for example, there was little attempt on the part of the participants to secure privacy for their various acts of anal intercourse or masturbation, although it is unlikely a secret trysting place was available for crewmen in any circumstance. They engaged in homosexual acts on the quarterdeck, which was probably manned 24 hours a day, below decks, and between bales of cargo. The number of witnesses who testified in the inquiry demonstrates that no effort was made to hide their conduct. In their era sexual acts were not performed as furtively as is presently the custom, and indeed there is no reason to suspect that sex acts in the seventeenth century were ordinarily performed in private. This was an age where the mass of men and women lived in close proximity to farm animals—always notorious for following their sexual inclinations with or without the presence of human or same-species audiences—and for most of the world's population the private bedroom had not yet been invented. In their homes, people ate, slept, worked, and copulated in the same space, and it is only natural to assume they would conduct themselves in the same manner aboard ships at sea. In the case of Captain Norman, the trial records do contain the information that the accused closed and locked the cabin door so that he would not be observed by the crew, an indication that although buggery among the men was not always a secret practice, one in a command position with the luxury of private accommodations nonetheless would prefer to engage in sexual practices unobserved by the rabble. Yet Norman knew, it must be assumed, that there are few secrets aboard a ship, and that sodomizing a cabin boy would be known by the crew in short order.

Homosexual Association and Identification

Examining patterns of sexuality three hundred years past against a corpus of data derived from modern research contains the same potential for over-extension and the drawing of unwonted conclusions inherent in pairing pirates and penitentiary inmates. But if a direct link between homosexuals past and present is dangerous, the method of approach offers some compensating qualities for illuminating the possibilities for diversity among homosexual or homosexually oriented groups. The social, intellectual, economic, and cultural variety characteristic of present-day populations engaged in homosexual activity was absent among the likes of those who became pirates, but Caribbean marauders were joined by other compelling social bonds, similar life experiences, privations endured, common economic problems, and the mastery of the same trades or techniques for survival. In this sense, they formed an interest community that went beyond sexually specified requirements, in contrast to the cliques of homosexuals frequently studied by sociologists and psychologists where there is no formal organization and only a sexual bond to unite them. Within such cliques, sex is clearly compartmentalized, and most members do not carry their homosexual associations on into their other business or leisure-time activities because of the risk of exposure and humiliation. But in seventeenth-century England, the risks were mimimal, and genuine communities composed of homosexuals evolved, although they could never be self-regulating due to the dominant heterosexual culture that pervaded the land.[13]

The lack of persecution and the ease of making homosexual contacts probably eliminated the need for social centers for pirate communities similar to modern gay bars or networks of gay coffee houses, baths, bookstores, record shops, gyms, restaurants, and other gathering places where homosexuals and those homosexually directed cannot only exchange information and make sexual contacts, but where the primary function is to reaffirm the patron's worth in a generally hostile environment. Although Randolph Trumbach traces the roots of a genuine homosexual subculture back into the closing decade of the seventeenth century, the men who became pirates were, for the

most part, gone from England by 1695, and those still in the homeland after that time were from levels of society far below the participants in the network of clubs, brothels, taverns, and meeting places
he describes. It is not likely there were any similarly functional institutions for males on the lowest social strata in seventeenth-century
and eighteenth-century England or the West Indies. The need
for such institutions was obviated by general acceptance of homosexual conduct and the opportunity for those involved to live with little
fear of the authorities and no concern over the hazards of public
exposure. There were of course sailors' grog shops, which were undoubtedly patronized by homosexuals and others similarly inclined,
but these differed from the gay bar in that they catered not specifically to men who sought out other men as sex partners but to a
clientele of sailors who happened to be homosexually oriented or
genuinely homosexual.[14] The same is probably true of other establishments. With the homosexual activity among lower-class males
considered to be ordinary behavior, one of the chief functions of the
gay bar, the establishment of the individual's personal value through
contact with other similarly oriented individuals, was not necessary.

Similarly, the problems of identification of potential sexual partners, sometimes a vexing exercise in the present day, was much less
complex for the potential buccaneer. Often the visible symbols of
class and occupation were sufficient for sexual classification, much
as occupation might indicate possible homosexual preferences today
for a hairdresser or an interior decorator. A sailor would likely be
receptive to homosexual advances, but a baker, owning his own shop,
with the need for a wife and children to aid him, and being a member of a class where heterosexuality was economically viable, would
be an unlikely prospect. Beyond these symbols, there is no evidence
from the seventeenth or eighteenth centuries to indicate that men
with homosexual proclivities or preferences from the pirate-producing
classes were recognizable by a system of secret signs or signals. The
literature is extensive on systems for identification among modern
homosexuals and men engaging in homosexual acts. The way glances
are exchanged, the manner of dress, a seemingly meaningless movement, the wearing of a pinky ring, Pall Mall cigarettes ("Wherever

Particular People Congregate") are understood only by the cognoscenti, while homosexual behavior obvious to the uninitiated is observable usually only in ten to 15 percent of the homosexual or homosexually oriented population.[15] One recent study maintains that among homosexuals in prison, isolated as they are in an all male community where homosexuality is an accepted part of daily life, recognizability rises to approximately 30 percent, but a prison environment is different in essential respects from English communities in the times of the later Stuarts and early Hanoverians, and it is distinct in essential respects from West Indian pirate communities as well.[16]

Communication and the Use of Specialized Language

The only possibility that there existed any systems to insure recognizability among homosexual pirates, beyond the indications presented by the facts of a seafaring life, was the maritime propensity for a secret language similar in some respects to the argot frequently used by members of homosexual cliques. Still, it is dangerous to place too heavy a burden of interpretative synthesis on such a factual base. Sailors, and thus pirates, have had for centuries their own speech patterns dealing with the details of seafaring. Landsmen unfamiliar with the language of the sea are pressed to remember if starboard is left or right and are lost amid references to hawsers and lifts or braces and yards. This sort of specialized nautical speech serves a function entirely different than the language of either homosexuals or homosexual pirates. It is a military language, a professional mode of expression necessary to deal with articles, practices, and procedures not encountered anywhere else, and it grew from necessity rather than to serve the purpose of concealment or identification. Modern homosexuals have their own dialogue, but as in the case of sailors, among underworld figures, in prisons, and with seafaring talk, the purpose is not to maintain secrecy but to classify and communicate common experiences. Among homosexuals, as among sailors, their private means of communication is not a language, but simply a limited set of words and expressions to communicate understanding in severely limited situations. Just as seafarer's language is extended to non-seafaring subjects only in metaphor and simile, the same is true with homosexual argot. The vocabulary that is exclusively homosexual is confined for the most part to activities that are exclusively homosexual.[17] As the terms binnacle and bowsprit have little use among men who do not make their living from the sea, so the expressions "slicklegging" or to pick up "trade" do not extend into heterosexual vocabulary.

Among pirates, the only unique portion of their vocabulary that survives, beyond seafaring terminology, is the regular use of nicknames. In this area, the practices of French and English buccaneers diverge somewhat. Nicknames relating to places of birth or residence were fairly common among the French. One of the most notorious pirate chiefs was Jean-David Nau, called L'Olonnais after his birthplace at Les Sables d'Olonnais, and pirates named in like manner were Michel le Basque and Pierre le Picard. Others carried titles that detailed their grisly physical appearance. Tête-d'Épingle and Pied de Bouc sailed with men like Bâbord-Amures, whose nose was noticeably directed toward the port side of his face. Tête-de-Mort had a nose half eaten away by an ulcer. Boisbrûlé and Gueule-de-Raie were merely ugly fellows, as one would assume was the case with Bille-en-Bois, but the character of other pirates was reflected in names such as Montbars the Exterminator or Pierre le Grand. English nicknames typically were less descriptive than those of the French. Common among them were more ordinary appellations like Black Bart, Blackbeard, Timberhead, or, in the case of one man, the simple and direct name, Bear. Both French and English nicknames sometimes carried sexual or homosexual implications. Tape-cul was so called in reference to his backside and surely Cœur d'Andouille must have occasionally detected a sly smile on the faces of those to whom he was introduced. Captain John Avery, as fierce as any who sailed in the eighteenth century, was known as Long Ben, not because of his height, and Louis Adhémar Timothée le Golif, known as Borgnefesse and who referred to his seafaring enemies as *bougres*, complained that the loss of a buttock to a caroming cannon ball made him an especially desirable partner to all manner of fellows. He of course preferred the company of his *matelot*, Pulvérin.[18]

Even though the buccaneers of Hispaniola used nicknames almost exclusively, leaving the planters who were married as the only island resident customarily employing real names, it is not likely their propensity to select new names after arriving in the Caribbean was functionally analogous to the practice of modern homosexuals, who frequently employ assumed names or operate on a first-name-only basis to conceal their identities.[19] If this was the purpose among pirates, their concern for remaining anonymous was to conceal their piratical activities rather than their sexual preferences or practices. Being known as a sodomite among seafarers was not a socially destructive bit of information, but being identified by name as a pirate could, with a measure of bad luck, send one to the gallows at a later date. More likely the use of nicknames was a combination of the desire to make prosecution more difficult and a lower-class propensity for the practice. Especially aboard pirate vessels, the use of nicknames would have a greater opportunity to become universal since there was no need to record complete names, as was the case on merchant or naval vessels. No pay records were kept among buccaneers and neither were there formal issues of clothing or other items. Pirates simply had no need for both given and surnames, and unlike other areas of society where both were needed, aboard buccaneering vessels the practice of using a single name was adopted for reasons unconnected with sexuality.

The use of feminine nicknames in some homosexual circles, especially the diminutive forms, in what Christopher Isherwood labeled "low camp," is part of a complex psycho-social situation that is not clearly defined or understood. While it is accepted by some, there is a hostile, almost pathological, rejection of the practice among groups who object to homosexual effeminacy. Pirates evidently would have been more in sympathy with the latter group, for although the use of assumed names was common among them, only one feminine name has survived. John Walden was called "Miss Nanney" by his cohorts, but it seems to have been conferred not because of effeminate behavior or the result of some particular sexual preference but because of his quick temper.[20]

Alcohol and Alcoholism

The excessive consumption of alcohol by pirates, when it was available in large quantities, and their predilection for debauchery, also played a part in increasing promiscuity and undermining the stability of couples. The conduct of buccaneers in port after returning from successful plundering expeditions is well chronicled, and tales of fortunes squandered, riotous excess, maniacal gaming, and lewd and drunken conduct are all substantially true. But pirate debauchery was not restricted to the rare occasions when their ships sailed into Jamaica's Port Royal and the whores and taverns of what was reputed to be the most wicked city in the western hemisphere were available to them. It was a regular feature in the lives of successful pirates who, like human beings everywhere, required a certain leaven of festival gaiety and took the opportunity for frolic whenever it was available. At the capture of a prize, if there were wine or brandy aboard, the time was at hand for celebration. On one such occasion, Captain Charles Vane and his men sailed to a deserted island, careened their ships for cleaning and maintenance, divided the spoils of their raid, and spent several days in wild debauchery.[21] In like fashion George Lowther and his men sailed a captured St. Christopher sloop to a small island where they cleaned their ships and amused themselves with "unheard of Debaucheries, with drinking, swearing and rioting, in which there seemed to be a kind of Emulation among them, resembling rather Devils than Men, striving who should outdo one another in new invented Oaths and Execrations."[22] Woodes Rogers described with amazement the intensity and enthusiasm of celebrating pirates. "I must add concerning these Buccaneers," he wrote, "that they liv'd without Government; so that when they met with Purchase, they immediately squander'd it away, and when they got Mony and Liquor, they drank and gam'd till they spent all; and during those Revels, there was no distinction between the Captain and Crew: for the Officers having no Commission but what the Majority gave them, they were chang'd at every Caprice, which divided them, and occasion'd frequent Quarrels and Separations, so that they cou'd do nothing considerable."[23]

Rogers did not understate his case when he noted that buccaneers were sometimes incapacitated by drunkenness. Captain John Coxon and his crew were reported on one occasion to have been too drunk to carry on negotiations with Governor John Vaughn for the release of prisoners in 1677, and some years later Coxon actually abandoned his own men after a drunken quarrel. William Dampier's crew once lost a rich galleon because they were too inebriated to fight, and accidents or disasters caused by alcohol-sodden sailors were not unusual. Not only are there records of prisoners escaping from pirates too drunk to guard them properly, but in what might have been the greatest buccaneer disaster attributable to excess consumption of liquor, a ship of 26 guns commanded by a Captain Bellamy ran aground off Massachusetts after the crew had consumed large quantities of Madeira. According to reports of the incident sent to London, 118 of 120 pirates aboard the ship perished in the accident.[24] Captain George Shelvocke blamed a mutiny aboard his ship on too much liquor, and there is evidence to indicate the supply of alcohol available to his sailors was sufficient to stoke considerable enthusiasm for a take-over. At one point, when an estimate was made for Shelvocke of the quantity of liquor aboard, there seemed to be enough for several years of voyaging. Either the estimate was incorrect or the capacity of the captain and his men was prodigious. Even though the spirits were diluted with water to make them last, the kegs were drained within the year. The captain himself was partially responsible for the rapid expenditure of their store. He was a regular partaker of "hipsey," a mixture of wine, brandy, and water, and his sailors later testified that often he had imbibed sufficient quantities to render him unable to command his ship. When Shelvocke had consumed all their alcoholic beverages, trouble started with crewmen complaining about the dull, flat character of sobriety. A mutiny followed shortly thereafter.[25]

The large quantities of brandy, Madeira, wine, or like beverages consumed by pirates when there was opportunity are everywhere substantiated by surviving evidence. The problems created by the unregulated drinking were recognized by commanders, and in the articles of agreement subscribed to aboard Captain Kidd's ship some attempt was made to control the immoderate use of alcohol. Any man drunk during an engagement or before prisoners were made fast was to be denied his share of the loot. Even on a ship like that of Bartholomew Roberts, a much more effectively disciplined vessel than Kidd's, strong drink also created problems. The crew was frequently drunk and disorderly, "every Man being in his own Imagination, a Captain, a Prince or a King." Captain Roberts attempted to restrain the revelry of his men by proclaiming that all lights had to be out by 8:00 P.M. and all drinking must be done on deck, but it was a mild measure and had little effect.[26]

Heavy doses of alcohol were a frequent feature of pirate celebrations, and drinking, when coupled with the grim remembrance that all present at any festivity might one day end their lives on the gibbet, exerted a discernible influence on their style of humor. Like any harassed minority, buccaneers evolved their own brand of wit, which was exceedingly well-suited to their circumstances.[27] A frequent feature of their revels was an activity containing all the terrors of their lives. Several accounts survive of pirates conducting mock judicial proceedings where days were spent trying one another for robbery, piracy, "ravishing Man, Woman and Child," or whatever charge came to mind. The judge one moment was a defendant the next, but the good humor of the occasions was obviously a veneer. The trials, whether held on deserted islands or aboard ships on the high seas, all seem to have a large measure of irony, a grim portentous quality. On one occasion, after a playful trial, a pirate was convicted, sentenced to death, and amid the laughter of his comrades, the sentence was carried out. The same style of humor was characteristic of Blackbeard, who after a prolonged drinking bout, laughed uproariously as he fired a pistol into the knee of his mate, Israel Hands, laming him for life.[28] There is no telling whether Edward Low was drunk when he captured a ship off Block Island, but with typical pirate humor, he sliced the ears from the captain's head and then supplying salt and pepper to improve the flavor, he gave his prisoner the order to eat, "which hard Injunction he comply'd with, without making a Word." Low's *"bon appetit"* was surely enough to ruin the digestion of any diner, but in this case the hapless prisoner might have considered himself fortunate. Roc Brasiliano, another buccaneer captain, once in a drunken frenzy began chopping off the arms and legs of bystanders.[29]

There is no reason to assume the relationship between pirate drunkenness and homosexuality in the seventeenth century was any closer than the slight connection between the two today. The depressive effects of alcohol and the resultant facilitation of sexual transference and the lessening of psychological repression are considerations of moment in evaluating or analyzing proscribed activities, but homosexual behavior among buccaneers did not fall into that category. Nor can any inference be drawn from the often observed conduct of drunken males comporting among themselves with coarse familiarity, indulging in excessive sentimentality, pawing each other, and singing college songs. Although alcohol may tend to release latency in some homosexuals, the quantum effect is not large. In one study of prisoners convicted of homosexual offenses, most insisted they were not drunk at the time of their offense. But even then, the easy acceptance and general practice of homosexuality by buccaneers reduced the effects of alcohol among them, making it less significant in inducing or promoting any manner of sexual conduct than might be the case in situations involving unmarried heterosexual couples when involved in legally or ecclesiastically proscribed sexual conduct. It is more likely that pirate drunkenness might well have been less frequent than drunkenness on the part of Britain's population in the later half of the seventeenth century. On an island where cereal grains grow everywhere, beer can be made and stored easily and in quantity by the members of any household affluent enough to own an ordinary crock or kilderkin, and both literature and public pronouncements from the reign of Henry VIII to the time of Queen Victoria contain a panoply of drunken characters and a torrent of tracts denouncing the excessive use of alcohol.[30] The poor drank beer and ale, those who could afford it poured down large quantities of Iberian wine or local brandies, and while intemperance was denounced by conforming Anglicans and in dissenting chapels with equal vigor, the admonitions had little effect. Student drunkenness was a fact of life at English universities, and in the Western Hemisphere it was "observ'd that upon all the New Settlement the Spaniards make, the first thing they do is to build a Church, the first thing the Dutch do upon a new Coloney is to build them a fort, but the first thing the English doe, be it in the most remote parts of the world or amongst the most Barbarous Indians is to set up a Tavern or drinking house."[31]

Drinking to excess at every opportunity was a hallowed pirate custom, but the opportunities to do so were not as frequent as the marauders might have wished. Surviving records dealing with pirate gastronomy reveal they were chronically short of bread, butter, cheese, and meat, the items basic to a seventeenth-century Englishman's diet. These commodities, along with alcoholic beverages, were acquired from the same sources of supply, and difficulty in obtaining one implied insufficient stocks of the other. Buccaneering vessels spent little time at anchor in island ports and sometimes weeks or even months would elapse before a ship was taken that carried any large stores of provisions.[32] Occasionally they attempted to keep chickens and pigs aboard their vessels to be slaughtered when needed, and in the absence of adequate supplies of meat, there was always the possibility of improvising. Bartholomew Sharp once reminisced that in 1681 on a ship under his command there was "a little sucking Pigg . . . which we kept on Board . . . for our Christmas days Dinner, which now was grown to be a large Hogg; so we killed it for Dinner, but thinking it not enough for us all, we bought a Spaniel-Dogg of the Quarter-Master for forty pieces of Eight, and killed him; so with the Hogg and the Dogg, we made a Feast, and we had some Wine left, which made us merry."[33] At the siege of Chagre in 1670, the attacking buccaneers were reduced to beating scraps of leather between stones, dampening them to scrape off the hair, roasting them in embers, cutting them into small pieces and then gobbling down the unchewable fragments. Another pirate on a southward voyage recorded what was for him the ultimate act of culinary degredation. When supplies ran out, he and his fellow crewmen were forced to eat penguin liver to stay alive.[34]

The price paid for the dog, perhaps the highest on record for a spaniel before the twentieth century, indicates that the demand for fresh meat far exceeded the supply among buccaneers, and the same was true for other food items. There are numerous instances of pirates attacking and capturing larger vessels with more men and guns aboard because they were driven by hunger to take exceptional risks and fight with the courage of desperation. In the absence of a reliable supply of "english victuals," pirates were forced to obtain sustenance from other sources, and they frequently replenished exhausted stocks with bananas, manioc, cassava, fish, turtles, and an occasional iguana, although the last could not have been particularly desirable to men who were queasy at the prospect of dining on penguin liver. All of these food items could be had by trading with natives, fishermen, and hunters, but when acquiring such supplies by trading or raiding isolated settlements on the coasts of obscure islands, the possibility of obtaining alcoholic beverages was slight. The failure of buccaneers to secure a regular supply of strong drink indicates that neither chronic alcoholism, the debilitating effects of decades of drunkenness, nor continual inebriation were a vital feature of their daily lives.[35]

Torture

An even more indelible aspect of the pirate image than their ill-deserved reputation for being regularly drunk is the commonly made association between pirates and sadism. In many works on buccaneering, the linkage apears over and again, and although at least one authority maintains the institutionalization of torture "in those early years, before the French colonizers shipped out the first cargo of women to Tortuga, . . . was a function of the way they lived together," there is no evidence that the brand of torture and cruelty they practiced correlated with buccaneer homosexuality or homosexual activities.[36] The methodical and intense infliction of pain for which pirates are known was not a figment of the imaginations of authors writing sea stories for an audience of adventure buffs. It was real and often ghoulish in the extreme, yet its causes are complex and clearly the result of conditions not directly related to sexual orientation.

The tendency to associate homosexuality and torture in a muddled cause and effect relationship is due in large measure to the willingness of many to classify homosexuality as pathological behavior. Pirates, involved as they were in both activities, provide an example, though incorrectly formulated, of a link between the two. Sadism is a facet of sexual activities involving members of both the same and opposite sexes, but violence among homosexuals is as rare as violence among heterosexuals, although it is often exaggerated in the popular mind. The equation of mental illness with selected modes of sexual expression has abated to some degree in recent years, but the personification of homosexuals and those who engage in homosexual acts as incarnations of psychosexual imbalance remains widespread.

In the seventeenth century there was apparently no tendency to associate sadism connected with homosexual manifestations with more virulent acts than those commonly connected with heterosexual activities. The sexual nature of the whippings administered to schoolboys was generally recognized by the reign of Charles II. An anonymous pamphleteer writing in 1699 complained not only of the futility of using punishment to correct academic deficiencies, but added a blast at "the immodest and filthy blows" upon the "secret parts" of youthful scholars. Thomas Shadwell touched on the same theme in his play *The Virtuoso*. An elderly man, one of Shadwell's characters, asks in a moment of sexual excitement for his mistress to fetch the birch rods. He explains to the audience that he had developed a taste for the rod when a lad at Westminster School. He then enjoins his woman, "Do not spare thy pains: I love castigation mightily."[37] Similarly, in a 1671 play entitled *The Country Revel*, a rural justice comments "If ye talke of skinnes, the best judgment to be made of the fineness of skinnes is at the whipping-post by the stripes. Ah! 'tis the best lechery to see 'em suffer correction. Your London aldermen take great lechery to see the poor wretches whipt at the court at Bridewell."[38] None of the practices mentioned were particularly gruesome by the standards of three hundred years ago, and indeed the rod was

used by both homosexuals and heterosexuals in their quests for gratification.

There are, of course, surviving examples of cruelty practiced by
obviously demented pirates, but individual acts seem to bear little
similarity to sadistic practices familiar to Restoration play-goers or to
other more ordinary instances of sadism. At the capture of Puerto
Cavallo, French buccaneer commander l'Olonnais comported himself with passionate cruelty toward his Spanish captives, hacking many
to bits, licking the blood off his sword, eating the heart out of one
disemboweled prisoner and threatening to do the same to others. Even
more ghastly was the incident where Mountbars the Exterminator,
another Frenchman, opened the abdomen of a captive, took out a
portion of the intestine, nailed it to a post, and then chased the prisoner with a firebrand, the intestine unraveling from his stomach as
he ran and danced about frantically trying to avoid the flame. On
another occasion, he beheaded every member of a captured Spanish
ship save one man who was kept alive to witness the executions and
then sent back to tell the Governor what had transpired. Torture of
this nature, the application of pain for the sake of pain, seems to
have been rare, the work of men who were genuine psychopaths.
There is only one surviving account of what is a likely act of pure
pirate sadism. In a 1683 incident, buccaneer Captain Nicholas Van-
horn whipped a Nicholas Browne to death for what Sir Thomas Lynch
described naively as no apparent reason.[39]

In harmony with naval and maritime practice everywhere in the
seventeenth century, torture was an accepted practice for insuring
order aboard ship. Whipping was the standard method of enforcing
obedience on merchant craft, but as in the navy where spread-eagling
and keelhauling were used, there were many variations. Pirates employed all of the usual methods and introduced a few of their own to
deal with recalcitrant crewmen. One method used on occasion by
buccaneers was called sweating. The malefactor to be punished by a
sweat was stripped naked and forced to run a gauntlet of his fellow
crewmen who struck him on the back, shoulders, and buttocks with
sail needles. Dripping with blood, he was then thrown into a sugar
cask amply stocked with cockroaches, the cask was covered with a

blanket, and the man was left bleeding amid the scurrying insects to endure the West Indian heat in a covered, unventilated barrel. Pirates who had fallen afoul of their shipmates were occasionally left on islands, marooned as it was known, either to die, live alone, or be picked up by another ship. The nature of the island and its location were vital factors in how drastic a punishment this was. A pirate left on a tiny, sand-covered bit of land would suffer an agonizing death by thirst and dehydration while another marooned at a more hospitable site might live in primitive comfort for years or be picked up in a short time if his island was along a frequently used shipping lane.[40]

A measure of the physical agony inflicted by buccaneers was in the nature of retaliation against similar treatment at the hands of the Spanish. The hatred of nationals of the two countries for one another was of long standing, and torture of captives was a frequent manifestation of their mutual aversion. As early as 1604, the Venetian ambassador to England wrote the information that two English vessels in the West Indies had been captured by Spaniards, and the crewmembers were relieved of their hands, feet, noses, and ears by their sword-wielding captors. They were then smeared with honey and tied to trees, allowing insects to conclude what humans had begun. Other tortures inflicted on the English by the Spanish in the West Indies were much less grim, but the practice seems to have been a part of Anglo-Spanish contact in the New World from the time of Elizabeth until over a century later when Captain Jenkins returned to London with his Spanish-severed ear in a container for all to see.[41]

The Restoration literature of flagellation, along with the fantasies it embodied and the practices it described was, like similar Victorian writings, a compromise with homosexuality and a defense against it. But there was little need for such psychological adjustments among pirates who had no need to reaffirm their sexual practices. With few exceptions, they seem to have carried out their torture systematically for the primary purposes of gaining booty or maintaining discipline among their own group. Gratuitous infliction of pain was not commonly practiced and when it was, it seemed to satisfy a need for hilarity rather than to serve as a sexual stimulant. Governor Thomas

Handasyd of Jamaica reported home that on at least one occasion he knew of pirates treating prisoners well when there was no opportunity for financial gain, and in encounters with natives where prisoners could be expected to yield no plunder, torture was rarely used.[42]

The most vivid and extensive accounts of pirate torture are those dealing with cruelty practiced by the victorious expeditions Morgan led against Gibralter, Porto Bello, Maracaibo, and Panama City. Morgan seems to have had no particular interest in torture as an activity with entertainment potential, but he directed his men in relentless and systematic brutality to learn where the Spanish citizenry of the captured towns had secreted their wealth. Whippings and beatings were the usual methods used by Morgan's men, but when more extreme measures were necessary, they were employed. Buccaneers lived in an age when the infliction of pain was an art form, and if the Spanish were to be victims, they were willing to employ techniques developed by others as well as a few of their own device. Fire was a favorite instrument with Morgan, and placing burning fuses between the fingers and toes of spread-eagled captives appeared to be a fairly effective technique for causing pain. Males and females were strappadoed, hung by the thumbs, stabbed repeatedly and left to die, roasted alive over small fires, and on occasion crucified. There is at least one case where a prisoner was hoisted aloft by rope wrapped around his genitals and then the genitals sliced off, but mutilation of captives' privy parts was not common, and when it was done, it was carried out with the business-as-usual attitude that corresponded with the purpose of pirate torture. A more usual method was the rack for extracting information. Its use was familiar to most pirates, and over the centuries it had proven its effectiveness. On occasion, however, pirates used some originality in devising their torments. A particularly maritime method of extracting information was known as woolding. To the sailor, woolding was rope wound tightly around a mast to give it added strength, but Morgan's men either discovered or learned from others than a rope wrapped around the forehead of a captive and then slowly twisted tighter and tighter produced unbearable agony along with forcing the victim's eyeballs to protrude like eggs. These tortures and others were often applied to prisoners over a period of several days to give them ample time to endure pain and reexamine their original decisions to remain silent. After Morgan's capture of Maracaibo, the torture and cruelty lasted for three weeks.[43]

The same purpose and purposefulness was the rule rather than the exception throughout the age of pirate depredations in the Caribbean. The record is full of cases like that of a Mrs. Trot who was barbarously murdered by buccaneers in an attempt to make her "confess where Col. Elding and his riches were,"[44] or the incident when the well-known Captain Edward England once threatened to sink the vessel of a captured seafarer and throw him overboard with a double-headed shot around his neck if he would not reveal the location of his money.

In circumstances where captives were taken by pirates and systematic torture was not inflicted, the treatment visited on the captives was nevertheless unpleasant in the extreme. Meanness, random clubbing, and what was described as "barbarous" actions are frequent in depositions. Incidents like that which occurred when Edward England took the *Calabar Merchant* of Bristol, beat and abused the master and his crew for nine weeks, then released them, returned their ship, and provided them with 21 Negroes as compensation for damage done are one of a kind.[45] Yet the frequency and intensity of buccaneer brutality was a symptom of the age rather than anything that can be associated especially with piracy or homosexuality. The severity of childhood upbringing in the seventeenth century, particularly the excessive brutality of the poor toward their offspring, according to Lawrence Stone, deeply affected the personality of large numbers of adults. Imprisonment in swaddling bands during the initial months of life, the continual application of physical punishment, and ejection from the home at an early age all combined to produce adults who were cold, hostile, suspicious, distrustful, cruel, unable to form close relationships with each other except under circumstances of extreme interdependence, and liable to sudden outbursts of aggressive behavior toward one another.[46]

Severe physical punishment was only a part of home life and child-rearing practice in the seventeenth century. Men who became pirates had been raised on what seem today to be instances of inexplicably cruel practices carried out regularly by local and national authorities in England and in the West Indies. A London man charged with blasphemy in 1656, for example, was pilloried four hours, the first two in London, and then shipped from London to Westminster for the second two. His tongue was then bored with a red-hot iron and he was branded on the forehead with the letter B. Despite his treatment, the man probably considered himself lucky to have escaped with so mild a series of punishments.[47] During the Restoration, public hangings occurred on a regularly scheduled basis, severe whippings were common, jail conditions were often the equivalent of capital punishment for the poor, and branding was occasionally used. In the first decade of the eighteenth century, Celia Fiennes attested to the merciful nature of English justice by describing the punishments inflicted by the authorities as relatively mild. To prove her case, she cited felons being taken to the gallows tied to their coffins to be dispatched in a reasonably rapid manner. Important persons who fell victim to the headsman's axe could have their heads sewn back onto their bodies for burial, and only whippings and brandings were employed for minor offenses. And traitors, after all, received their just desserts, she explained. They were hanged until near expiration, then cut down while barely alive, disemboweled, the heart removed, and presiding officials took up the organ, announced that here was the heart of a traitor, and the "body . . . cutt in quarters and hung up on the top of the great gates of the City."[48]

The list of grim treatment of criminals by the authorities could be continued almost without end, and literally tens of thousands of specific cases could be adduced as examples of the brutality of the age. There would be no sweatings or wooldings in the list of punishments meted out by the English system of justice, but the severity of the punishments applied to persons from petty thief to traitor was no less brutal than the tortures buccaneers visited on their captives. They represent nothing that could be labeled socially or sexually pathological within the context of their environment. The abuse of prisoners by pirates surely went beyond legally inflicted agonies, but not too far beyond them, and like the sentences prescribed by English law, pirate tortures were designed to serve a purpose rather than simply to entertain.

In other respects, the agonies inflicted by pirates could be considered mild when compared to the practices commonly employed for the discipline and training of slaves in the West Indies. Plantation owners were within their legal rights in perpetrating the most grisly forms of torture they could imagine if the victim were a troublesome black. One traveler in the Caribbean in the early eighteenth century reported a slave being nailed to the ground and burned with a firebrand from his feet toward his head. Castration of slaves was also a common practice—usually to make them more tractable rather than for punishment—but mutilation, whipping with salt rubbed into the wounds, dripping melted wax on the skin and several other exquisite torments were the lot of the troublesome bondsman. Later in the eighteenth century, legislation was enacted on several islands preventing planters from killing, mutilating, or dismembering slaves, but this was half a century after the last pirate had disappeared from the Caribbean, and even then it was unlikely that slaves were awarded damages by the courts for injuries sustained at the hands of their masters or that planters were ever assessed the maximum penalty of 12 months in jail and fined £100 for mistreating their blacks.[49] Indeed, if there is any puzzle about the relationship between buccaneers and the tortures they meted out, it is to be found not in the fact that physical abuse was used by them but instead it is in the difficulty of explaining why in the vast numbers of depositions, narratives, journal accounts, newspaper reports, and other sources of information on piratical depredations there are so many that do not mention torture and so few that do. Although it is likely some buccaneers were sadists and derived sexual pleasure from torturing captives, the limited, structured, and purposeful use of pain only to extract information and locate booty indicates sadism was not a general characteristic of buccaneer sexuality. If it had been so, torture would have been a regular feature of piracy, practiced in more than carefully limited circumstances.

Effeminacy and the Pirate Role

Not only is sadism difficult to find among buccaneers, but effeminacy, another characteristic often associated with homosexuality and
homosexual practices, seems to be absent from their communities.
Aside from a few captains noted for their ornate dress, no more ornate really than that of upper-class gentlemen during the Restoration,
they were garbed rather plainly in whatever was available, usually
jerkin and britches of sail cloth or any other clothing they might have
captured. Gold earrings, commonly worn by at least some buccaneers, were clearly a part of their fashion rather than distinctly effeminate, and on at least one occasion, a battle fought in the waning
hours of daylight, the reflection of the last remaining rays of the sun
on the earrings enabled the pirates to identify each other in the thick
of combat.[50] Incidents of pirates sashaying or parading in costume
always carry with them the enthusiasm of a successful fight or the
capture of a ship carrying elaborate clothing. Captain John Evans
wrote in 1728 of his experiences as a captive aboard a pirate ship,
and at one point he related that after rummaging his cabin, immediately after he was captured, "the Fellows . . . met with a Leather
Powder Bag and Puff, with which they had powder'd themselves from
Head to Foot, walk'd the Decks with their Hats under their Arms,
minced their Oaths, and affected all the Airs of a Beau, with an
Awkwardness [that] would have forced a Smile from a Cynick."[51]
Père Labat, the pirate priest, relates a similar story of pirates having
captured a hoard of rich clothing being a "comical sight as they strut-
ted about the island in feathered hats, wigs, silk stockings, ribbons
and other garments."[52] But this was obviously playfulness and celebration rather than a longing for effeminate trappings, and indeed
the powder bag and puff were masculine rather than feminine ac-
coutrements three hundred years ago.

The only recorded incident of pirates bedecking themselves for a
non-festive occasion was in the case of Dennis Macarty and Thomas
Morris, both of whom appeared unusually ornamented. Macarty wore
long blue ribbons at his neck, wrists, knees, and cap, while Morris
appeared in much the same style, but with red ribbons rather than

the blue. The occasion, however, was the hanging of the two men along with several others for piracy, and to interpret their behavior on this occasion as effeminate could hardly be sustained.[53]

The lack of effeminate pirates or effeminate behavior among them on any known occasion does not diminish the intensity or frequency of pirate homosexual contact or orientation. Even in modern western society where sexual relationships are assumed to be male-female encounters, the larger number of homosexuals reject effeminacy not only because it is a threat to their own masculinity but there seems to be a preference for feminine-appearing homosexuals only among a limited proportion of homophiles. In the brief and furtive encounters characteristic of many homosexual experiences, there is no gender consciousness, and neither should any be expected. The effeminate gay cannot be assumed to hold universal attraction to men for whom women as sexual partners have little appeal. In fact, feminine identification among male homosexuals, while often the most conspicuous manifestation of homosexuality to the heterosexual world, is demonstrably rare. Most often it is the result of a maturational environment where masculine identification was difficult or impossible to establish, hardly the case for a wandering lad or apprentice boy in the seventeenth or eighteenth centuries.[54] Research by psychologists, sociologists, and even works of knowledgeable homosexual fiction reject the effeminate gay as anywhere near typical. The ordinary homosexual is a rather ordinary man, adopting neither a feminine style nor of the manner of swaggering, leather-clad motorcyclists or hulking weight-lifters. To be sure, the homosexual hustler is often hyper-masculine, exhibiting the badge of his saleable sexuality much as a female prostitute exhibits herself, but the need for the male image to sell the product indicates the direction of most homosexual preference. In one survey of sexual practices in the military it was found that effeminacy among homosexual psychopaths was exceedingly high, almost 50 percent of those surveyed, but significantly, in the same study among those examined and determined to be free from psychopathological symptoms, homosexuals with effeminate characteristics fell to two percent of the sample.[55] Among pirates in cases where indications of psychosexual pathology are absent, there is no reason to assume the rate of effeminacy would be particularly high. On the few occasions where pirates comment on effeminate behavior it is condemned, although not with a viciousness that indicated overcompensation. Effeminate characteristics, in fact, were usually ascribed to the hated Spanish, and lumped in with other unpirately qualities such as cowardice and passivity. "But we may confidently presume that these American Spanyards, are an idle, cowardly, and effiminate people, not exercised, nor brought up, in Warlike discipline," observed one Englishman.[56] Another commentator, with close ties to French pirates, characterized Brazilian slaves pejoratively as indolent and effeminate, and added a gratuitous comment that the monks he observed were even worse. They were not only ignorant of Latin, but in their excesses pursued women and strove "even to out-vie the Sodomites in their Debaucheries."[57]

But the matter of effeminacy in the age of piracy, whether connected with homophile sexuality or simply as a sartorial abberation, was an oddity rather than grotesque or mortally sinful. If seafarers had chosen or been inclined to divide or to constitute their groupings into male and female moieties with a relatively full range of identifiable sexual characteristics, they could have done so with considerably less difficulty than would have been possible in the nineteenth or twentieth centuries. While it may have been impossible in the Royal Navy or aboard merchant vessels, among pirates there would literally have been no impediment to such practice. But in fact effeminate behavior was no part of pirate society. Masculinity was not diminished by homosexuality among buccaneers, as is the case in social circumstances where an emotional commitment has been made to the normality of heterosexual activity. Pirates who preferred homosexuality as well as those who partook in it as the only sexual outlet available practiced their proclivity for men without the social or psychological necessity for creating the appearance of heterosexual engagement.

Buccaneers cultivated the masculine attributes of physical toughness, courage in combat, endurance, and comradeship, but these virtues were valued in every member of the community from *matelot* and carpenter's boy all the way up to captain. No pirate crewmen were exempt from battle or received special protection due to weakness or lack of the will or desire to fight. They exalted instead the virtues of physical strength, bravery, endurance, and military skill. On occasions when pirates boasted of their exploits, toughness, hostility, and fierceness were emphasized in every case. Nowhere did buccaneers make any pretensions of effeminacy, and even those rovers known to fancy fashionable attire took the part of the lord rather than the fool. There is nothing remarkable in their behavior. Buccaneers following ordinary human patterns internalized the social roles with which they were familiar and those they were required to assume by circumstance. The exaggerated female "role" did not become associated with homosexual behavior in England until the closing years of the seventeenth century, but if it had emerged earlier, it remains unlikely it would have been assumed by Caribbean buccaneers. In situations where the effeminate homosexual role is a recognized feature of society, it appears to have some effect on the distribution of homosexual conduct, but such conduct is not widely practiced by men involved in homosexual behavior. West Indian pirates had no need to assume a cast of effeminacy even if it had been available. Their own roles required the very opposite style of conduct. The necessary qualities for continued existence were stamina, courage, and a cruelly competitive spirit, and sodomitical pirates, like men everywhere, cultivated attributes necessary for survival.[58]

Sexual relations between pirates were an ordinary activity, condemned by no one among them and denigrated only by those classes with whom they had little contact and less familiarity. Their homosexual contact was in no way a unique thing, made more tantalizing for them by the knowledge that they participated in behavior condemned socially, ecclesiastically, and by civil statute. Church, government, and English society were far removed from their daily life and exerted little influence. Nor were there among them a particular class of sex objects, specially effeminate pirates whose duty it was to provide sexual services for the remainder of the company. There is no evidence to indicate pirates regarded sexual activity as something necessarily conducted between human beings who differed from one another in attitude, conduct, or personality. From them, it was an activity engaged in by men; there was no attempt to ape the practices of heterosexual society. No special vocabulary was required for identification purposes or to perpetuate secrecy for this ordinary part of their life. It was only in dealing with women, a rare and exotic feature of their lives, that sexual difficulties arose. In this respect there were two general types of problems that relate to the pirates' own sexual orientation. Among the complete homosexuals, of course, female contact was probably avoided completely, but among other pirates there were those whose alienation from the heterosexual world was only partial, sufficient to enable them to attempt marriage and fail or at best to sustain contacts only with those females who could not pose a threat to their masculinity or to their social being. Their women must of necessity be drawn from groups that could be dominated: those adjudged racially inferior, captives, or prostitutes. Heterosexual skills were insufficiently developed for them to succeed with women on an equal basis. A pirate forced into a situation of equality with a female would undoubtedly have been as uncomfortable as would have been the case had he been miraculously transported from the deck of his ship to Whitehall Palace and set down to dinner with the king.

A gigantic chasm of three hundred years separates the present from the seventeenth century and to postulate truths on the nature of human actions and interactions over three hundred years when such truths are based on severely limited amounts of evidence is clearly impossible. Even the intemperate or the foolish who were not intimidated by the passage of so great a length of time would hesitate to conclude that the society evolved by buccaneers living independently of socially imposed constraints on their sexuality indicates in some way that if only heterosexuals could suppress their hostility and accept homosexuals as full-fledged members of the human community then, perhaps, with the dissipation of the opprobrium directed against them, homosexuals would be transformed into equal participants in modern society. This may be so, but adequate evidence to substantiate it is still not available. What can be drawn from a study of those features of pirate society that make it truly distinctive is not that homosexual and heterosexual can function comfortably together, but that

homosexual communities can function virtually independent of heterosexual society. Aside from the production of children, homosexuals alone can fulfill satisfactorily all human needs, wants, and desires, all the while supporting and sustaining a human community
remarkable by the very fact that it is unremarkable. The almost universal homosexual involvement among pirates meant homosexual
practices were neither disturbed, perverted, exotic, nor uniquely desirable among them, and the mechanisms for defending and perpet-
uating such practices, those things that set the modern homosexual
apart from heterosexual society, were never necessary. The male engaging in sexual activity with another male aboard a pirate ship in
the West Indies three centuries past was simply an ordinary member
of his community, completely socialized and acculturated. The appearance and institutions of his society were substantial reflections of
the heterosexual England that produced him, and the functional ac-
comodations made to adjust for homosexuality were minor. The lives
of the pirates were ordinary within the context of their chronological
period and their economic requirements, and instances of antisocial,
depraved, or pathological behavior were not noticeably more common than in concomitant heterosexual society.

NOTES

PREFACE

1. *Calendar of State Papers. Colonial Series. America and the West Indies*, 5:636, 7:236; *Interesting Tracts Relating to the Island of Jamaica Consisting of Curious State Papers, Councils of War, Letters, Petitions, Narratives, etc. . . . from Its Conquest, Down to the Year 1702* (St. Jago de la Vega [Spanish Town], Jamaica, 1800), p. 116.

INTRODUCTION

1. For a comprehensive account of the trials and condemnation, see Arthur N. Gilbert, "The *Africaine* Courts-Martial: A Study of Buggery and the Royal Navy," *Journal of Homosexuality* 1 (1974): 111–122.

2. More complete discussions of societal reaction theory are found in Kenneth Plummer, *Sexual Stigma: An Interactionist Perspective* (London: Routledge and Kegan Paul, 1975), pp. 1–92; Edwin M. Schur, *Labeling Deviant Behavior: Its Sociological Implications* (New York: Harper and Row, 1971). For a short discussion of societal reaction theory and its uses in dealing with homosexuality, see John I. Kitsuse, "Societal Reaction to Deviant Behavior: Problems of Theory and Method," *Social Problems* 9 (Winter, 1962): 247–256. For analysis of societal reaction theory and its relation to historical research see Kenneth Kenniston, "Psychological Developments and Historical Change," in *Explorations in Psychohistory*, ed. Robert Jay Lifton (New York: Simon and Schuster, 1974), pp. 149–164; despite the title, Robert F. Berkhofer, Jr.'s *A Behavioral Approach to Historical Analysis* (New York: Free Press, 1969) also contains a fine discussion of societal reaction theory in Chapter II. An example of societal reaction as a base for historical analysis can be found in Kai T. Erikson's *Wayward Puritans: A Study in the Sociology of Deviance* (New York: Wiley, 1966).

1. SODOMY AND PUBLIC PERCEPTION: SEVENTEENTH-CENTURY ENGLAND

1. Peter Laslett, *The World We Have Lost* (New York: Scribners, 1965).
2. Frederick Pollock and Frederic W. Maitland, *The History of English Law Before the Time*

of Edward I (Cambridge: Cambridge University Press, 1895), 2:554–555; A.L. Rowse, *Homosexuals in History: A Study of Ambivalence in Society, Literature and the Arts* (New York: Macmillan, 1977), pp. 24–25; J.S. Cockburn, *A History of the English Assizes, 1558–1714* (Cambridge: Cambridge University Press, 1972), pp. 127–133; J.H. Baker, "Criminal Courts and Procedure at Common Law, 1550–1800," *Crime in England, 1550–1800* (Princeton: Princeton University Press, 1977), pp. 43–44; M.J. Ingram, "Communities and Courts: Law and Disorder in Early Seventeenth-Century Wiltshire," ibid., p. 110. For an excellent survey of assorted sexual practices during the seventeenth and eighteenth centuries, see Vern L. Bullough's compendious *Sexual Variance in Society and History* (New York: Wiley, 1976), Chapter XVI. H. Montgomery Hyde's *The Other Love, An Historical and Contemporary Survey of Homosexuality in Britain* (London: Heinemann, 1970) is also exceedingly useful; Hyder Rollins and Herschel Baker, "Richard Barnfield," in *The Renaissance in England* (Boston: D.C. Heath, 1954), pp. 396–397.

3. Anthony Fitzherbert, *Loffice et Auctority de Iustices de Peace* (London, 1606), folio 50; William Lambarde, *Eirenarcha, or Of The Office of the Justices of Peace in Foure Bookes* (London, 1610), pp. 224–225; Retha M. Warnicke, *William Lambarde, Elizabethan Antiquary* (London: Phillimore, 1973), pp. 61, 70–72; Lambarde's same absence of concern was evident in Michael Dalton's *Countrey Justice* published over half a century later in 1655. Dalton barely touched on the crime, although he did extend it to include sex acts involving only women and several unspecified heterosexual practices (pp. 340–341); Sir Edward Coke, *The Third Part of the Institutes of the Laws of England* (London, 1644), pp. 58–59; Coke, *The Twelfth Part of the Reports of Sir Edward Coke* (London, 1658), pp. 36–37.

4. A.L. Rowse, *Homosexuals in History*, pp. 48–66.

5. Ibid., p. 67; Lawrence Stone, *The Family, Sex and Marriage in England 1500–1800* (New York: Harper, 1977), pp. 492–493.

6. Chester Quarter Sessions 21/3, p. 174a.

7. [Anon.], *The Tryal and Condemnation of Mervin, Lord Audley Earl of Castle-Haven* (London, 1699).

8. Ibid., p. 9.

9. Ibid., p. 4.

10. Ibid., pp. 10–12. On sodomy indictments see also the anonymously written *Faithful Narrative of the Proceedings in a Late Affair . . . to which is Prefixed A Particular Account of the Proceedings Against Robert Thistlethwayte for a Sodomical Attempt upon Mr. W. French* (London, 1739), p. 30.

11. [Anon.], *Tryal and Condemnation of . . . Lord Audley*, pp. 22–31.

12. There is no evidence in accounts of the trial to indicate the execution of Castlehaven's two servants is proof, as one authority contends, of the revulsion toward sodomy held by members of the court. See Caroline Bingham, "Seventeenth-Century Attitudes Toward Deviant Sex," *Journal of Interdisciplinary History* 1 (Spring 1971): 463–465. Even though Bingham suggests homosexuality was considered an abomination early in the century, she concedes, significantly, that this was not the case seventy years later (ibid., pp. 464–468).

13 Nicholas Bernard, *The Penitent Death of John Atherton* (Dublin, 1641), p. 15.

14. Ibid., pp. 15, 26, *et passim*; Atherton's accuser was hanged some days or weeks before Atherton (ibid., p. 26); *DNB*, I, pp. 689–690.

15. John White, *The First Century of Scandalous, Malignant Priests* (London, 1643), preface, pp. A2 (recto, verso), A3, 1–2, 11, 23–24, 28; [Lionel Gatford], *Public Good Without Private Interest* (London, 1657), p. 16.

16. William Wycherly, *The Country Wife*, in *The Complete Plays of William Wycherly*, ed. Gerald Weales (New York: New York University Press, 1966), Act III, scene 1.

17. Thomas Killigrew, *The Parson's Wedding* in *Comedies and Tragedies by Thomas Killigrew* (London, 1664), Act I, scene 2.

18. Ibid., Act I, scene 1.

19. Ibid., Act III, scene 5.

20. Ibid., Act II, scene 7; Act I, scene 3.

21. Ibid., Act II, scene 2.

22. Montague Summers, Introduction to *Restoration Comedies* (London: Jonathan Cape, 1921) p. xxxi.

23. Charles Johnson, *The Successful Pyrate* (London, 1713).

24. John Wilmot, Second Earl of Rochester, "A Satyr on King Charles II," in *Collected Works of John Wilmot, Earl of Rochester*, ed. John Hayward (London: Nonesuch Press, 1926), p. 104.

25. *London Gazette*, November 22–25, 1680.

26. Wilmot, *Sodom or the Quintessence of Debauchery* (Paris: Olympia Press, 1957), Act V, scene 2.

27. Samuel Pepys, *The Diary of Samuel Pepys*, eds. Robert Latham and William Matthews (Berkeley: University of California Press, (1970–   ), 9: 2, 247, 293. This was apparently true even into the next century (J. Jean Hecht, *The Domestic Servant Class in Eighteenth-Century England* [London: Routledge and Kegan Paul, 1956], pp. 201–204).

28. William Prynne, *Histrio-Mastix: The Players Scourge* (London, 1633), pp. 75–76.

29. Ibid., p. 211.

30. Ibid., pp. 208–214.

31. Ibid., p. 135.

32. Arthur Bedford, *The Evil and Danger of Stage Plays Showing Their Natural Tendency to Destroy Religion and Induce a General Corruption of Manners* (London, 1706), p. 139; "Copies of Several Presentments of the Grand Juries, Against the Play House Lately Erected in the City of Bristol" (1704–1706), in Bedford, *Evil and Danger of Stage Plays*, pp. 222–227; *Middlesex County Records, Calendar of Session Books, 1689–1709*, ed. W.J. Hardy (London: Richard Nicholson, 1905), p. 347; John Dennis, *The Critical Works of John Dennis*, ed. Edward N. Hooker (Baltimore: Johns Hopkins University Press, 1943), I, 153, 156, 473, II, 311, 314, 315, 396, 510–511; Dudley W.R. Bahlman, *The Moral Revolution of 1688* (New Haven, Conn.: Yale University Press, 1957), pp. 4–5.

33. Pepys, *Diary*, 3: 159–160. Neither did Mrs. Pepys accept the notions of sexual promiscuity common to the court. Exceedingly jealous, she raged at her husband's infidelities, real and imagined, almost destroying their marriage (ibid., 9: 337–338 ff.).

34. Ibid., 8: 596.

35. Ibid., 4: 209.

36. Ibid.

37. Ibid., 4: 210.

38. Ibid., 3: 66, 206–207, 4: 382.

39. John Evelyn, *The Diary of John Evelyn*, ed. E.S. DeBeer (London: Oxford University Press, 1955), 4: 234.

40. Applebee's *Original Weekly Journal* (London), April 2, 1715, August 23–30, 1718, August 8, 1719, April 2, 1720; *Proceedings of the King's Commission of the Peace and Oyer and Terminer and Jail Delivery of Newgate . . . 1699* [1698] (London, 1698), pp. 4, 6; Narcissus Luttrell, *A Brief Relation of State Affairs from September 1678 to April 1714* (Oxford: Oxford University Press, 1857), 1: 156, 4: 97, 127, 130, 245, 474–475, 6: 603, *et passim*; *Account of the Proceedings on the King's Commissions of the Peace and Oyer and Terminer, and Gaol Delivery of Newgate Held for the City of London, and The County of Middlesex, June 1698*

(London, 1698), pp. 1–2, 5. *Middlesex County Records, Rolls, Books, and Certificates*, ed. John Cordy Jeaffreson (London: Chapman and Hall, 1888), 3: xxii–xxiii, 11, 97, 207, 252, 4: 146, 152, 169, 239, 243.

41. Luttrell, *Brief Relation*, 4: 192.

42. *Middlesex Records, Calenders*, pp. xiii, 5, 8, 21, 128, 133, 136, 139, 151, 156, 175.

43. Ibid., 6: 38; Max Beloff, *Public Order and Popular Disturbances 1660–1714* (London: Frank Cass, 1963), p. 27.

44. David Ogg, *England in the Reigns of James II and William III* (Oxford: Clarendon Press, 1955), pp. 100–101; Luttrell, *Brief Relation*, 3: 521; *Applebee's Original Weekly Journal*, February 26, 1715, March 12, 1715, August 2, 1718, December 19, 1719, January 23, 1720.

45. Ibid., September 15, 1716, February 20, 1720; Luttrell, *Brief Relation*, 1: 113–114, 2: 24.

46. Ibid., 4: 461–462; *Applebee's Original Weekly Journal*, November 30, 1717. The situation evidently had not improved almost half a century later. Thomas Andrews, convicted of an "unnatural crime" in 1760, was pardoned the following year "to the astonishment of nine persons in ten who knew anything of the case." *Newgate Calender: Or Malefactor's Bloody Register*, ed. Sandra Lee Kerman (New York: Capricorn Books, 1962), pp. 192–194.

47. *Applebee's Original Weekly Journal*, December 6, 1718; June 6, 1719.

48. Luttrell, *Brief Relation*, 1: 41, 51, 53.

49. David Ogg, *England in the Reign of Charles II* (Oxford: Clarendon Press; 1956), p. 592; Luttrell, *Brief Relation*, 1: 55; *London Gazette*, September 16–20, 1680; *London Sessions Records 1605–1685*, ed. Dom Hugh Bowler (London: Publications of the Catholic Record Society, 1934), pp. 298–300, 319–320. Mrs. Cellier may have been Elizabeth Cellier, a midwife convicted of popery in 1680 (ibid., p. 297).

50. Ogg, *Reign of Charles II*, p. 604; [Anon.], *The Narrative of Col. Tho. Blood Concerning the Design . . . Against the . . . Duke of Buckingham* (London, 1680); Titus Oates, *An Exact and Faithful Narrative of the Horrid Conspiracy of T. Knox* (London, 1680); [Anon.], *A Letter to A Friend in the Country Concerning the Duke of Buckingham* (London, 1679?): The charges against the Duke were apparently for heterosexual rather than homosexual buggery, but English law regarded both crimes with an equal degree of seriousness. See the case of Thomas Davis accused of buggering spinster Charity Parot (*Proceedings of the Kings Commission of the Peace Held in the Old Bailey October 11–14 1699*, p. 4).

51. Evelyn, *Diary*, 4: 234; Luttrell, *Brief Relation*, 1: 248.

52. [Anon.], *Narrative of Col. Tho. Blood*, pp. 15, 30–31, *et passim*; J.H. Wilson, *A Rake and His Times: George Villiers, Second Duke of Buckingham* (New York: Farrar, Straus, and Young, 1954), p. 256; Luttrell, *Brief Relation*, 1: 44–45.

53. Ibid., pp. 461–462.

54. Henri Van Der Zee and Barbara Van Der Zee, *William and Mary* (New York: Knopf, 1973), pp. 422–424.

55. *London Gazette*, December 11–14, 1699; William III, *A Proclamation for Preventing and Punishing Immorality and Prophaneness*, December 9, 1699.

56. [Anon.], *Tryal and Condemnation of . . . Lord Audrey*, Preface.

57. Luttrell, *Brief Relation*, 6: 226.

58. John Bunyan, *The Pilgrim's Progress* (New York: New American Library, Signet Classic, 1964), p. 155.

59. Ibid., p. 91.

60. Ibid., pp. 102–103.

61. Ibid., p. 255.

62. [Anon.], *A Full and True Account of a Dreadful Fire That Lately Broke Out in the Pope's Breeches* (London, 1713).

63. [Anon.], *Sober Advice to Mockers Shewing the Unspeakable Danger of Scoffing at Any of Christs Faithful Ministers* (London, 1692).

64. [Anon.], *Answer to the Satyr Upon the French King* (London, 1697).

65. [Anon.], *Trick for Trick; or The Hasty Cuckold* (London, 1714); [Anon.], *A Funeral Elegy in Commemoration of the Sadly Deplored and Much-Lamented Death of that Unfortunate Knight Sir John Johnston* (London, 1790); George Sinclair, *Satan's Invisible World Discovered* (Edinburgh, 1685), unnumbered page; Thomas Wright, *The Glory of Gods Revenge and Detestable Sins of Murther and Adultry Expressed in 30 Tragic Histories* (London, 1688). The same harshness toward sex offenders was also practiced in Scotland during the period. See John Lamont, *The Diary of John Lamont of Newton, 1649–1671* (Edinburgh: John Clark, 1830), pp. 28, 53, 82, 111, 218.

66. *Applebee's Original Weekly Journal*, July 25, 1719. It was not only sex offenders who were endangered by the spectators. In 1725, a particularly famous robber was pelted with stones and dirt on his way to Tyburn. When the executioner allowed too much time for the man to make his peace with God, the mob threatend to lynch the criminal and the executioner as well (*Newgate Calender*, p. 94).

67. Ogg, *Reign of Charles II*, p. 595; Beloff, *Public Order and Popular Disturbances*, p. 150.

68. Luttrell, *Brief Relation*, 1: 34.

69. *Applebee's Original Weekly Journal*, July 25, 1719; Randolph Trumbach, "London's Sodomites: Homosexual Behavior and Western Culture in the 18th Century," *Journal of Social History* 11 (Fall 1977): 15, 20, 23.

70. Quarter Session Rolls Q/SR 49, Taunton, 1622, Somerset Record Office, Taunton, Somersetshire.

71. Linda Auwers Bissell, "Family, Friends, and Neighbors: Social Interaction in Seventeenth-Century Windsor, Connecticut," Ph.D. Diss., Brandeis, 1973, pp. 123–129. For a trenchant examination of the complete range of proscribed sexual practices involving homosexual acts and bestiality in early New England, see Robert F. Oaks's "Things Fearful to Name: Sodomy and Buggery in Seventeenth-Century New England," *Journal of Social History* 12 (Winter, 1977): 268–281.

72. *Records of the Colony of New Plymouth in New England*, ed. Nathaniel B. Shurtleff (Boston: William White, 1855), 1: 64, 2: 35–36, 146, 148, 3: 37; John Demos, *A Little Commonwealth: Family Life in Plymouth Colony* (New York: Oxford University Press, 1970), pp. 157–158.

73. John Winthrop, *The History of New England from1630 to 1649*, ed. James Savage (Boston: Little Brown, 1853), 2: 324.

74. Ibid.

75. *Minutes of the Council and General Court of Virginia*, ed. H.R. McIlwaine (Richmond: The Colonial Press, 1924), pp. 33–34, 47, 85, 93.

76. Marvin K. Opler, "Anthropological and Cross-Cultural Aspects of Homosexuality," in *Sexual Inversion: The Multiple Roots of Homosexuality*, ed. Judd Marmor (New York: Basic Books, 1965), p. 70; C.A. Tripp, *The Homosexual Matrix* (New York: McGraw-Hill, 1975), p. 68.

77. Ibid., p. 90; Evelyn Hooker, "Male Homosexuals and their Worlds," in *Sexual Inversion: The Multiple Roots of Homosexuality*, ed. Judd Marmor, p. 90.

2. TO TRAIN UP A BUCCANEER

1. The table is available in Peter Laslett's *World We Have Lost*, pp. 32–33. For estimates of King's general reliability see D.V. Glass, "Gregory King's Estimate of the Population of

England and Wales, 1695," *Population Studies*. 3 (December 1950): 338–374; "Gregory King and the Population of England and Wales at the End of the Seventeenth Century, *Eugenics Review* 37 (January 1946): 170–183.

2. Laslett, *World We Have Lost*, p. 90.

3. Ibid., pp. 14–15.

4. One authority argues that the economic position of the single agricultural laborer was strong during the period. There was a scarcity of workers, but the rise in the cost of manufactured goods was not reflected in a corresponding increase in the price of food products. The position of the unmarried laborer was also strengthened by the usual failure of the authorities to use the Act of Settlement against him. Once married, the laborer soon found that the adequate wage he once earned was no longer sufficient for the needs of a family. Children were a burden under the circumstances, but when they reached the age where they could be employed in agriculture, it was easy to expel them from the household and inject them into the bustling labor market (Beloff, *Public Order and Popular Disturbances*, pp. 14–15). See also Laslett, *World We Have Lost*, pp. 12–13; *Middlesex Records, Calendars*, p. xi; M. Dorothy George, *London Life in the Eighteenth Century* (New York: Capricorn Books, 1965), pp. 230, 243–244; *Middlesex Records, Calendars, passim*; *Middlesex Records, Rolls, Books, and Certificates, passim*; *Records of the County of Wilts, Being Extracts from the Quarter Sessions Great Rolls of the Seventeenth Century*, ed. Howard Cunnington (Divizes, Wilts.: George Simpson, 1932), *passim*.

5. For additional information on beggar bands and methods adopted to control or reduce the number of wandering and homeless children see Ivy Pinchbeck and Margaret Hewett, *Children in English Society*, Vol. I, *From Tudor Times to the Eighteenth Century* (Toronto: University of Toronto Press, 1969), pp. 106, 108, 133–135, 146–148; *An Account of the General Nursery or the Colledge of Infants Set Up By The Justices of the Peace for the County of Middlesex* (London, 1686); *Applebee's Original Weekly Journal*, June 11, 1715, May 26, 1715; Abbot Emerson Smith, *Colonists in Bondage: White Servitude and Convict Labor in America, 1607–1776* (New York: Norton, 1971), p. 12; Ogg, *Reign of Charles II*, p. 125; *London and Middlesex Archeological Transactions* 7 (1936): cited in Beloff, *Public Order and Popular Disturbances*, p. 33.

6. Laslett, *World We Have Lost*, p. 31.

7. *North Riding of the County of York Quarter Sessions Records*, J.C. Atkinson (London: North Riding Records Society, 1889), pp. xii, 184, 188–189; A.L. Beier, "Vagrants and the Social Order in Elizabethan England," *Past and Present* 64 (August 1974): 19–20; D.C. Coleman, "Labour in the English Economy of the 17th Century," *Economic History Review*, n.s., 7 (1956): 291.

8. For additional information on beggar bands and contemporary assessments of their composition, the dangers they posed, and their sexual practices, see [Thomas Dekker], *The Belman of London: Bringing to Light the Most Notorious Villanies That Are Now Practiced in the Kingdom* (London, 1608), *passim*; Thomas Harman, *The Fraternity of Vagabonds* (London, 1575), *passim*.

9. Irving Bieber, *et al.*, *Homosexuality: A Psychoanalytic Study* (New York: Random House, 1962), pp. 8, 173, 311, 399; Harry Stack Sullivan, *The Interpersonal Theory of Psychiatry* (New York: Norton, 1953), pp. 192, 248, 249. Beier, "Vagrants and the Social Order," p. 6; Pinchbeck and Hewett, *Children in English Society*, p. 143; *Middlesex Records, Calendars*, pp. 124, 347, *et passim*; *Wilts Records*, pp. 241, 268, 269, *et passim*. The same concern with vagrancy is present in the records of almost every county for the Tudor and Stuart eras.

10. Steven R. Smith, "The Social and Geographical Origins of the London Apprentices, 1630–1660," *The Guildhall Miscellany* 4 (April 1973): 196–198; "London Apprentices as Seventeenth-Century Adolescents," *Past and Present* 61 (November 1973): 153–156, 160.

11. Erving Goffman, *Asylums: Essays on the Social Situation of Mental Patients and Other Inmates* (New York: Doubleday, 1961). For an extended discussion of homosexuality and homosexual frequency in all-male institutions see Peter C. Buffum, *Homosexuality in Prisons,* publication of the National Institute of Law Enforcement and Criminal Justice (PR 72–3), February, 1973, pp. 4–18.

12. Abbott Payson Usher, "The Growth of English Shipbuilding, 1572–1922," *Quarterly Journal of Economics* 42 (May 1928): 467, 472–73, 478; T.S. Willan, *The English Coasting Trade, 1600–1740* (New York: Augustus M. Kelley, 1967), pp. 173, 175; Ralph Davis, *The Rise of the English Shipping Industry in the Seventeenth Century* (London: Macmillan, 1962), pp. 15–17.

13. Violet Barbour, "Dutch and English Merchant Shipping in the Seventeenth Century," *Economic History Review* 2 (January 1930): 269, 282–283. In 1670 Dutch tonnage stood at approximately 586,000 tons. Thirty years later, despite rapid expansion, English tonnage was still only one-third to one-half the Dutch total. E.E. Rich and C.H. Wilson, *The Economy of Expanding Europe in the Sixteenth and Seventeenth Century,* vol. 4 in *The Cambridge Economic History of Europe* (Cambridge: Cambridge University Press, 1967), pp. 210–211.

14. Willan, *English Coasting Trade,* pp. 14–16; Davis, *Rise of the English Shipping Industry,* pp. 71, 73; John Ehrman, *The Navy in the War of William III, 1689–1697* (Cambridge: Cambridge University Press, 1953), p. 110.

15. Ibid., pp. 109–110; Davis, *Rise of the English Shipping Industry,* pp. 71, 73, 114–115, 135–137.

16. Ibid., pp. 4, 114–115; Barbour, "Dutch and English Merchant Shipping," pp. 263–265; Willan, *English Coasting Trade,* pp. xiv, 178.

17. Luttrell, *Brief Relation,* 1: 592, 607; Pepys, *Diary,* 4: 284; L.A. Wilcox, *Mr. Pepys' Navy* (New York: A.S. Barnes, 1968), pp. 102–106. Edward Barlow, who was employed as a sailor for over four decades, once complained that merchant service was less desirable than naval employment. The advantages of serving the King that he enumerated were: (a) better food aboard warships, (b) surer pay, (c) no deductions from pay resulting from damaged cargo, (d) pensions for service-incurred disabilities, (e) easier work, and (f) clothing did not wear out as fast in naval service. Despite these advantages, Barlow preferred to sail aboard merchant ships, as his record of voyages indicates (Edward Barlow, *Barlow's Journal of His Life at Sea in the King's Ships, East and West Indiamen and Other Merchantmen from 1659 to 1703* [London: Hurst and Blackett, 1934], p. 426).

18. Ogg, *Reign of Charles II,* pp. 263–265; Beloff, *Public Order and Popular Disturbances,* p. 123.

19. Ibid., Ehrman, *The Navy in the War of William III,* pp. 110, 112. The table is constructed using the Navy's formula for calculating the necessary crewmen per vessel based on the amount of ordnance carried by each ship. This system placed the number needed to man a first rate, the largest warship in the Navy, at between 600 and 780 men, depending on specific armament. The smallest warship, the sixth rate, required only fifty to eighty-five men using the same formula. Since warships were chronically undermanned, the number serving on shipboard was probably somewhere between ten and twenty percent below theoretical requirements, but the reduced figures hardly diminish the dramatic nature of the Navy's increase in size over a brief period of time.

20. Pepys, *Diary,* 7: 196.

21. Ogg, *Reign of Charles II,* p. 264.

22. Davis, *Rise of the English Shipping Industry,* p. 116.

23. Beier, "Vagrancy and the Social Order," pp. 6–9.

3. THE CARIBBEE ISLES

1. Large numbers of females were evidently part of the population of Spanish colonies from the earliest times of settlement. See Peter Boyd-Bowman, "Patterns of Spanish Emigration to the Indies until 1600," *Hispanic American Historical Review* 56 (December 1976): 580–604. This was confirmed later for at least one rude coastal village by Sir William Beeston, a governor of Jamaica, who wrote in 1671 that at "Trinadadoe," where his ship had docked, "There are many women, which is as I judge all the delights they have." ("Journal of Sir William Beeston," Additional Manuscript 12,424, British Museum, London).

2. Violet Barbour, "Privateers and Pirates of the West Indies," *American Historical Review* 16 (April 1911): 531–535; C.H. Haring, *The Buccaneers in the West Indies in the Seventeenth Century* (London: Methuen, 1910), pp. 13, 42.

3. For an explanation of the role of land policies in creating a viable society from a commercial colony, see Sigmund Diamond, "From Organization to Society: Virginia in the Seventeenth Century," *American Journal of Sociology* 63 (March 1958): 457–475. Even with the Virginia Company actually sending women to the colony, the sex ratio was probably not immediately altered to any great degree. John Smith recorded in 1619 that of 1,216 persons sent over on 11 ships, only 90 were young women (John Smith, *Captain John Smith's History of Virginia*, ed. David Freeman Hawke [Indianapolis: Bobbs-Merrill, 1970], p. 147). The absence of women among the early Virginia colonists and their apparent lack of interest in them led the Indians to conclude, according to one resident, that the settlers "were not borne of women, and therefore not mortall" (Edmund S. Morgan, *American Slavery, American Freedom* [New York: Norton, 1975], p. 38.

4. Richard S. Dunn, *Sugar and Slaves: The Rise of the Planter Class in the English West Indies, 1624–1713* (New York: Norton, 1973), pp. 118–119.

5. Ibid., p. 50.

6. Ibid., p. 56.

7. Richard Ligon, *A True and Exact History of the Island of Barbados* (2nd ed.; London, 1673), pp. 5, 9, 13.

8. Ibid., p. 107. Apparently Ligon was not the only Englishman for whom perspiration had an anti-aphrodisiacal effect. After a visit to the West Indies late in the seventeenth century, Edward Ward wrote humourously of the latitudes near Jamaica, "Kissing here grew out of Fashion; there's no joyning of Lips, but your Noses would drop Sweat into your Mouths" (*A Trip to Jamaica; With a True Character of the People* [London, 1700], p. 12).

9. Ligon, *True and Exact History*, p. 57.

10. Ibid., pp. 46–47; Jerome S. Handler, "The Amerind Slave Population of Barbados in the Seventeenth and Early Eighteenth Century," *Caribbean Studies* 3 (1969): 38–39; C.S.C. Higham, *The Development of the Leeward Islands Under the Restoration* (Cambridge: Cambridge University Press, 1921), p. 125. A recent estimate of the sex ratio of slaves in the Caribbean places the women at 40 percent of the slave population (Robert W. Fogel and Stanley L. Engerman, *Time on the Cross: Economics of American Negro Slavery* [Boston: Little-Brown, 1974], pp. 26, 156. See also Sidney W. Mintz and Richard Price, *An Anthropological Approach to the Afro-American Past: A Caribbean Perspective*, No. 2 in Institute for the Study of Human Issues Occasional Papers in Social Change (Philadelphia: Institute for the Study of Human Issues, 1976), p. 2.

11. Ligon, *True and Exact History*, pp. 21, 35, 101.

12. Ibid., pp. 90, 93, 110, 113–115; Richard Blome, *A Description of Jamaica with Other Isles and Territories in Jamaica* (London, 1672), pp. 16–18.

13. A.E. Smith, *Colonists in Bondage*, p. 169.

14. Ibid., pp. 169–170. After the Restoration, the possibility of sending colonists was again

discussed. In March of 1661, the Council of Foreign Plantations considered shipping "1000 able men to Jamaica." No mention was made of females (*C.S.P. Colon.*, 7: 19). See also ibid., 9: 541 for a proposal to send males to the islands.

15. A.E. Smith, *Colonists in Bondage*, p. 169.

16. Ibid., p. 167.

17. Frank Wesley Pitman, *The Development of the British West Indies, 1700–1763* (New Haven, Conn.: Yale University Press, 1917; reprinted, New York: Archon, 1967), p. 45. Beggar bands also appeared in the West Indies. Laws were passed to regulate them on several occasions by authorities on Barbados. Given island demographic conditions, the wandering vagrants were even more heavily male than similar groups in England (*Acts of the Assembly Passed on the Island of Barbados From 1648–1718* [London, 1722], pp. 39, 40, 71).

18. A.E. Smith, *Colonists in Bondage*, pp. 152, 164–165, 192.

19. J.H. Bennett, "The English Caribbees in the Period of the Civil War, 1642–1646," *William and Mary Quarterly* 24 (July 1967): 360–361, 376–377; Dunn, *Sugar and Slaves*, p. 121.

20. Christopher Jeaffreson, *A Young Squire of the Seventeenth Century*, ed. John Cordy Jeaffreson (London: Hurst and Blackett, 1878), 1: 211, 2: 18, 19, 36–37. See also Luttrell, *Brief Relation*, 3: 31–32; Dunn, *Sugar and Slaves*, p. 164; *London Gazette*, September 4– September 8, 1690; Carl and Roberta Bridenbaugh, *No Peace Beyond the Line: The English in the Caribbean, 1642–1690* (New York: Oxford University Press, 1872), p. 182; *C.S.P. Colon.* 7: 142, 19: 495; *Interesting Tracts*, pp. 96–97.

21. *C.S.P. Colon.*, 9: 367, 10: 266; Higham, *Development of the Leeward Islands*, p. 148. Figures given by Richard Blome are: Barbados, 10,000 fighting men, Jamaica, 3,000 fighting men, privateers, sloop and boatmen (*Description of Jamaica*, pp. 42, 66).

22. A.E. Smith, *Colonists in Bondage*, pp. 96–98; A.G.L. Shaw, *Convicts in the Colonies* (London: Faber and Faber, 1966), p. 33; Barbour, "Privateers and Pirates," p. 541.

23. Jeaffreson, *Young Squire*, 2: 6–7, 116, 157–158; *C.S.P. Colon.*, 9: 346.

24. Jeaffreson, *Young Squire*, 2: 44–45, 47, 58–59, 72–73, 118, 150–151, 192.

25. Ibid., pp. 126, 184–185, 192, 195.

26. Ibid., pp. 197–198.

27. *Middlesex Records, Rolls, Books, and Certificates*, 3: 283, 287, 291, 293, 296; *Mist's Weekly Journal* (London), January 19–March 9, 1717.

28. A.E. Smith, *Colonists in Bondage*, pp. 104–106; *C.S.P. Colon.*, 15: 341, 541, 543, 559, 560, 567.

29. Jeaffreson, *Young Squire*, 1: 317–318.

30. Ibid., 1: 317–319, 2: 3–5; William Bullock, *Virginia Impartially Examined and Left to Public View* (London, 1649), p. 47 (mispaged p. 39); *Middlesex Records, Rolls, Books, and Certificates*, 3: 330–331.

31. John Latimer, *The Annals of Bristol in the Seventeenth Century* (Bristol: William George's Sons, 1900), p. 254.

32. Ibid., pp. 254–256.

33. [Gatford], *Public Good Without Private Interest*, pp. 4–5; Bullock, *Virginia Impartially Examined*, pp. 4–5; N. Dermott Harding, ed., *Bristol and America: A Record of the First Settlers in the Colonies of North America, 1654–1685* (Orig. pub. London, 1929; Baltimore: Genealogical Publishing Company, 1967), pp. viii–ix; Mildred Campbell, "Social Origins of Some Early Americans," *Seventeenth-Century America: Essays in Colonial History*, ed. James Morton Smith (New York: W.W. Norton, 1959), pp. 78, 80; David W. Galenson, " 'Middling People' or 'Common Sort'? The Social Origins of Some Early Americans Examined," *William and Mary Quarterly* 35 (July 1978): 504.

34. Campbell, "Social Origins,", pp. 68–78. The number of youths and unskilled laborers

may have been substantially higher than these figures according to David W. Galenson ("'Middling People' or 'Common Sort'?", pp. 505–507, 522). Mildred Campbell maintains Galenson's higher figures are not accurate (ibid., pp. 525–540). The most complete portion of the tabulation in the Bristol record is a segment including not only the names of migrants but some indication of social class. It is complete only for approximately 3,000 people who went to America during the first seven years the record was kept. The information on social class has been omitted from Harding's edition of Bristol and America, although there is no indication in the printed work that this vital data even exists in the manuscript.

35. A.E. Smith, Colonists in Bondage, pp. 62–66.

36. Haring, Buccaneers in the West Indies, p. 143; Ruth Bourne, Queen Anne's Navy in the West Indies (New Haven, Conn.: Yale University Press, 1939), p. 31.

37. A.E. Smith, Colonists in Bondage, pp. 142–143.

38. Ibid., p. 285.

39. Thomas Walduck to James Petiver, November 12, 1710, Journal of the Barbados Museum and Historical Society 15 (November 1947–1948), pp. 48–49; Acts of the Assembly, pp. 23–24. In Virginia, where the proportion of female servants was higher than in the Caribbean, one planter complained it was impossible to keep men away from even the ugliest serving women (Bullock, Virginia Impartially Examined, p. 54). There is no way of estimating how many serving women in the West Indies were illegally impregnated, but research on the subject for servants in Charles County, Maryland indicates the figure was approximately 20 percent for the period from 1658 to 1705. The sex ratio for whites in the colony for this period ranged from two to three males per female (Lois Green Carr and Lorena S. Walsh, "The Planter's Wife: The Experience of White Women in Seventeenth-Century Maryland," William and Mary Quarterly 34 [October 1977]: 543, 548); C.S.P. Colon., 8: 495; Dunn, Sugar and Slaves, pp. 108–110; A.E. Smith, Colonists in Bondage, p. 30; Blome, A Description of Jamaica, p. 85.

40. Ibid., pp. 99–103; Dunn, Sugar and Slaves, pp. 122–123, 127, 131, 148. Only on St. Christopher was the number of males and females roughly equal during this period. There were on the island 695 men and 539 women. Antigua had the greatest sexual disparity with 1,236 men and 544 women (ibid., p. 127).

41. Ibid., pp. 155, 165; Michael Craton and James Walvin, A Jamaica Plantation: The History of Worthy Park, 1650–1970 (Toronto: University of Toronto Press, 1970), pp. 21–22; Pitman, Development of the British West Indies, pp. 48–50; Bridenbaugh and Bridenbaugh, No Peace Beyond the Line, pp. 208 ff.; Laws of Jamaica (St. Jago de la Vaga [Spanish Town], Jamaica: 1792), p. 80; C.S.P. Colon., 7: 65, et passim; 8: 52, 9: 141, 285–286, 349.

42. Henry Cadbury, "Conditions in Jamaica, 1687," Jamaica Historical Review 3 (1966), pp. 25–35; R.B. [Nathaniel Crouch], The General History of Earthquakes (London, 1694), preface, pp. 143, 150; [Anon.], The Truest and Largest Account of the Late Earthquake in Jamaica (London, 1693), p. 9; [Ward], A Trip to Jamaica, p. 16; C.S.P. Colon., 8: 104, 306, 711; Craton and Walvin, Jamaica Plantation, p. 22; Dunn, Sugar and Slaves, pp. 179–181; David Buisseret and Michael Pawson, Port Royal, Jamaica (Oxford: Clarendon Press, 1975), pp. 24, 98, 103, 119, 184–185, Appendix A; Haring, Buccaneers in the West Indies, p. 273; Cadbury, "Quakers and the Earthquake at Port Royal, 1692," Jamaica Historical Review 8 (1971): 19–31.

43. C.S.P. Colon., 9: 318–320, 10: 216–219, 11:270, 14:257, 639, 15: 41–42, 179–180, 16: 140–141, 455, 474: The growth of official hostility toward piracy is particularly apparent from 1690 to 1700 (C.S.P. Colon., 15–18: passim).

44. Peter Gerhard, Pirates of the West Coast of New Spain, 1575–1742 (Glendale, Calif.: Arthur H. Clark, 1960); C.S.P. Colon., 10: 606, 11: 287–288, 471–472, 473, 12: 20–21, 15: 113, 336, 362, 379, 381, 468, 538, 552, 16: 477, 17: 539, 18: 256, 19: 372, 22: 712, 23: 24–

25, 26: 231, 30: 57, 31: 271, 354–356, 32: 11–12, *et passim*; Haring, *Buccaneers in the West Indies*, p. 271.

45. *C.S.P. Colon.*, 12: 50, 15: 73, 356, 17: 60, 307, 412–414, 18: 35–137, 19: 89–90, 20: 454, 464, 21: 100, 155.

46. Ibid., 20: 464–465; 21: 694–695, 29: 53–54, 140–141, 338, 31: 8, 32: 74–75.

47. Bridenbaugh and Bridenbaugh, *No Peace Beyond the Line*, p. 337; Dunn, *Sugar and Slaves*, pp. 76–77, 172.

48. Ibid., pp. 228, 252–253; Pitman, *Development of the British West Indies*, pp. 24, 28.

49. Jeaffreson, *Young Squire*, 1: 79.

50. Ibid., p. 89.

51. *C.S.P. Colon.*, 10: 329–330.

52. Walduck to Petiver, November 12, 1710, p. 50.

53. R.B., *General History of Earthquakes*, p. 150; [Anon.], *Truest and Largest Account*, p. 9; *C.S.P. Colon.*, 8: 49–51; [Ward], *A Trip to Jamaica*, p. 16; Dunn, *Sugar and Slaves*, pp. 125–126; *Massachusetts Historical Society Proceedings*, 2nd Ser., 5: 106. In the Tudor era and in the early part of the seventeenth century, Englishmen understood Sodom's sins to include bestiality and child molestation along with homosexual contacts, but by the time of the Restoration, the term sodomy without qualifying description was commonly used to refer only to sex relations between members of the same sex.

4. BUCCANEER SEXUALITY

1. See Buffum, *Homosexuality in Prisons*; Donald Clemmer, *The Prison Community* (New York: Holt, 1940); J.F. Fishman, *Sex in Prison* (London: John Lane, 1935); Gresham Sykes, *The Society of Captives* (Princeton: Princeton University Press, 1958). A bibliography of periodical literature dealing with prison homosexuality is included in Buffum. A survey of recent research on homosexuality and homosexual conduct in penitentiaries is included by William Simon and John Gagnon in *Sexual Conduct* (Chicago: Aldine, 1973), pp. 235–249.

2. Prison life in fact contains many cues for homosexual behavior. Youths grown to adulthood in penal systems, whether homosexual or willing to engage in homosexual acts in the absence of other sources of sexual contact, are attuned to an elaborate series of sex-inducing situations unique to reformatories and prisons.

3. Phillip Gosse, *Pirate's Who's Who* (London: Dulan, 1924), p. 21.

4. Gardner Lindzey, Charlotte Tejessy, and Harold Zamansky, "Thematic Apperception Test: An Empirical Examination of Some Indices of Homosexuality," *Journal of Abnormal and Social Psychology* 57 (January, 1958): 74.

5. Ibid.; Bieber, *Homosexuality*; Lawrence Ross, "Odd Couples: Homosexuals in Heterosexual Marriage," *Sexual Behavior* 2 (1972): 42–49; Laud Humphreys and Brian Miller, "Identities in the Emerging Gay Culture," in *Homosexual Behavior: A Modern Reappraisal*, ed. Judd Marmor (New York: Basic Books, 1980), p. 152; Alan P. Bell and Martin S. Weinberg, *Homosexualities: A Study of Diversity Among Men and Women* (New York: Simon and Schuster, 1978), pp. 55, 161, 174–175; A.O. Exquemelin, *The Buccaneers of America* (Orig. pub. 1678; Baltimore: Penguin, 1969), pp. 111, 138, 199.

6. Richard Simpson, "Richard Simpson's Voyage to the Straits of Magellan and the South Sea in the Year 1689," Sloane MSS. 86 or 672, British Museum, London, folio 56, p. 107.

7. Alexander Winston, *No Man Knows My Grave* (Boston: Houghton Mifflin, 1969), p. 22.

8. [William A.] Cowley, *Capt. Cowley's Voyage Round the Globe* in *A Collection of Original Voyages*, ed. William Hacke (London, 1699), pp. 6–7.

9. D.J. West [Michael George Schofield], *Homosexuality* (London: Duckworth, 1955), pp.

264–265; Hooker, "Male Homosexuals," p. 88; Paul Gebhard, *et al., Sex Offenders: An Analysis of Types* (New York: Harper and Row, 1965), pp. 300, 591, 857.

10. C.H. Firth, *Naval Songs and Ballads* (London: Navy Records Society, 1908), p. 167.

11. Daniel Defoe, *A General History of the Robberies and Murders of the Most Notorious Pyrates*, ed. Manuel Schonhorn (Orig. pub. 1724; Columbia, S.C.: University of South Carolina Press, 1972), p. 76.

12. *C.S.P. Colon.*, 30: 146–150; Charles B. Driscoll, "Finale of the Wedding March," *American Mercury* 14 (July, 1948): 358.

13. Ibid., p. 357; Defoe, *General History of the Pyrates*, p. 95.

14. *C.S.P. Colon.*, 20: 442–446, 28: 119; Winston, *No Man Knows My Grave*, pp. 26–27.

15. *C.S.P. Colon.*, 27: 335; Haring, *Buccaneers in the West Indies*, p. 271.

16. Woodes Rogers, *A Cruising Voyage Round the World: First to the South-Seas thence to the East-Indies, and Homewards by the Cape of Good Hope* (London, 1713), p. 6; Henry Teonge, *The Diary of Henry Teonge, Chaplain on Board His Majesty's Ships* Assistance, Bristol, *and* Royal Oak, *Anno 1675–1679*, ed. G.E. Manwaring (London: George Routledge and Sons, 1927), pp. 29, 36–38, 79.

17. One hundred years later, the attitude scarcely seems to have changed. Writing during the Napoleonic Wars, William Robinson explained that it was "not the happiest moment of a sailor's life, when he has to part with his Nancy, but grieving's a folly, and, upon these occasions they generally throw grief and a temporary affection over the taffrail, as commodities they do not take to sea with them." Jack Nastyface [William Robinson], *Memoirs of an English Seaman* (orig. pub. 1836; Annapolis, Md.: Naval Institute Press, 1963), pp. 100–101; Gosse, *Pirates' Who's Who*, pp. 109, 280; Defoe, *General History of the Pyrates*, p. 494.

18. William A. Cowley, "The Voyage of William Ambrose Cowley," Sloane MS. 54, British Museum, London, folio 49, p. 98; Bartholomew Sharp, "A Journal Kept By Capt. Bartholomew Sharp of Passages in Going Over Land to the South Seas from the Island Called the Golden Island in April 1680," Sloane, MSS. 64A, British Museum, London, p. 2; William Betagh, *A Voyage Round the World Being an Account of a Remarkable Enterprise Begun in the Year 1719* (London, 1728), p. 219.

19. Rogers, *Cruising Voyage Round the World*, p. 256.

20. Cowley, "Voyage of William Ambrose Cowley," folio 48, p. 96. For the temporary nature of such cavorting, see Exquemelin, *Buccaneers of America*, pp. 219–223.

21. Exquemelin, *Buccaneers of America*, pp. 54, 82, 219.

22. Defoe, *General History of the Pyrates*, p. 342; Stanley Richards, *Black Bart* (Llandybie, Carmarthenshire: Christopher Davies, 1966), p. 67, from H.C.A. 41/104.

23. Betagh, *Voyage Round the World*, p. 121.

24. Ibid., p. 123; *C.S.P. Colon.*, 15:614.

25. Gosse, *Pirates' Who's Who, passim*, James Burney, *History of the Buccaneers of America* (London: Swan Sonnenschein, 1891), pp. 372ff.

26. Winston, *No Man Knows My Grave*, pp. 56–57; Exquemelin, *Buccaneers of America*, pp. 137, 177.

27. Ibid., p. 210.

28. *C.S.P. Colon.*, 7: 232–233; Bartholomew Sharp, *The Voyages and Adventures of Capt. Bartt. Sharp* (London, 1684), preface. Exquemelin does state at one point that Spanish women were raped at Panama (*Buccaneers of America*, p. 201). See also note 31, below.

29. Rogers, *Cruising Voyage Round the World*, pp. 178–179; *C.S.P. Colon.*, 8: 322, 24: 123, 281, 531–532.

30. Basil Ringrose, *Buccaneers of America, The Second Volume Containing the Dangerous Voyage and Bold Attempts of Captain Bartholomew Sharp, and Others, Performed upon the*

Coast of the South Sea for the Space of Two Years (London, 1685), p. 163. Ringrose also mentions that information obtained from the prisoners indicated that some of the English pirates taken by the Spaniards some time before were alive and well. The Spanish captives explained that the Englishmen were being treated civilly by all sorts of people but especially by women. There is no surviving data on the actual treatment received by the English prisoners, but information on how they were treated by the Spanish, when furnished by Spaniards in the hands of English captors, cannot be given much weight (ibid.).

31. Sir William Beeston, "A Narrative of Sir William Beeston, of the Descent on Jamaica by the French," in *Interesting Tracts*, pp. 252, 255, 258. The French buccaneers' aversion to living women, implied in the Beeston account does not coordinate easily with Exquemelin's numerous descriptions of French and Dutch planters and pirates regularly engaging in fornication and rape (*Buccaneers of America*, pp. 54, 81, 102, 104). Exquemelin's accounts of the French and Dutch treatment of captive women is also in marked contrast to his descriptions of their treatment at the hands of English pirates. The English rarely raped, murdered, or tortured females—unless it was suspected they had knowledge of hidden wealth (ibid., pp. 130–131, 137–138, 147, 199). The only systematic brutalization of women prisoners by Englishmen occurred after the capture of Panama, according to only one report by Exquemelin, when some of Morgan's men, reinforced it should be noted by a large contingent of French buccaneers, starved and beat women who would not be seduced (ibid., p. 201).

32. Peter K. Kemp and Christopher Lloyd, *The Brethren of the Coast* (London: Heinemann, 1960), p. 57; Defoe, *General History of the Pyrates*, p. 82.

33. William Dampier, *A New Voyage Round the World* (Amsterdam, 1698; reprint ed., London: Argonaut Press, 1927), pp. 174–175.

34. Ibid., pp. 342–344.

35. Ibid., pp. 346–366: An interest in lads was not confined to captains commanding shiploads of marauders. Edward Barlow recorded the purchase of a "pretty" boy by his own captain off the Malibar Coast in 1697 (Barlow, *Journal*, p. 468).

36. Haring, *Buccaneers in the West Indies*, p. 72; [Anon.] *News From the Sea, or The Takeing of the Cruel Pirate* (London, 1674), p. 7; Kemp and Lloyd, *Brethren of the Coast*, p. 57; C.S.P. Colon., 12: 226, 315, 19: 736, 23: 262: In another case, a lad who had served as a witness against a crew of 44 pirates was given a cash award to sustain him when he complained to the court that he had no clothes or shoes. Still, whatever information he offered could not have been vital to the prosecution. At a time when it required four pence per day to maintain a prisoner in Newgate, the witness received less than a shilling (P.R.O. Adm. 1/3666, pp. 49, 232).

37. Defoe, *General History of the Pyrates*, p. 212.

38. Gebhard, *et al.*, *Sex Offenders*, pp. 307, 308, 319, 336–339; J.W. Mohr, R.E. Turner, and M.B. Jerry, *Pedophilia and Exhibitionism* (Toronto: University of Toronto Press, 1964), pp. 68–70, 94–95.

39. Gebhard, *et al.*, *Sex Offenders*, p. 32; Evelyn Hooker, "The Homosexual Community," reprinted in *Sexual Deviance*, eds. John H. Gagnon and William Simon (New York: Harper and Row, 1967), p. 207; B. Apfelberg, Carol Sugar, and Arnold Pfeffer, "A Psychiatric Study of 250 Sex Offenders," *American Journal of Psychiatry* 100 (May 1944): 766; Mohr, Turner, and Jerry, *Pedophilia and Exhibitionism*, pp. 13, 54, 68; B.R. Burg, "Legitimacy and Authority: A Case Study of Pirate Commanders in the Seventeenth and Eighteenth Centuries," *American Neptune* 37 (1977): 40–49.

40. Buffum, *Homosexuality in Prisons*, pp. 15–17; see also Simpson, "Richard Simpson's Voyage," folio 39, pp. 73–74.

41. Bridenbaugh and Bridenbaugh, *No Peace Beyond the Line*, pp. 114–115; Exquemelin, *Buccaneers of America*, pp. 53–54, 82, 104.

42. Louis Adhémar Timothée Le Golif, *Memoirs of a Buccaneer*, eds. G. Alaux and A. t'Serstevens (London: Allen and Unwin, 1954), pp. 103–110, 141.

43. West, *Homosexuality*, pp. 228–229.

44. Defoe, *General History of the Pyrates*, pp. 224–225.

45. Simpson, "Richard Simpson's Voyage," folio 56, p. 107.

46. Defoe, *General History of the Pyrates*, pp. 640–641; *C.S.P. Colon.*, 30: 438.

47. William Dampier, *A Vindication of His Voyage to the South-Seas in the Ship St. George* (London, 1707?), p. 1.

48. Betagh, *Voyage Round the World*, p. 36.

49. Ibid., p. 209.

50. Stone, *Family, Sex and Marriage*, pp. 93–102, 268–269.

51. In his study of World War I, Paul Fussell explains the need for love to mitigate the horror of combat by using Proust's perception of war provoking "an almost tropical flowering of sexual activity behind the lines which is the counterpart to the work of carnage which takes place at the front" (*The Great War and Modern Memory* [London: Oxford University Press, 1975], pp. 270–271): See also C. Anderson, "Conscious and Unconscious Homosexual Responses to Warfare," *British Journal of Medical Psychology* 20 (1944): 170–174.

52. Gebhard, *et al.*, *Sex Offenders*, pp. 345–367: See also Donald Webster Cory, *The Homosexual in America: A Subjective Approach* (New York: Greenberg, 1951), pp. 339–341; Donald Webster Cory and John P. LeRoy, *The Homosexual and His Society* (New York: Citadel Press, 1963), pp. 11–16; Bell and Weinberg, *Homosexualities*, p. 69.

53. Leslie A. Fiedler, "Come Back to the Raft Ag'in Huck Honey," in *An End to Innocence* (Boston: Beacon, 1955), pp. 145–146. The sea or the wilderness as a setting for the "Sacred Marriage of Males" also provides a setting for working out a metaphor of the relationship between races in America. Natty Bumppo is undefiled by women but he also boasts of "no cross" in his blood. The bonds of love unite both Dana and Ishmael with natives, and the most obvious instance is the journey down the Mississippi aboard the raft by Huckleberry Finn and Nigger Jim (ibid., pp. 143–148).

54. Ibid.

55. Bell and Weinberg, *Homosexualities*, pp. 107–111.

56. Evelyn, *Diary*, 4: 234.

57. Wilmot, "Satyr on King Charles II," p. 104; Oates, *Exact and Faithful Narrative*, p. 8.

58. Quick and furtive encounters between male homosexuals may not be as common as was once supposed, according to Bell and Weinberg, (*Homosexualities*, p. 80); Cory and LeRoy, *Homosexual and His Society*. Cory and LeRoy maintain that anal intercourse will become more common as homosexual encounters become more easily realized with the removal of tension that often accompanies them (p. 172).

59. Martin Hoffman, *The Gay World: Male Homosexuality and the Creation of Evil* (New York: Basic Books, 1968), pp. 36–37; Stone, *Family, Sex and Marriage*, p. 486. Another authority who maintains that oral-genital sex may have been substantially absent among the unwashed classes is *Kinsey Report* co-author Wardell Pomeroy (Discussion with Pomeroy, Center for Sex Research, California State University, Northridge, Inaugural Weekend Program, November, 1976).

60. Mohr, Turner, Jerry, *Pedophilia and Exhibitionism*, p. 20; Gebhard, *et al.*, *Sex Offenders*, pp. 293, 320. The most viable objection to this, based again on studies of homosexuals made since World War II, is that even among sex offenders whose primary sexual experiences are with children and youths, anal penetration is the least common sort of contact. Masturbation is the most usual type of contact, with the adult maturbating the child rather than the reverse. Masturbation accounts for approximately half of the contacts, with approximately 40 percent involving fellatio, and buggery being employed in less than ten or 11 percent of cases.

5. THE BUCCANEER COMMUNITY

1. Goffman, *Asylums*, pp. xiii, 5–6; V. Aubert and O. Arner, "On the Social Structure of the Ship," *Acta Sociologica* 3 (1958), pp. 200–201; Warren H. Hopwood, "Some Problems Associated With the Selection and Training of Deck and Engineer Cadets In The British Merchant Navy," in *Seafarer and Community*, ed. Peter H. Fricke (London: Croom Helm, 1973), p. 102; Jan Horbulewicz, "The Parameters of Psychological Autonomy of Industrial Trawler Crews," ibid., p. 68.

2. Fricke, *Seafarer and Community*; Buffum, *Homosexuality in Prisons*, p. 7; David Sonnenschein, "The Ethnography of Male Homosexual Relations," *Journal of Sex Research* (May 1968): 73; John Durival Kemp, Viscount Rochdale, *Committee of Inquiry into Shipping* (Cmd. 4337), Parliamentary Papers of the House of Commons and the Papers Presented by Command (London: H.M.S.O., 1970); Aubert and Arner, "Social Structure of the Ship," p. 211; T.L. Wilmon and T.G. Rich, "Report on the General Health and Morale of the Officers and Crew During a 30-Day Simulated War Patrol Aboard A Snorkel Submarine," Report No. 3 on BuMed Research Project NM 002 009 "Effect of Snorkelling on Submarine Personnel," Medical Research Laboratory Report 140a, U.S. Naval Submarine Base, New London, Connecticut (4 November 1948), pp. 2–4; Benjamin B. Weybrew, "Psychological Problems of Prolonged Marine Submergence" in Neal M. Burns, Randall M. Chambers, and Edwin Hendler, *Unusual Environments and Human Behavior: Physiological and Psychological Problems of Man in Space* (Glencoe, Ill.: Free Press, 1963), pp. 107–108.

3. Goffman, *Asylums*, pp. ix–x; Willmon and Rich, "Report," p. 3; Viscount Rochdale, *Committee of Inquiry* (Cmd. 4337); Hopwood, "Some Problems Associated With The Selection and Training of Deck and Engineer Cadets," p. 103; Fricke, "Family and Community: The Environment of the Ship's Officer," in *Seafarer and Community*, p. 147; J.H. Earls, "Human Adjustment to an Exotic Environment: The Nuclear Submarine," *Archives of General Psychiatry* 20 (1969):121; Aubert and Arner, "On The Social Structure of the Ship," p. 205; G.E. Ruff, E.Z. Levy, and V.H. Thaler, "Studies of Isolation and Confinement," *Aerospace Medicine* 30 (August, 1959): 601; C.S.P. Colon., 29: 141, 31: 10; Exquemelin, *Buccaneers of America*, pp. 70–73, Haring, *Buccaneers in the West Indies*, p. 69; Jean-Baptiste Labat, *The Memoirs of Père Labat* (London: Constable and Co., 1931), pp. 36–37.

4. C.S.P. Colon., 5: 622, 633, 7: 7, 49–51, 11:395. In a study of seafarers attitudes commissioned by the Rochdale Committee (*Committee of Inquiry* [Cmd. 4337] 1970), 24 percent of the group questioned gave evidence of discomfort when among landsmen. Officers and men aboard oil tankers, where parallels between the crew and buccaneers are more exact in that the level of impermeability is especially great in both situations, reported a higher rate of discomfiture ashore than men serving on conventional merchant vessels. The sub-group claiming the greatest difficulties getting along with the non-nautical population were the deck officers in the survey, the segment of the maritime population most likely to have been rigorously and systematically socialized into shipboard life at an earlier age than other seamen. Most joined ships directly from school or nautical college and only one out of five had previous non-maritime employment experience, in contrast to 75 percent of the engineering officers who had worked on land before going to sea. The effects of the total institution in this situation were evidently more profound on those with longer and more intensive socialization experiences (Bryan Nolan, "A Possible Perspective on Deprivation" in *Seafarer and Community*, pp. 94–95). See also Joseba Zulaika's *Terranova: The Ethos and Luck of Deep-Sea Fishermen* (Philadelphia: Institute for the Study of Human Issues, 1981) for acculturation problems of married Spanish fisherman on voyages with frequent visits to ports.

5. Fricke, "Family and Community," p. 33; Hopwood, "Some Problems Associated With The Selection and Training of Deck and Engineer Cadets," p. 103; Nolan, "A Possible Perspective on Deprivation," pp. 89–90, 94–95.

6. *The Laws, Ordinances, and Institutions of the Admiralty of Great Britain, Civil and Military* (London: 1746), I, p. 70.

7. P.R.O., H.C.A. 1/5, 52, 53, 121, and an unnumbered sheet. Hewitt's case is cited by Evelyn Berckman in *Victims of Piracy, The Admiralty Court* (London: Hamish Hamilton, 1979) pp. 51–52. Berckman also cites the case of a sailor aboard the *Surety* in 1608 who was acquitted of buggery despite his confession, a further indication seventeenth-century Englishmen were not outraged over homosexual acts (ibid). For Stone's case, see H.C.A. 1/7, 164, 171; H.C.A. 1/32, p. 10; H.C.A. 1/48, 234; H.C.A. 1/50, p. 87.

8. P.R.O., H.C.A. 1/9, pp. 37–38, 41; H.C.A. 13/142, pp. 15–16.

9. P.R.O., H.C.A. 1/64, p. 17.

10. *The Piratical Seizure of the Van-Herring* (London: T. Davies, 1681), II, p. 3.

11. P.R.O., H.C.A. 1/17, pp. 162, 184; H.C.A. 1/30, pp. 151–152, 170; H.C.A. 1/55, p. 21; Buffum, *Prison Homosexuality*, p. 17.

12. Dampier, *New Voyage Round the World*, pp. 38, 54, 74; John Cox, "John Cox His Travills over the Land into the So. Seas from thence Round the South parte of America to Barbados and Antegoe," Sloane MSS. 49, British Museum, London, folio 8; Sharp, "Journal," pp. 21, 61; Ringrose, *Buccaneers of America, The Second Volume*, pp. 2, 4, 121, 137.

13. M. Lenzoff and W. A. Westley, "The Homosexual Community," in *Sexual Deviance*, eds. Gagnon and Simon, p. 185; Hooker, "The Homosexual Community," pp. 171–172; Hooker, "Male Homosexuals and Their Worlds," pp. 93–94.

14. *C.S.P. Colon.*, 29: 94–99. See also Nancy Achilles, "The Development of the Homosexual Bar as an Institution," in *Sexual Deviance*, eds. Gagnon and Simon, pp. 228–244; Thomas J. Noel, "Gay Bars and the Emergence of the Denver Homosexual Community," *Social Science Journal* 15 (April 1978): 59–74; and Trumbach, "London's Sodomites," pp. 1–33.

15. Gebhard, *et al.*, *Sex Offenders*, p. 642; John Gerassi, *The Boys of Boise: Furor, Vice, and Folly in an American City* (New York: Macmillan, 1966), p. 42; Cory, *Homosexual in America*, pp. 80, 117; Hooker, "Homosexual Community," p. 175.

16. Gebhard, *et al.*, *Sex Offenders*, p. 63. By the end of the seventeenth century, a distinct homosexual subculture had evidently developed in London with stress on effeminacy, transvestism, enactment of childbirth, and marriage rituals. Several clubs were formed, and by the first half of the eighteenth century, the exposé of a number of homosexual coteries had created serious scandals. The rudimentary subculture, with its nicknames and recognized cruising areas, was distinct from lower class and seafarers' homosexuality. It was clearly an upper- and upper-middle-class business and was a reaction against heterosexual society rather than an alternate form of sexual expression (Mary McIntosh, "The Homosexual Role," *Social Problems*, 16 [2, 1968]: 187–188; see also Trumbach "London Sodomites," pp. 15, 17, 23).

17. M.M. Lewis, *Language in Society* (New York: Social Science Publishing, 1948), p. 141; Gordon Westwood, *Society and the Homosexual* (London: Gollancz, 1952), pp. 126–217; Sykes, *Society of Captives*, p. 85.

18. Exquemelin, *Buccaneers of America*, pp. 67, 86, 93, 114, 178; Gosse, *Pirates' Who's Who*, pp. 153, *et passim*; Hans Sloane, *A Voyage to the Islands of Madera, Barbados, Nieves, S. Christophers and Jamaica* (London, 1707), 1: lxxxvii; Le Golif, *Memoirs of a Buccaneer*, pp. 88–89, 98–100, 102, 114–115, 166, 168, 192, 201. In seventeenth-century usage, the term "bougre" referred to a practitioner of sodomy. It was not used to denominate a "blackguard" as was its meaning in the eighteenth century and after. See Peter N. Moogk, " 'Thieving Buggers' and 'Stupid Sluts': Insults and Popular Culture in New France," *William and Mary Quarterly* 36 (October 1979): 539.

19. Haring, *Buccaneers in the West Indies*, p. 69.

20. Hooker, "Homosexual Community," pp. 181–182; Gosse, *Pirates' Who's Who*, p. 313; Richards, *Black Bart*, p. 74.

21. Exquemelin, *Buccaneers of America*, pp. 81–82; Defoe, *General History of the Pyrates*, p. 135.

22. Ibid., p. 312.

23. Woodes Rogers, *Cruising Voyage Round the World*, p. xvii.

24. Kemp and Lloyd, *Brethren of the Coast*, p. 154; Cox, "John Cox His Travills Over The Land Into The So. Seas," folio 42; *C.S.P. Colon.* 9: 121; 10: 606; 29: 360.

25. George Shelvocke, *A Privateer's Voyage Round the World* (Orig. pub. 1726; London: Jonathan Cape, 1930), pp. 30, 40; Betagh, *Voyage Round the World*, 22–25, 155, 186.

26. *C.S.P. Colon.*, 9: 430, 17: 12–13, 18: 199, 27: 332–335, 29: 211–213, Defoe, *General History of the Pyrates*, pp. 211, 222, 224.

27. Richard Hauser, *The Homosexual Society* (London: Bodley Head, 1965), p. 33.

28. Defoe, *General History of the Pyrates*, pp. 292–294.

29. Ibid., pp. 84, 334.

30. Karl Abraham, "The Psychological Relationship between Sexuality and Alcoholism," in *Selected Papers* (London: Hogarth, 1949), p. 87; Gebhard, *et al.*, *Sex Offenders*, pp. 292, 353.

31. Walduck, "T. Walduck's Letters," p. 35.

32. Exquemelin, *Buccaneers of America*, p. 190.

33. Sharp, "Journal Kept by Capt. Bartholomew Sharp," pp. 108–110; Sharp, *Voyages and Adventures*, pp. 108–109.

34. Exquemelin, *Buccaneers of America*, p. 188; Simpson, "Richard Simpson's Voyage," folio 21, p. 38.

35. Although alcoholism or the excessive consumption of alcohol is frequently associated with homosexual behavior by many in modern America, there seems to be little basis for linking the two. See Marcel T. Saghir and Eli Robins, *Male and Female Homosexuality: A Comprehensive Investigation* (Baltimore: Williams and Wilkins, 1973), pp. 119–120.

36. Jack Beeching, Introduction to Exquemelin, *Buccaneers of America*, p. 11.

37. Stone, *Family, Sex and Marriage*, pp. 439–440.

38. John Aubrey, *Brief Lives, Chiefly of Contemporaries, Set Down By John Aubrey, Between the Years 1669 and 1696*, ed. Andrew Clark (Oxford: Clarendon Press, 1898) 1:395.

39. Exquemelin, *Buccaneers of America*, pp. 91, 106–107; *C.S.P. Colon.*, 11: 396.

40. Betagh, *Voyage Round the World*, p. 26; Shelvocke, *Privateer's Voyage*, p. 32; Defoe, *General History of the Pyrates*, pp. 75, 352–355; *C.S.P. Colon*, 29: 213.

41. Haring, *Buccaneers in the West Indies*, p. 54; *C.S.P. Colon.* 11:364, 27: 144–149.

42. Stone, *Family, Sex and Marriage*, pp. 439–440; Steven Marcus, *The Other Victorians: A Study of Sexuality and Pornography in Mid-Nineteenth Century England* (New York: Basic Books, 1964), p. 260; *C.S.P. Colon.*, 24: 486.

43. Exquemelin, *Buccaneers of America*, pp. 11, 99, 101, 130–137, 138, 147, 150–151, 200. See also *C.S.P. Colon.*, 5: 50–51.

44. Ibid., 24: 531–532.

45. Ibid., 30: 263–264, 410, 32: 272, 319.

46. Stone, *Family, Sex and Marriage*, pp. 81, 101–102, 194–195, 470–478.

47. Latimer, *Annals of Bristol*, p. 270; Evelyn, *Diary*, 4: 140–141.

48. Celia Fiennes, *The Journeys of Celia Fiennes*, ed. Christopher Morris (New York: Chanticleer Press, 1949), pp. 310–312.

49. Sloane, *Voyage to the Islands*, p. lvii; *Code Noir of Jamaica* (London: 1788), p. 4.

50. Le Golif, *Memoirs of a Buccaneer*, p. 46; Neville Williams, *Captains Outrageous* (London: Barrie and Rockliff, 1961), p. 152.

51. Defoe, *General History of the Pyrates*, pp. 69–70.

52. Labat, *Memoirs of Père Labat*, pp. 239–240.

53. Defoe, *General History of the Pyrates*, pp. 659–660.

54. Hoffman, *Gay World*, pp. 23–24, 51; Hooker, "Male Homosexuals," p. 87; Cory and LeRoy, *Homosexual and His Society*, pp. 77–78.

55. Hooker, "Homosexual Community," pp. 182–183; Gore Vidal, *The City and the Pillar* (New York: Grosset and Dunlap, 1948), p. 106. An excellent collection of short works that demonstrates this point is *Different: An Anthology of Homosexual Short Stories*, edited with an introduction by Stephen Wright (New York: Bantam, 1974); L. H. Lieser, "The Sexual Psychopath in Military Service," *American Journal of Psychiatry* 102 (1945): 95.

56. "Mercurius Americanus, A Brief Journall or a Succinct and True Relation of the Most Remarkable Passages Observed in That Voyage Undertaken by Captaine William Jackson to the Westerne Indies or Continent of America," Sloane MS. 793 or 894, British Museum, London, folio 23; (Anon.), *The Voyages of Captain William Jackson, 1642–1645*, ed. Vincent Harlow, Camden Miscellany, Vol. XIII (London: By the Society, 1923), p. 30.

57. [Francois] Froger, *A Relation of a Voyage Made in the Years 1695, 1696* (London, 1698), p. 56.

58. McIntosh, "Homosexual Role," p. 192; Trumbach, "London's Sodomites."

BIBLIOGRAPHICAL ESSAY

One of the most pleasurable aspects of research on homosexual buccaneers of three centuries past has been the opportunity to delve into
widely divergent but equally fascinating subject areas. Stuart England, early European settlement in the Caribbean, homosexuality,
and seafaring all contain sufficient problems to occupy legions of researchers for an indeterminate period. Trying to integrate them into
a coherent study has been an exercise in both frustration and joy.
The frustrations were occasioned by those things that are the bane of
scholars working on seventeenth-century topics and on projects dealing with human sexuality. There is never enough material and it
often is not of the sort required. The joys were produced by the writings of men who during the great days of piracy recorded what they
saw and did, and by others who came after and wrote about England,
America, and the sea. Without either of these groups, both the first-
hand observers and the more recent scholars, completion of my study
would have been impossible. The works mentioned in this essay represent in no way a complete catalog of those consulted. The titles
included are only a small fraction of the mass of material available,
but they are, in almost every case, the items that proved to be of
greatest value.

Piracy

Over the past centuries, there have been scores of published accounts detailing activities of the pirates and buccaneers who plundered the Caribbean and the Spanish Main from the restoration of Charles II in 1660 to the first decades of the eighteenth century. The most convenient and comprehensive bibliography of piracy, although far from complete, is *Piracy and Privateering,* published as volume four of the *National Maritime Museum Catalog of the Library* (London: H.M.S.O., 1972). The basis of the volume is the extensive collection of material on piracy compiled by the late Philip Gosse and acquired by the Museum in 1939, but considerable material is included in the catalog that was not part of the Gosse collection. Some of the earliest accounts of West Indian piracy to appear in print were the narratives and journals of men who sailed and fought as pirates and later returned to Europe and wrote of their adventures. The most notable of these early first-hand descriptions is *De Americanenche Zee-Roovers* written by Alexander O. Exquemelin and published in Holland in 1678. Exquemelin is thought to have been born in France at Harfleur, but beyond this information and the probable date of his birth in 1645, little is known of his early life. By 1666, he was in the West Indies as an employee of a French company on Tortuga, and three years later he joined the buccaneers, serving with Henry Morgan's expeditions against Porto Bello, Maracaibo, and Panama City. His book-length narrative of the piratical exploits of Morgan and his men was an instant success. Within a decade after its publication it had been translated into English, German, Spanish and French. By 1700, there were four English editions, indicating the work was read by Englishmen with as much interest and enthusiasm as they had read Richard Hakluyt's *Principal Navigations of the English Nation* one hundred years before. For the sake of convenience, I have used an easily available paperback edition of *The Buccaneers of America* (Baltimore: Penguin, 1969). Extended discussions of the various editions are included in *Piracy and Privateering* (pp. 49–60) and in C.H. Haring's *Buccaneers in the West Indies in the Seventeenth Century* (orig. pub. 1910; Hamden, Conn.: Archon Books, 1966), pp. 277–280.

Throughout the seventeenth and into the early eighteenth century, narratives of piratical and semi-piratical voyages to the New World were published in quantity. In many cases the authors were men who had operated on the fringes of buccaneering and had, most often, at least quasi-legal justifications for their depredations. Their accounts were usually written to justify their own conduct rather than recount adventures. Such works are William Betagh's *Voyage Round the World, Being an Account of a Remarkable Enterprize Begun in the Year 1719* (London, 1728); William Dampier's two books, *A New Voyage Round the World* (orig. pub. 1697; London: Argonaut Press, 1927) and *A Vindication of His Voyage to the South-Sea in the Ship St. George* (London, [1707?]); Basil Ringrose, *The Dangerous Voyage and Bold Attempts of Captain Bartholomew Sharp, and Others Performed Upon the Coasts of the South Sea* (London, 1685); William Ambrose Cowley's *Capt. Cowley's Voyage Round the Globe* in *A Collection of Original Voyages*, ed. William Hacke (London, 1699); Bartholomew Sharp's *The Voyages and Adventures of Capt. Bart. Sharp* (London, 1684; George Shelvocke's *A Privateer's Voyage Round the World* (orig. pub. 1726; London, Jonathan Cape, 1930); and Lionel Wafer's *A New Voyage and Description of the Isthmus of America* (London, 1699). In the same genre, but with less direct involvement in piracy, is Woodes Rogers's *A Cruising Voyage Round the World: First to the South-Seas, Thence to the East-Indies, and Homewards by the Cape of Good Hope* (London, 1713).

In 1724, *A General History of the Robberies and Murders of the Most Notorious Pyrates* went on sale in London. Four years later a second volume appeared, containing more detail on several of the men mentioned in the earlier effort, accounts of additional pirates, and a lengthy tale of a fictional Madagascar freebooter named Captain Misson. Although the title pages of the volumes attributed authorship to a Captain Charles Johnson, the author of both books was Daniel Defoe. Defoe was primarily a journalist and an author of fiction, but he was also a prolific writer of the rogue literature that had wide appeal to English popular taste. His accounts of piracy were compiled with attention to accuracy and detail that was seldom found in the work of eighteenth-century journalists. He carefully authenticated his material, comparing newspaper stories with one another, regularly interviewing participants in the adventures he chronicled, and examining indictment and trial records to make his accounts as close to the truth as possible. Despite the occasional inclusion of a fictional buccaneer or manufactured background data, Defoe's work is sufficiently accurate so that along with Exquemelin and narratives by seafarers Basil Ringrose, William Dampier, Bartholomew Sharp and Lionel Wafer, it has served as a basic source for most tales of piracy written during the past two hundred and fifty years. An account of the various editions of *General History of the Pyrates* is included in *Piracy and Privateering* (pp. 83–97). The best available edition for scholarly purposes is that edited by Manual Schonhorn (Columbia, S.C.: University of South Carolina Press, 1972). Schonhorn includes a perceptive introductory essay, a carefully researched investigation of Defoe's sources, and indices of pirates, places, subjects, and ships, the value of which is hard to overestimate. Two works similar in content to Defoe but dealing with individual pirates rather than with large numbers of them are the anonymously written *Arraignment, Tryal, and Condemnation of Capt. John Quelch and Others of His Company* (London, 1705) and *The Grand Pyrate: Life and Death of Capt. George Cusack The Great Sea-Robber* (London, 1676).

The most widely known modern researcher in the field of piracy was Dr. Philip Gosse, who produced two major works on the subject: *The Pirates' Who's Who* (London: Dulan, 1924) *and The History of Piracy* (New York: Tudor, 1934). Both works contain vast amounts of information about individuals, incidents, and the nature of piracy. Unfortunately, there is no indication as to where Gosse obtained his material, and while his works are generally accurate, researchers must be careful when using them. Probably the most valuable single recent work on piracy by a modern scholar is Haring's *Buccaneers in the West Indies*. In addition to the works by Gosse and Haring, there are large numbers of books on piracy available. Most are written from

Exquemelin or Defoe and add little to our knowledge of buccaneering. Their quality depends on the literary skill of the authors rather than on content.

The manuscript holdings of the British Museum, the Public Record Office, the National Maritime Museum at Greenwich, and other repositories of nautical survivals for the period of full-dress piracy in the Caribbean are vast. Most materials deal with the operational aspects of piracy, however, or attempts to encourage or restrict depredations in the West Indies or in the East. There is little that is concerned with the day-to-day lives of pirates, their society, or their sexuality. Even the manuscript journals kept by seafarers during the period have little to offer. Sailors' diaries for the most part deal with those things that are the business of sailors: headings, winds, tides, harbors, landfalls, and cargoes. They rarely wrote about other of their activities. Accounts and depositions of pirate captives, assessments of pirate strengths or weaknesses, and other information on piracy are included in the *Calendars of State Papers, Colonial Series, America and the West Indies*. The *Calendars* are organized chronologically and indexed by subject, making them easy to use. Microfilm or copies of complete documents in the *Calendars* are usually available from the Public Record Office at an extortionate rate.

One other buccaneer narrative requires mention in any essay on sources. Captain Louis Adhémar Timothée le Golif's *Memoirs of a Buccaneer*, eds. G. Alaux and A. t'Serstevens (London: Allen and Unwin, 1954) is without a doubt the finest extant pirate narrative. It is unfortunate, given the quality of the work, that there is the possibility it is a fraud. Not only is it in the nature of something too good to be genuine, but the existence of the putative author of the volume cannot be established from any other source. Nor have the owners of the manuscript been willing, at least at this writing, to subject it to the scrutiny of scholars able to establish its authenticity. Despite my own doubts about its genuineness, I have on occasion been unable to resist the temptation to quote or cite it. Where it is used, it provides only an additional example of pirate practice; no substantial points are based on evidence from Le Golif. If it were verified, needless to say, it would have been used much more heavily.

Homosexuality

The literature on homosexuality has grown prodigiously since World War II. The most useful bibliographic tool in dealing with it is Vern L. Bullough, Barrett W. Elcano, W. Dorr Legg, and James Kepner's two-volume *Annotated Bibliography of Homosexuality* (New York: Garland, 1976). Sections on the behavioral sciences are particularly valuable for historical research, and the comprehensive nature of the work makes it especially useful in tracing obscure articles, monographs, and papers. The bibliography also contains a list of pseudonymous authors, a handy feature in evaluating several works on homosexuality. Another essential research aid is Martin S. Weinberg and Alan P. Bell's *Homosexuality: An Annotated Bibliography* (New York: Harper, 1972). Although less comprehensive than Bullough *et al.*, the annotations are longer and more descriptive. Sections on homosexuality in history, non-western societies, and special settings are helpful, but the primary emphasis of the book is on etiology and treatment rather than on social or sociological aspects of homosexuality.

The works any researcher on homosexuality finds most useful are those closely attuned to his theoretical perspective, and I am not an exception. But beyond theoretical harmony, the truly valuable studies for research on buccaneers were those that could be characterized most accurately as tentative, experimental, or uncertain rather than the many dogmatic products that form the core of the literature. Perhaps the ablest researcher in the field of homosexuality, at least for my purposes, is Evelyn Hooker ("An Empirical Study of Some Relations Between Sexual Patterns and Gender Identity in Male Homosexuals," in *Sex Research: New Developments*, ed. John Money [New York: Holt Rinehart and Winston, 1965], pp. 24–52; "The Homosexual Community," in *Sexual Deviance*, eds. John H. Gagnon and William Simon [New York: Harper, 1967], pp. 167–184; and "Male Homosexals and Their Worlds," in *Sexual Inversion: The Multiple Roots of Homosexuality*, ed. Judd Marmor [New York: Basic Books, 1965], pp. 83–107). Hooker has conducted one of the few longitudinal studies of homosexuals, and although in historical terms the chronological span is woefully abbreviated, it remains one of the out-standing recent research products on homosexuality done in the last three decades. The conclusions reached by Hooker are presented as the findings of careful investigation rather than as the divinely or-dained truths often encountered in studies on homosexuality. She is also aware, unlike many of the psychologists and therapists working in the field, that homosexuality, like heterosexuality, is a complex of behavioral patterns created by convoluted and intertwined patterns of biological and social considerations.

Easily available discussions of the origins and evolution of sexuality are found in John Gagnon's *Human Sexualities* (Glenview, Ill.: Scott Forseman, 1977) and Herant A. Katchadourian and Donald T. Lunde's *Fundamentals of Human Sexuality* (2nd ed.; New York: Holt, Rinehart and Winston, 1975). Another valuable work on the devel-opment of homosexuality is *Sex Offenders: An Analysis of Types* by Paul H. Gebhard, John H. Gagnon, Wardell B. Pomeroy, and Cor-nelia V. Christenson (New York: Harper, 1965). The investigation deals with 14 types of sex offenders, three of which are homosexual. There are among the three types of offenders (offenders against chil-dren aged 12 or under, against youths aged 12 to 15, and against adults aged 16 or over) general patterns of childhood development, according to the authors. The studies were carried out with convicts rather than with members of the general population, but the findings are nonetheless valuable for historical work. Of some additional value is Alan P. Bell and Martin S. Weinberg's *Homosexualities: A Study of Diversity Among Men and Women* (New York: Simon and Schu-ster, 1978).

Studies that were occasionally helpful for integrating homosexual-ity with patterns of social behavior are Wainwright Churchill, *Homo-sexual Behavior Among Males, A Cross-Cultural and Cross Species Investigation* (Englewood Cliffs, N.J.: Prentice Hall, 1971); Clellan S. Ford and Frank A. Beach, *Patterns of Sexual Behavior* (New York: Harper, 1952); and Marvin K. Opler, "Anthropological and Cross-Cultural Aspects of Homosexuality," in *Sexual Inversion*, pp. 108–123. Two especially useful works on the integrated nature of sexuality and society are A.E. Ashworth and W.M. Walker, "Social Structure of Homosexuality: a Theoretical Appraisal," *British Journal of Sociology* 23 (1972): 146–158 and E. William Monter, "La sodomie à l'époque moderne en Suisse romande," *Annales: E.S.C.* 29 (1974): 1023–1033. Monter's work was particularly valuable in illuminating the nexus between sodomy and accusations of sundry political offenses.

A single compendium of work on homosexuality in prisons is Peter C. Buffum's *Homosexuality in Prisons* (National Institute of Law Enforcement and Criminal Justice Publication PR 72–3, 1973). It is the result of a national conference on prison homosexuality held in Philadelphia in 1971, and although it does not attempt to review all aspects of prison homosexuality, the summary of the papers presented by a distinguished list of participants contains in its pages numerous provocative insights. Buffum's discussion of the non-sexual function of homosexuality is particularly enlightening and obviously applicable to seventeenth-century pirate communities. The concern expressed for seeking solutions to problems of prison homosexuality—institutional rather than individual therapy—appears as an obligatory inclusion, but the contributors to the symposium were generally psychologically oriented and could naturally be expected to exhibit a need to articulate solutions no matter how outlandish. The requirement for "solutions" to prison homosexuality is also the result of the sponsoring agencies. The Pennsylvania Prison Society and the National Institute of Law Enforcement and Criminal Justice are organizations that expect some return from their investment in terms of recommendations, formulae, treatment strategies, and suggested administrative responses.

The most useful historical works for illuminating social conditions and their impact on sexuality are Vern L. Bullough's *Sexual Variance in Society and History* (New York: Wiley, 1976) and Lawrence Stone's *The Family, Sex and Marriage in England* 1500–1800 (New York: Harper, 1977). Bullough's meticulously researched and compendious study covers far more than England in the seventeenth and eighteenth centuries. It is a cross-cultural and historical investigation of sexual practice for a substantial segment of the recorded human past. It ranges in scope from sexual variations among the ancients, around the world to describe practices in the Orient, and on to an informed examination of opportunities for further research. The depth and breadth of Bullough's research makes his work the standard reference for historians dealing with sex and sex-related matters for almost every period and geographical area. It is the starting point for any investigation of variant sexual practice in earlier eras. Lawrence Stone's work is by far the most ambitious theoretical and interpretative examination of the origins and motives for a portion of sexual practices in Stuart and Hanoverian England. It is thesis history in some respects, and is masterfully done. Homosexuality is only one aspect of the work, a minor phase at that, but the discussions are informed, carefully constructed, and thoughtful. Stone has avoided the pitfall of relying on psychological methodology to produce a historical study, and this alone makes his work more comprehensible than the usual psycho-historical-sexual monograph. Some challenge may emerge in the future to his classifications of affective and non-affective family relationships or his explanation of the roots and early evolution of pre-Victorian sexual repression, but his theoretical constructs are of the sort that provide foundations for other scholars to build upon rather than simply serving as targets for revisionist assaults.

Historical works dealing exclusively with homosexuality fall into two general patterns, rosters of famous homosexuals such as A.L. Rowse's *Homosexuals in History: A Study of Ambivalence In Society, Literature and the Arts* (New York: Macmillan, 1977) and other books that attempt to attribute homosexuality to every major figure in the past. The first type are usually no more than lists of names with little understanding and less value. Of the second type, the one word that most accurately characterizes them is pathetic. Two exceptions to the above categories, both works that have considerable utility for research on English homosexual behavior, are H. Montgomery Hyde's *The Other Love, An Historical and Contemporary Survey of Homosexuality in Britain* (London: Heinemann, 1970) and Randolph Trumbach's "London's Sodomites: Homosexual Behavior and Western Culture in the 18th Century," *Journal of Social History* 11 (Fall 1977): 1–33.

An interesting work, although with limited value for a study of Caribbean pirates, is Jonathan Katz's *Gay American History* (New York: Crowell, 1976). The volume is a pioneering documentary collection of materials relating to homosexuals in America, and although only a small portion deals with the seventeenth and early eighteenth centuries and none with the West Indies, it stands as an example of what can be done by a devoted and judicious scholar. It is marred occasionally by uncalled-for ideological infusions and by stridency where none is necessary, but neither fault diminishes its importance as a signal contribution to the history of human sexuality.

Homosexual first-person accounts, exposés, and fiction must be used judiciously by historians, especially when dealing with earlier periods. As a rule, they are self-serving, apologistic, polemical, and often painful to read. Two of the best narratives of the "gay world" are those by Donald Webster Cory (in reality Edward Sagarin) with his collaborator on the second work, John P. LeRoy. The first, *The Homosexual in America: A Subjective Approach* (New York: Greenberg, 1951) contains all of the abovementioned faults, and is best characterized by its own subtitle. The second work, done with LeRoy, is in the nature of a sympathetic exposé, and does contain much of value, although like Cory's earlier effort, it must be used with considerable care. The difficulties of relying heavily on homosexual fiction are obviated in dealing with a time three centuries past simply because such fiction did not exist as a sub-classification of English literature until at least the nineteenth century. The problems of incorporating material from homosexual novels, short stories, plays, and poetry are approximately the same as those encountered by any scholar using fiction as a source for historical writing. With care, understanding, and a venturesome spirit, positive results can occasionally be obtained.

Although not concerned directly with homosexuality, the literature on men confined to limited areas other than prisons contains much that is relevant to Stuart-era seafarers. Most of the difficulties encountered as a result of isolation aboard modern commercial vessels were magnified for men in the age of sail. Peter H. Fricke's anthology, *Seafarer and Community: Towards a Social Understanding of*

Seafaring (London: Croom Helm, 1973), contains a number of articles that are directly pertinent to the pirate community. Fricke's own contribution to the book, also entitled "Seafarer and Community" (pp. 1–7), is especially valuable as is "The Parameters of Psychological Autonomy of Industrial Trawler Crews" (pp. 67–84) by Jan Horbulewicz. Warren H. Hopwood's "Some Problems Associated with the Selection and Training of Deck and Engineer Cadets in the British Navy" (pp. 97–116) helped in understanding the role of previous conditioning for men struggling to adapt to life at sea. Other works that aided in various ways are V. Aubert and O. Arner, "On the Social Structure of the Ship," *Acta Sociologica* (No. 3, 1958): 200–219; J.H. Earls, "Human Adjustment to an Exotic Environment: The Nuclear Submarine," *Archives of General Psychiatry* 20 (January 1969): 117–123; G.E. Ruff, E.Z. Levy, V.H. Thaler, "Studies of Isolation and Confinement," *Aerospace Medicine* 30 (August 1959): 599–604; Benjamin B. Weybrew, "Psychological Problems of Prolonged Marine Submergence," in Neal M. Burns, Randall M. Chambers, Edwin Hendler, *Unusual Environments and Human Behavior: Physiological and Psychological Problems of Man in Space* (Glencoe, Ill.: Free Press, 1963), pp 87–125; T.L. Willmon and T.G. Rich, "Report on the General Health and Morale of the Officers and Crew During a 30-Day Simulated War Patrol Aboard a Snorkel Submarine," U.S.N. Med. Res. Lab. Rep. No. 140a (New London, Conn., 1948). The most provocative work on "total institutions" is that by Erving Goffman, who coined the term. His *Asylums* (New York: Doubleday, 1961) has provided much more than the few citations in the footnotes reveal. Knut Weibust's *Deep Sea Sailors: A Study in Maritime Ethnology* (2nd ed.; Stockholm: Nordiska Museets, 1976) describes many typically homosexual behavior patterns among nineteenth-century sailors, but does not explore their sexual behavior, either homosexual or heterosexual.

The English West Indies in the Seventeenth Century

One of the finest travel accounts written by a seventeenth-century Englishman is Richard Ligon's *True and Exact History of the Island of Barbados* (2nd ed.; London, 1763). Few of even the smallest details escaped Ligon's sharp eye, and he recorded what he saw with charm and considerable literary skill. Equally valuable but less skillfully written is Christopher Jeaffreson's *Young Squire of the Seventeenth Century* (London: Hurst and Blackett, 1878), a two-volume diary edited by John Cordy Jeaffreson. The work contains large numbers of letters written by Jeaffreson to officials, employees, and acquaintances in the Leeward Islands. Since most of the correspondence deals with business matters it is a trove of information about agricultural practices, the hopes and problems of planters, and the difficulties in putting colonies on a paying basis.

Migration to the West Indies is partially recorded in several contemporary records. I have relied most heavily on *Bristol and America: A Record of the First Settlers in the Colonies of North America 1654–1685*, ed. N. Dermott Harding (orig. pub. 1929; Baltimore: Genealogical Publishing Company, 1967). The lists of migrants it contains can be profitably supplemented with materials on the city's social history from John Latimer's *Annals of Bristol in the Seventeenth Century* (Bristol: William George's Sons, 1900), an incomplete but nonetheless admirable compendium. Additional information on migration is contained in Mildred Campbell's "Social Origins of Some Early Americans" in *Seventeenth-Century America: Essays in Colonial History*, ed. James Morton Smith (New York: Norton, 1959), pp. 63–89 and in David W. Galenson's " 'Middling People' or 'Common Sort?': The Social Origins of Some Early Americans Reexamined," *William and Mary Quarterly* 35 (July 1978): 499–524. Also useful was John Camden Hotten's *Original Lists of Persons . . . Who Went from Great Britain to the American Plantations 1600–1700* (Rpt. from 2nd ed.; Baltimore: Genealogical Publishing Company, 1962). This book is particularly helpful on migration to Barbados.

Seventeenth-century records from the West Indies are to be had only in restricted quantity. Some of the most easily available are the *Acts of the Assembly Passed in the Island of Barbados, From 1648–1718* (London, 1722) and the *Laws of Jamaica: Comprehending All the Acts in Force Passed Between the Thirty-second Year of the Reign of King Charles and the Thirty-third Year of the Reign of George the*

Third (St. Jago de la Vega [Spanish Town], 1792). An early compilation of records from seventeenth-century Jamaica, containing copies of materials long ago lost or destroyed, is *Interesting Tracts Relating to the Island of Jamaica Consisting of Curious State Papers, Councils of War, Letters, Petitions, Narratives, . . . from Its Conquest, Down in the Year 1702* (St. Jago de la Vega [Spanish Town], 1800).

General works dealing with broad West Indian topics are Frank Wesley Pitman, *Development of the British West Indies 1700–1763* (orig. pub. 1917; Hamden, Conn.: Archon, 1967); C.S.S. Higham's *Development of the Leeward Islands Under the Restoration 1660–1688* (Cambridge: Cambridge University Press, 1921); Carl and Roberta Bridenbaugh's *No Peace Beyond the Line: The English in the Caribbean 1624–1690* (New York: Oxford University Press, 1972); and the exceedingly important work by Richard B. Sheridan, *Sugar and Slavery: An Economic History of the British West Indies* (Baltimore: Johns Hopkins University Press, 1974).

Although Abbott Emerson Smith's *Colonists in Bondage: White Servitude and Convict Labor in America 1607–1776* (orig. pub. 1947; New York: Norton, 1971) is dated in many respects and deals primarily with the colonists on the North American mainland, it is still especially useful on general patterns of indentured servitude, convict labor, and prisoners of war. It also includes some valuable information on servitude in the English Caribbean.

One of the most incisive scholars writing on the Caribbean is Richard S. Dunn. His pioneering article on "The Barbados Census of 1680: Profile of the Richest Colony in English America," *William and Mary Quarterly* 27 (January 1969): 3–30, is of particular usefulness, but by far his primary contribution is the finely wrought monograph *Sugar and Slaves: The Rise of the Planter Class in the English West Indies, 1624–1713* (New York: Norton, 1973). The book explores large areas of Caribbean social, political, and economic growth to substantiate the author's arguments, and the investigation is conducted with skill, sagacity, and occasionally with verve. Another monograph dealing with only Jamaica but the equal in quality to Dunn's work is Michael Craton and James Walvin's *Jamaica Plantation: The History of Worthy Park* (Toronto: University of Toronto

Press, 1970). There is a considerable corpus of material available on Port Royal, a good part of which is of dubious quality. Writers on the early history of the city were fascinated most often by its reputation as the wickedest spot in the Western Hemisphere, and their reports are filled with tales of roistering buccaneers and accounts of fleshpots that never existed. The only work with a balanced and scholarly treatment of the town for the period before the earthquake of 1692 is David Buisseret and Michael Pawson's *Port Royal, Jamaica* (Oxford: Clarendon Press, 1975), a general history that covers much more than the seventeenth century.

Two bibliographies for the West Indies from the seventeenth to the nineteenth centuries are *Biblioteca Jamaicensis: Some Account of the Works on Jamaica in the Library of the Institute* (Kingston: Institute of Jamaica, 1895) and *Biblioteca Barbadiensis: A Catalog of Materials Relating to Barbados 1650–1860 in the Boston Public Library* (Boston: Boston Public Library, 1968).

Seventeenth-Century England

Even the most perfunctory survey of materials that have been of use concerning Stuart and early Georgian England would be far beyond the scope of an abbreviated bibliographical essay. The works that follow represent only those that were relied upon continually or offered limited but uniquely valuable information or perceptions. I have borrowed heavily from works by Peter Laslett. His *World We Have Lost, England Before the Industrial Age* (New York: Scribner's, 1965), despite severe criticism and a particularly ill-tempered review by Christopher Hill in *History and Theory* 6 (1967), pp. 117–127, contains material admirably suited to research in lower-class male groups. The studies contained in his *Family Life and Illicit Love in Earlier Generations: Essays in Historical Sociology* (Cambridge, Cambridge University Press, 1977) are useful as is the article he wrote in collaboration with John Harrison, "Clayworth and Cogenhoe" in *Historical Essays Presented to David Ogg*, eds. H.E. Bell and R.L. Ollard (New York: Barnes and Noble, 1963). Another work of the same methodological persuasion that is of some utility is E.A. Wrigley's *Popula-*

tion and History (New York: McGraw-Hill, 1969). As mentioned before, Stone's *Family, Sex and Marriage* provided substantial material and analysis of seventeenth-century social conditions.

Other than the vast number of quarter sessions records available, the contemporary sources containing helpful material are those generally used by historians and students of English literature. The single work containing most material on daily life, at least for wealthy London society, is *The Diary of Samuel Pepys*, 9 vols., eds. Robert Latham and William Matthews (Berkeley: University of California Press, 1970–). Like Pepys's *Diary*, *The Diary of John Evelyn*, 6 vols., ed. E.S. DeBeer (London: Oxford University Press, 1955) is a standard source for studies dealing with the period, although Evelyn's account is shorter, contains less data on ordinary events, and lacks the intriguing asides and fascinating anecdotes of Pepys. John Aubrey's collection of biographies of notable figures, *Brief Lives, Chiefly of Contemporaries, Set Down By John Aubrey, Between the Years 1669 and 1696*, ed. Andrew Clark, 2 vols. (Oxford: Clarendon Press, 1898) has long been an object of derision for historians. Aubrey was denounced as a gossip, a charge certainly true. His biographies were criticized as inaccurate and incomplete, another charge that was undoubtedly true. Yet sandwiched between tidbits of scandal, pages of tedious detail on Thomas Hobbes, and assorted ramblings, there is a wealth of small treasures about the way things were in England under the later Stuarts. The most neglected of the multi-volume diarists of three hundred years ago is Narcissus Luttrell, whose *Brief Historical Relation of State Affairs from September 1678 to April 1714*, 6 vols. (Oxford: Oxford University Press, 1857) is a singularly lackluster piece in an age of literary brilliance. Luttrell's chronicle was written largely from newspapers and broadsides, with little added by the author about either himself or events. The judgments on the news entered into the *Historical Relation* are few, the events recorded are repetitious, and only by reading Luttrell and discerning patterns in his entries does his work assume considerable value. That indefatigable recorder of things English, Daniel Defoe, produced one of the finest of the many travel accounts published in late seventeenth- or early eighteenth-century England. His *"Tour Thro' The Whole Island of Great Britain* (orig.

208 BIBLIOGRAPHICAL ESSAY

pub. 1724–1726; New York: Augustus M. Kelley, 1968) is a wonderfully written account of his travels; Defoe was also a careful observer of economic conditions, trading patterns, and the growth of the nation's commerce and manufacturing.

The works dealing with apprentices, wanderers, beggars, vagrants, criminals, and the like that have provided the preponderant amount of material for this study deal with the Elizabethan as well as Stuart eras. Two early sources, as valuable for the views of the authors as for their accounts of evil-doing, are Thomas Dekker's *The Belman of London: Bringing to Light The Most Notorious Villanies That Are Now Practiced In The Kingdom* (London, 1608) and Thomas Harmon's *Fraternity of Vagabonds* (London, 1575). One of the few scholarly pieces on vagabondage is A.L. Beier's carefully researched "Vagrants and the Social Order in Elizabethan England," *Past and Present* 64 (August 1974): 3–29. For a synthesis on lower-class mayhem after the Restoration, Max Beloff's *Public Order and Popular Disturbances, 1660–1714* (London: Frank Cass, 1963) is the best available monograph. Three articles by Steven R. Smith provide much information about apprentices and apprentice culture. His "London Apprentices as Seventeenth-Century Adolescents," *Past and Present* 61 (November 1973): 149–161; "Religion and the Conception of Youth in Seventeenth-Century England," *History of Childhood Quarterly* 2 (Spring 1975): 493–516; and "The Social and Geographical Origins of the London Apprentices, 1630–1660," *The Guildhall Miscellany* 4 (April 1973): 195–206, are all particularly valuable.

The literature on England, ships, and sailing is almost as boundless as the seas themselves, and much of it is navigated only by the most intrepid of scholars. The truly dangerous rocks and shoals are those dealing with the minutiae of ships, their construction, operation, and the processes of navigating them from port to port. I have left sailing on voyages where such hazards are encountered to more courageous captains. The passages I have traveled deal with economic and institutional structure of English maritime activity, subjects more appropriate for the stay-at-home sailor. The only comprehensive study of the Royal Navy for the period after the Glorious Revolution is John Ehrman's splendid *The Navy in the War of Wil-*

liam III (Cambridge: Cambridge University Press, 1953). The work is no mere military history with accounts of heroes, dissertations on the caliber of ships' guns, and a bevy of battle maps. It contains these things, and everything else anyone could possibly want to know about the Navy's organization, administration, operation, and effect. A study of comparable quality dealing with merchant shipping is Ralph Davis's *The Rise of the English Shipping Industry in the Seventeenth and Eighteenth Centuries* (London: Macmillan, 1962). Also valuable on the same subject is Abott Payson Usher's "The Growth of English Shipping, 1572–1922," *Quarterly Journal of Economics* 42 (May 1928): 465–478. Ruth Bourne's *Queen Anne's Navy in the West Indies* (New Haven, Conn.: Yale University Press, 1939) is a useful study, and of primary importance for understanding maritime employment patterns is T.S. Willan's *The English Coasting Trade 1600–1750* (New York: Augustus M. Kelley, 1967).

INDEX